# DAY LATE, DOLLAR SHORT

# Day Late, Dollar Short

## The Next Generation and the New Academy

*edited by*
*Peter C. Herman*

*State University of New York Press*

Published by
State University of New York Press, Albany

© 2000 State University of New York

Printed in the United States of America

For information, address State University of New York Press
State University Plaza, Albany, New York 12246

Production by Dana Foote
Marketing by Dana E. Yanulavich

**Library of Congress Cataloging-in-Publication Data**

Day late, dollar short : the next generation and the new academy /
edited by Peter C. Herman.
p. cm.
Includes bibliographical references and index.
ISBN 0–7914–4679–4 (alk. paper) — ISBN 0–7914–4680–8 (pbk. : alk. paper)
1. English literature—Study and teaching (Higher)—United States. 2. American literature—Study and teaching (Higher)—United States. 3. Literature—Study and teaching (Higher)—United States. 4. Criticism—United States—History—20th century. 5. Literature teachers—Training of—United States. 6. English teachers—Training of—United States. 7. Criticism—United States—Forecasting. I. Herman, Peter C., 1958–

PR51.U5 D39 2000
801′.95′0973—dc21

00–032929

10 9 8 7 6 5 4 3 2 1

# Contents

*v*

# ACKNOWLEDGMENTS

First and foremost, I am deeply grateful to all the contributors for bearing with this project through its various trials, tribulations, and incarnations. I am, however, particularly indebted to Jeff Williams, who in many ways has been the shadow editor of this volume. If *Day Late* has any merit, he deserves the credit. I gladly take all the blame. I also want to thank Jeffrey Di Leo for our discussions about jazz and for publishing several of these essays in *symplokē 3.1* (1995) as well as Michael Bristol of McGill University for his initial enthusiasm for this idea.

I am also grateful to the editors of *College Literature* and the *Michigan Quarterly Review* for their assistance with essays that first appeared in their journals.

# Introduction

# '60s Theory/'90s Practice

## Peter C. Herman

This volume seeks to explore the ways in which the recent shifts in the material conditions affecting the academy have influenced the theory and praxis of the Next Generation of literary critics. Generations are, of course, notoriously difficult to define, and academic ones are no different. Whereas in an earlier era one could probably rely on a strictly chronological rubric, assuming that "the next generation" refers to critics who grew up in the '70s and went to grad school in the '80s, the fact of people returning to the profession after some years of doing something else makes the chronological approach less than entirely satisfactory. Generally, I have in mind critics who are now at the beginning of their careers, people who are in graduate school or are assistant professors. If tenured, then tenured only recently. The common denominator, however, is that everyone in the next generation received the various approaches and epistemologies signified by the shorthand term *Theory,* second-, if not thirdhand. Theory is something we (and it should be understood that *we* means *my* sense of "we"; others disagree with these views) are taught in graduate school, not something that we discovered for ourselves at its originary moment. Theory, in other words, for the next generation does not have the sense of bold discovery that reading Foucault or Derrida might have had in the late '60s or early '70s. Rather, theory is something that comes along with graduate education, a body of knowledge and a language to be mastered. It is, in this sense, institutionalized, packaged, and commodified. While the ideas themselves have not lost their potency or relevance, theory now comes to us in a different mode than it did initially. Consequently, someone born in 1968 belongs to the same *professional* generation as someone born in 1958.

It has become a critical commonplace that interpretation both reflects and shapes its particular cultural moment. Terry Eagleton, for example, has demonstrated how the social conditions of the 1920s and 1930s shaped the formation of New Criticism,[1] and much has been done on how shifts in historical and ideological contexts resulted in shifts in the interpretations of various texts. The disillusionment after World War I, for instance, made possible the first skeptical interpretations of Shakespeare's *Henry V,*[2] and the influence of the '60s on theoretical developments is taken for granted (if not yet subjected to sustained scrutiny). But the symbiotic relationship between culture and criticism leads directly to the problem that this collection seeks to reveal and address.

Since the next generation faces an entirely different scene, socially, politically, materially, and professionally, than previous generations, how does our social moment and the changes in university culture inflect *our* criticism? our sense of the profession?

our modes of scholarship? How do we receive paradigms that originated in an historical moment other than our own? What paradigms of our own have we produced?
How has the corporatization of the academy affected those at the beginning of their
careers, and how will it shape those careers? The same question obtains for the
influence of computers, the Internet and the various proposed "virtual" universities.
What kinds of criticism will we write—indeed, are currently writing? In sum, if the
'60s produced "theory," what are the '80s and '90s producing?

One of the most salient distinctions between the critics who came of age in the
'60s and those of my (chronological) generation lies in our attitude toward our predecessors. Our teachers often fought tooth and nail with their own, declaring their independence by adopting a variety of texts and authors that their teachers probably did
not understand, or if they did, did not like. Yet the next generation has largely adopted
the same texts our teachers used as guideposts and authorities for our own work.[3] The
irony of this phenomenon is that the critical practice of forefathers and foremothers
originated in a visceral, if not vicious, *rejection* of their own teachers' work. Faced with
critical practices often emphasizing unity and social hierarchy, critical practices that
have their roots in World War II and the Cold War, the most influential '60s generation critics devised methodologies that exposed fissures, questioned unspoken
assumptions, and generally adopted a "hermeneutics of suspicion" toward literature
and criticism. "Literature" turned into "texts," and these "texts," no longer "read," are
"challenged" or "interrogated."

Curiously, most of the next generation has uncritically and unproblematically
accepted these theoretical paradigms.[4] A quick glance over the bibliographies and
indices from books produced by critics and graduate students who belong both professionally and chronologically to the next generation shows that we accept the
"hermeneutics of suspicion" *without* much suspicion; we rarely "interrogate" the notion that texts ought to be read against the grain. The same figures who guided our
teachers' work guide our own: Foucault and Derrida, Raymond Williams and
Lawrence Stone, Clifford Geertz and Victor Turner figure in our bibliographies as
much as, say, Greenblatt's or Louis Montrose's.[5] We are not reading anything or anybody new or different from those voices who inspired and guided the previous generation's work. We often continue to fight the same critical battles as our teachers, as
evidenced by the continuing denunciation (among '90s generation early modern
scholars) of the New Critical lack of historicity or E. M. W. Tillyard's mistaking *an*
Elizabethan World Picture for *the* Elizabethan World Picture.[6] And even when we criticize our elders, it is generally done on their own terms and for not following through
on their insights, not from the standpoint of a radically new theoretical approach. For
example, the New Historicism is often castigated for not going far enough; that is, for
not including gender among its objects of analysis, a point that was made almost con-
temporaneously with this movement's conception.[7]

What's wrong with us? Are we just a bunch of Greenblatt wannabes? of unre-
constructed deconstructionists discovering the instability of the text over and over
again?

Perhaps, but then again, maybe the problem does not lie with us. The kind of generational warfare between, say, the old and new historicists, does not look particularly edifying or useful from our perspective. And one might also ask what law demands that each generation must without fail or exception denounce their predecessors and come up with something they think is brand new? Does each generation, in other words, have to repeat the Oedipus story in order to achieve critical independence? Perhaps we do not have to violently reject what the previous generation believed, but can simply proceed, making our differences known without hostility or polemics, continuing the discussion rather than trying to create an entirely new one, producing finer grained analyses rather than entirely novel ones.

Yet there are also good historical and professional reasons for what might be called our lack of originality. To state the obvious, the '60s marked a watershed in American, indeed world, life and culture, and the theories produced in the '60s, as Walter Cohen and Don E. Wayne have said, were part of a much larger rethinking, *oppositional* rethinking, of values.[8] No such cultural upheaval marks the '80s and '90s; consequently, no such upheaval marks our writing. Furthermore, unlike in the '60s, aside from the standard tensions between parents and children, nothing like the "generation gap" separates us from our parents, professional or otherwise, and the criticism of my generation reflects this sad or happy, depending on one's perspective, cultural fact. Interestingly, this preference for marked trails, this reticence toward striking out on our own, also characterizes the recent resurgence in conservative thought. As an article in *The New York Times Magazine* (12 February 1995) makes clear, many of the newer voices of conservatism are the *sons* of important conservatives (Norman Podhoretz and Midge Decter produced John Podhoretz, Irving Kristol is the father of William Kristol, Adam Bellow the son of Saul, etc.).[9] For those of us who chronologically belong to the next generation, on both sides of the left/right chasm we by and large see little reason to reject our fathers and mothers.

Yet there is also a less benign element shaping the next generation's perspectives—the pressure of the job market. As everyone knows, and as Bettina Huber's statistics in the *MLA Newsletter* reiterate with depressing precision, each year brings fewer and fewer positions,[10] and the downturn in opportunities is matched by an upswing in almost absurdly qualified candidates.[11] The resulting fierce competition for these ever-decreasing slots hardly encourages bold departures from the norm, as the next generation depends far too much upon the good will of our teachers and superiors to risk much in the way of critical disagreement. Even the common adoption of the language of contestation constitutes a bow toward our elders, as they more or less invented this language. We need their approval for letters of recommendation, and we need hiring committees (generally drawn from the senior ranks of the department who, obviously, will constitute the majority in any vote) to like us so we will get the offer. We need to publish in journals our elders edit and with presses they control in order to stay hired, and we need their further approval to get tenure. In sum, thumbing our nose at our teachers risks alienating precisely the generation upon whom our professional survival depends. And as an unfortunate number of my friends and colleagues are learning all too well, once out of the profession, it is exceedingly hard, if not impossible, to get back in.

The result is not only an emphasis upon sociability, but increasing, if subtle, pressure to write not what we feel, but what we think we ought to say, to paraphrase the last lines of *King Lear.* Granted, such pressures have always existed. New criticism created a scandal in its own day, and there are instances of '60s generation critics, such as Colin McCabe, having employment problems due to their theoretical orientation. Yet the contraction of the market has, I think, rendered this generation particularly risk-averse. When there are anywhere from 250 to 500 applicants for every position (rumor has it that Berkeley once received 900 applicants for an Americanist position), taking on an entire critical tradition, as, say, Jonathan Dollimore did in *Radical Tragedy* or Stanley Fish in *Surprised by Sin,* would seem especially ill-advised for someone who would probably face representatives of that tradition in a job interview or a tenure review. We do not have the luxury of assuming that if we do not get X job, there will probably be Y job.

A marvelous anecdote Annabel Patterson recounts concerning one of her early job searches puts into stark relief the different pressures faced by the next generation: "In the early 1980s, I greatly disconcerted a director of undergraduate studies at an Ivy League school by declaring, as a candidate for a job, that I would not teach their standard course in metaphysical poetry."[12] Although opportunities declined in the early '80s, it is worth remembering that Patterson uttered this statement before she became the "star" she is today and when the market consisted of between thirteen hundred and fifteen hundred positions in English literature. We face significantly fewer positions (about one thousand advertisements in the 1995–96 *Job Information List,* and a good number of these jobs either never materialized or were canceled, so the actual number is probably around eight hundred to nine hundred) and I doubt that many of us on the market over the last couple of years would have taken such an iconoclastic position toward a hiring committee, Ivy League or otherwise. Certainly I did not.

Hence a certain sameness starts to creep into scholarship, a certain predictability about conclusions, a certain reticence toward taking positions that might either lead to rejection at journals with considerable professional capital (e.g., *ELR, ELH, Representations, Modern Philology, Texas Studies in Literature and Language*) or alienating influential people and hiring committees. To put the matter another way, there is implicit pressure to produce work that we *think* will be professionally advantageous in terms of either getting or keeping a job (I emphasize "think" because we are not always right and neither publishing nor hiring decisions are neatly predictable). And if nothing else, when Alan Sokal published his mock essay in *Social Text,* he proved that it is more than possible to write in a theoretical mode one does not believe in solely for the purpose of getting published.

But at exactly the same time, there are other, more optimistic perspectives on the next generation's position. I like to compare the next generation's literary criticism with the present state of jazz, which has gone through a similar evolution. To simplify greatly, jazz developed from the formalism of New Orleans style playing and the swing era to the unlacing of structures by Miles Davis et al., to the complete atonality of free jazz. Stricter forms ceded place to looser forms, which ceded in turn to no form at all. The question facing postsixties jazz musicians is where does one go after the squeaks, honks, and bleats of late Coltrane and Ornette Coleman? If one defines music as organized sound, how does one progress after sound has been completely disorganized? One cannot push the envelope of harmony or form any further because the envelope no longer exists.

Somewhat analogously (I recognize that the correspondences are more evocative than exact), literary criticism has progressed, if that is the appropriate term, from the formalism of New Criticism to the mandarin freedom of Derridean and de Manian deconstruction and of Barthesian *jouissance*. We have gone from an absolute and unquestioned faith in the connection between text and author, a faith shared with nonspecialists, to an equally absolute faith in the separation between sign and signified, between statement and understanding. Indeed, according to de Man, understanding does not exist, only misunderstanding.[13] Significantly, many have claimed that jazz lost its audience when it lost its swing. In other words, when jazz turned away from popular acceptance and toward the harsher sounds of the avant garde, people stopped listening and stopped buying. Jazz thus became the music of an elite, a coterie, rather than a popular idiom. Most people knew Duke Ellington's "Mood Indigo," for instance; comparatively few listen to John Coltrane's "Live in Japan," let alone Anthony Braxton's, Cecil Taylor's, or John Zorn's work. And as the academy's detractors have pointed out, in place of using a language understandable by a general, intelligent audience, many literary critics adopted a style difficult even for initiates to penetrate (e.g., "As an articulation of displacement and dislocation, it is now possible to identitfy 'the cultural' as a disposal of power, a negative transparency that comes to be agonistically constructed *on the boundary* between frame of reference/frame of mind").[14] Whereas Ellington and Irving Howe reached a broad, popular audience, most academic critics today speak only to those within their immediate circles.[15]

What to do? Interestingly, both jazz musicians and the next generation of literary critics have reacted in parallel ways, and, I think, for similar reasons. The first has to do with improving public relations and trying to reach a wider audience. Eschewing the kind of public arrogance cultivated by Miles Davis, Wynton Marsalis has become a kind of roving ambassador for jazz, trying to reach not only a wider audience through becoming the director of Lincoln Center's jazz program, but also trying to proselytize to nonjazz listeners and children through his radio, television, and video programs. In essence, Marsalis has turned himself into the Leonard Bernstein of jazz, spreading the word and popularizing what had been perceived as an elite music. Analogously, a highly visible minority of literary critics are trying to break through to a nonacademic audience by publishing in such less rarified (yet still intellectual) venues as *Harper's, VLS, The New Yorker,* and *The New York Times.* Also, a number of important critics, including Stephen Greenblatt, have contributed to *What's the Word,* "a series of radio programs designed to promote understanding of the work done by language and literature teachers."[16] In other words, academic critics are increasingly trying to write for the public sphere; that is, the intellectual world outside the immediate confines of their particular disciplines. Like Marsalis proving that jazz is accessible and jazz musicians are neither misanthropes nor drug-addicted eccentrics, when such critics as Michael Bérubé, Henry Louis Gates, and Jeffrey Williams write for nonacademic readers, they demonstrate that English (or cultural studies) professors are neither tenured barbarians nor modern versions of Mr. Chips. Furthermore, they demonstrate that contemporary critical approaches can be applied to difficult topical issues in ways that everyone who cares to can understand.

Second, Marsalis and those following in his wake (e.g., Roy Hargrove, Christian McBride, Brad Mehldau, Terence Blanchard, and Joshua Redman, an admittedly arbitrary list but these are my favorites) confronted the problem of originality by quite deliberately combining the "old" and the "new," by going backward and reinserting swing, melody, tonality, *and* atonality into their improvisations. A similar movement is, I propose, constitutive of much '90s generation literary criticism. Like Marsalis and others, we cannot go any further in terms of dissolution of form or interpretive freedom. Once the Author does not exist, we cannot prove that the Author is even deader than Foucault believed. We can either go backward and recover authorial intention or provide further proof for Foucault's essay by recovering the seemingly mundane details of book production, and the like.[17] Either way, this development leaves us open to charges of unoriginality and timidity. Yet one can look at the matter in yet another way.

When Marsalis plays a solo, he employs the entirety of jazz history in his music. Similarly, both Joshua Redman and James Carter combine within the space of one solo Ben Webster's breathy romanticism, Sonny Rollins's improvisational rigor, and the very late Coltrane's explosions of sound.[18] The originality of these musicians lies in their recombinative and synthetic skills, in using the elements of the past to create something new and, to my ears, entirely wonderful.[19] Similarly, the next generation of literary critics can use the insights of new historicism, feminism, new criticism, deconstruction, indeed the entirety of literary theory, however we feel like and in whatever measure seems appropriate.

What does such scholarship actually look like? Claire McEachern's *The Poetics of English Nationhood: 1590–1612,* published by Cambridge University Press in their highly prestigious series, Cambridge Studies in Renaissance Literature and Culture, exemplifies these developments.[20] McEachern was born in 1963, thus she fits chronologically within the next generation, and she studiously adopts a *via media* in describing her methodology. Navigating between the Scylla of '60s generation new historicism ("For many literary critics, the historical event often functions as the prefatory point of departure, the warrant cited in passing") and historians, for whom "literature functions as a kind of high cultural flourish, a nice epigraph, a poetic way of saying what must be proven first less glamorously" (3), McEachern situates herself right in the middle and unapologetically takes from both what she needs:

> Studies which attempt to negotiate between these two evidentiary standards are doomed to fall, as it were, between two schools. . . . Nonetheless, this is the most interesting place to be. The function of the "non-literary" in this account is not a determinative one—the literary texts here are not read as reflections of contexts, or even, in that conveniently vague new historicist term, interrogations of them. But nor, to suggest the other extreme, is this a source study, an account of authors freely choosing their terms from inert predecessors. (3)

McEachern's next generational approach also manifests itself in her relationship to the state and to previous scholarship. Significantly, McEachern differntiates her work from Richard Helgerson's on specifically generational grounds. The new historicism (in all its fuzziness) is, as I have said, a product of the '60s, and as one would expect, its practitioners generally take a rather dim view of the state. McEachern, though, belongs to the next generation, and our experience does not include Vietnam, student riots, and Alabama sheriffs sicking dogs on civil rights protesters. Her view of the state is correspondingly different:

> What Helgerson shares with his own generation of literary critics is a conviction of the ultimately hegemonic determination of the state in this period, and by extension, of the "more dutiful" nation constructed for it. The governing new historicist understanding of the Tudor-Stuart state is of a system absolutist in ambition if not in accomplishment, one in which the interest and power of a few sought to control the interest and agencies of the many (20–21).

McEachern proposes a more irenic, more inclusive, and certainly more benign view:

> What I am suggesting is not that we work harder to defend the boundary between literature and propaganda, or literature and the state—that would be to argue for the subversive agency of literature. On the contrary, I would argue for the fellowship of literature and propaganda, and the expression in both alike of the *state itself as a utopian structure:* to entertain the idea that the state was indeed, upon occasion, a place where (imaginatively speaking) "many a captain kissed the queen's hand" (and not just, as Marx said of Spenser, her arse). In other words, I would urge less that we work to "save literature" from propaganda than that we save propaganda from pettiness, and hegemony from a unequivocally coercive construction. (23; emphasis in the original)

In other words, while McEachern uses the theoretical tools devised by '60s generation critics, she adapts them to create a vision of the early modern period more in keeping with the next generation's experience (and, interestingly, more in keeping with the nostalgic view of the Renaissance expressed by E. M. W. Tillyard and C. S. Lewis, precisely the people Helgerson et al. reacted against).[21] If her book lacks the fiery polemical edge enlivening, say, Jonathan Dollimore and Alan Sinfield's 1985 anthology *Political Shakespeare* (considered the foundational text for cultural materialism, the harder-shell Marxist cousin of American new historicism), that is in large part because the next generation also lacks that polemical edge.

Yet this irenic position, this freedom to combine older and new critical paradigms, while producing interesting and important work (such as McEachern's), nonetheless also demonstrates that nothing really matters anymore in whatever theory one chooses to use. In *Cultural Capital: The Problem of Literary Canon Formation,* John Guillory suggests, inter alia, that the canon wars are entirely beside the point because literature itself, and by extension, the paradigms used to study it, have become entirely beside the point. The fact is, literature has lost the cultural capital that once made reading it an essential activity:[22]

> The decline of the humanities was never the result of newer noncanonical courses or texts, but of a large-scale "capital flight" in the domain of culture. The debate over what amounts to the supplementation (or modernization) of the traditional curriculum is thus a misplaced response to that capital flight. . . . Since both canonical and noncanonical works constitute at base, despite their apparent conflict, the same *kind* of cultural capital, the social forces displacing this kind of capital will sooner or later strand the participants in the canon debate on an ever shrinking island within the university itself.

Clearly, Guillory is not wrong, and part of the work of the next generation must be the reinvigoration, assuming that is possible, of both the canon and literary studies, if for no other reason than self-preservation. For that, we must ask ourselves and those who came before us why exactly we are doing what we are doing and then translate the answers into some kind of public program (or programs, since it is highly unlikely that a single program could adequately represent the diversity of this profession). In other words, for both jazz musicians and literary critics, the rapprochement between the generations has become a matter of survival. For jazz musicians, the audience, the *paying* audience, for their work had dwindled to the point that it was simply impossible to make a living. Even so, for literary critics, the matter is a little different.

Perhaps the most important difference between the next generation and its forebears lies in the changes within the academy itself, the increasing emphasis on corporatization and corporate values (one chancellor of the California State University system, for instance, liked to refer to himself as the CEO, nor is he alone in doing so),[23] and another chancellor (or CEO) of the CSU, Charles B. Reed, asserted that "Cal Poly and the other 22 institutions of the CSU [California State University] all are in the same business that business and industry are in."[24] Faced with dwindling state and private support, many university administrations have turned to private corporations to make up the difference, with the result that education (at all levels) is increasingly viewed as an exploitable market by business interests. Furthermore, the confluence between education and business is being encouraged, to put it mildly, by administrators who want to turn the university into a corporation of sorts.[25] Hence the steady attacks on tenure (under the rubric of "flexibility"), the decline in tenure-track positions, and the alarming increase in the use of adjuncts to teach both basic and advanced courses.[26] But also, the corporatization of the academy dehumanizes the students (or "customers," as they are often now referred to). Reed, for example, compares the summer break to factories or "plants [that] are down two or three months of the year," which implies that students are commodities no different than widgets.[27]

It is in this context that we need to see the phenomenal (and for the most part, entirely uncritical) drive toward wiring the academy. Certainly, computers have aided research by speeding things up exponentially. Instead of paging through volume after volume of the MLA Bibliography, one can now use a CD-ROM, or even access the bibliography from one's home computer if one's institution has it online. In place of writing letters, we can now email each other, thus speeding up communications. Furthermore, the various listservs and discussion groups make discussion between those with like interests much easier. The question remains, though, whether "faster" means "fundamentally different." Doubtless, we can communicate with each other much more quickly, but that does not mean that the kinds of criticism we produce has actually changed. No doubt, computers are having an effect on the next generation, but it may not be the expected one.

An increasing percentage of decreasing dollars available for higher education is being devoted to technology, with the result that less money goes to maintaining libraries or funding tenure-track positions. In fact, some even maintain that conventional libraries are a thing of the past, and so purchasing books and journals is as outdated as investing in the horse and buggy.[28] Yet despite the hype, the bulk of our research is still done using printed materials, and the bulk of university press books and older archives are not available online. As Edward Rothstein, author of the *New York Times* technology column, writes: "The Internet will not come close to replacing even the most ordinary library until every book of importance is published in digital form, financial arrangements are worked out with publishers, and search engines become as powerful as the index in back of a reference book. Right now, even the most limited local library has much the Internet cannot touch."[29] One can also add the problem of planned obscelesence in archiving technology (older CD-ROMS, for instance, cannot be read by newer CD-ROM machines, and CD-ROMS themselves will doubtless be replaced eventually), which means that one is always upgrading and replacing, even though library budgets are dwindling. Furthermore, computers also threaten to exacerbate the job crisis, since, in the zero-sum game of university funding, money spent on technology means less money for tenure-track positions. Florida Gulf Coast University and the Arizona International Campus represent the confluence of these trends, as both are new institutions devoted to long-distance learning and without tenure-track positions. But even more traditional universities are starting to combine computer-based, long-distance learning with for-profit education.[30]

I would therefore suggest that the move toward recovering more traditional concepts and modes of interpretation by the next generation constitutes in part a *de-*

*fensive* move. After one has deconstructed the author and demonstrated the imperialist roots of disciplinary boundaries, it becomes increasingly difficult to then argue for more tenure-track lines in literature to administrators who see little monetary value in such courses, who see the at times inflammatory rhetoric emanating from literature departments driving away state or private contributor dollars (see Barbara Riebling's chapter in this volume), and who regard the traditional classroom as expensive and outmoded. And there is the further irony in how arguments for the importance (read continuing funding) of the humanities often reiterate precisely the language that the new historicism and its allied approaches made so unstylish. Whereas the previous generation invented "strategic essentialism," the next generation might have to adopt "strategic conservatism" simply in order to survive.

Moreover, the corporatization of university life has made life even more uncertain for the nontenure track, as Kalí Tal discovered. Professor Tal, lured to the Arizona International Campus with all sorts of promises, made the unfortunate mistake of critiquing the "school's" provost and discovered that she could be fired without any chance for appeal, since "the University of Arizona's standard terms for the 'non-tenure-eligible' . . . stipulate that renewal decisions are made solely by the dean or provost and are 'not subject to further administrative review.'"[31] While Professor Tal ultimately prevailed in her legal battle (she was reinstated), the popularity of "tenure reform," which usually means attempts to get rid of tenure, argue that her experiences are symbolic of the new realities facing the next generation. Others finding themselves in her position may not be as fortunate.

While I certainly would agree that the greater part of the work produced by any generation is derivative, there is a new element at work with this group. The greater caution and the lack of pathbreaking thinking among the next generation results, I propose, in part from the extremely vulnerable position of the humanities and its practitioners in the shifting culture of the academy, and the move toward a greater presence in the nonacademic public sphere results from our need to ensure continued funding. Moreover, the move to consolidate older and newer approaches has some of its roots in a perception that we need to do so in order to preserve our tenure-track lines that might otherwise go to more "productive" departments. The same applies to the increasing rhetoric over reprivileging teaching. Universities under financial and political pressure want to ensure that students are getting value for their tuition dollars and legislators are getting value for the money they put into higher education (the definition of *getting value,* of course, like the definition of *productivity,* is highly problematic, and shifts dramatically among different constituencies; in my experience, at least, university administrators define these terms very differently than the faculty do). Publishing an article in *PMLA* may justify one's existence within the confines of the profession, but teaching courses with large enrollments tends to be a more persuasive justification outside the profession. It is no accident, as David Galef demonstrates below, that rhetoric/composition studies, as well as creative writing, have become growth industries in academia, a development one might not want to celebrate.

Concomitantly, the seeming unoriginality of the next generation also reflects the pervading sense of insecurity and changing criteria for raises. At many schools, financial advancement and professional development are not divorced: publish a book, get a raise. Get a good review, get an even larger raise. And while this often still applies, at other schools, mainly the nonelite ones that most of us work at, committee work, community service, and teaching classes with large enrollments rather than publication are swiftly becoming the primary avenues toward raises and even tenure.[32] Furthermore, as several of the contributors point out, the popularity among administrators for modeling the university after the corporation entails a radical devaluation of scholarship's worth. James F. Carlin, for example, the chairman of the Board of Higher Education of Massachusetts, an insurance and real estate magnate with no academic credentials other than a B.S. in business administration, announced that "Professors should teach more than 12 hours a week, and 'meaningless research' should be banned; 50 percent of research outside the hard sciences was 'a lot of foolishness.'"[33]

Needless to say, under such pressure, there is a decreasing sense of reward for doing scholarly work. Teaching may very well represent the next generation's opportunity for distinguishing itself, as Gerald Graff suggests, but many of us are being pushed there by the lack of understanding of and sympathy for traditional scholarship that does not necessarily have an immediate business application.

In sum, the next generation faces a myriad of institutional pressures that did not exist for our teachers. Until fairly recently, corporate America was not considered an appropriate model for higher education, and there was little sense that teaching literature or literary theory had to be justified on purely economic grounds. The next generation's irenic moves, in other words, stem in good measure from our need to appear unthreatening to those holding the purse strings as well as from our need to change our image in the public's eye. Furthermore, our continuing along previously forged critical paths results, again in part, from pressures to teach more and to defend ourselves to nonacademic audiences. Many of us do not, in other words, have the time—that is, the reduced course loads—or the psychic space to worry about inventing new theoretical paradigms.

Yet at the same time, the defensiveness of the next generation is also a prelude to taking the offensive, as several of the contributors emphasize the profession's ongoing commitment to social change and social action, both inside and outside academia (see the essays by Bartolovich and Swan as well as Bérubé's epilogue), although both the goals and the means have become much more practical. Furthermore, while Riebling may condemn the overheated rhetoric that sometimes overtakes the humanities, her goal is actually the same as the more overtly politically committed essays. Riebling's argument is that to effect change, one must first be heard. The difference between her and Swan or Bartolovich lies in means, not ends. Consequently, an important element of the next generation's work will be striving to improve the working conditions of our colleagues in the knowledge industry through joining unions, among other means, in addition to worrying about the workers in other industries, while at the same time we carry on our more traditional objects of study. And it is likely that we will be spending more time doing public writing, that is to say, responding to negative stories about us in the media with letters to the editor and putting our own views forward in the popular media (e.g., newspapers) about the conditions of university teaching using arguments and language that nonspecialists not only will understand, but find persuasive.[34] "Strategic conservatism," in other words, my admittedly provocative phrase, constitutes a strategy for effecting change, not a call for retreat or quietism.

To be sure, not all the contributors agree with this assessment—some passionately disagree with it—but these differences are consistent with my sense of the next generation's overall suspicion of totalizing or grand schemes. As the essays below will show, the next generation puts forward no overarching critical approach. To assert, as Paul de Man infamously did, that deconstruction (or any other critical methodology) will constitute the work of *all* future literary criticism is simply risible, if not conceptually impossible.[35] Having before us the rise and fall of so many critical empires, we are rightly skeptical of anyone promising an all-encompassing critical dogma. Yet, that does not mean that we are entirely rudderless or have no sense of where we want to go.

Jeffrey Williams coins the term *posttheory* to define this generation's position both theoretically, "its seeming lateness on the scene, coming after the monumental successes of the great Theories," and professionally—that is, we inhabit "a job-traumatized field, after the post-Fordist reconfiguration of the university and university labor." Williams defines our critical work thus: "the project of posttheory seems to have shifted to localized units of production, similar to microbreweries, away from large-scale, totalizing concepts such as class, or race or sex for that matter." Yet Williams also notes that a distinguishing characteristic of our theoretical moment may be the move toward more public forms of discourse, publishing, say, in the *VLS* or *The New Yorker* as much as *ELH* or *English Literary Renaissance*.

Sharon O'Dair's "Stars, Tenure, and the Death of Ambition" addresses the conditions under which the next generation works. In recent years, much has been written, most of it negative, about the emergence of a star system or cult of celebrity in literary and cultural study. And even more, perhaps, has been written about the collapse of the job market in literary and cultural study. O'Dair ties the two together by suggesting that the emergence of the star system is symptomatic, the result of the collapse. The collapse of the job market, in turn, is not about a fall-off in absolute numbers of tenure-track jobs, but rather about a collapse in a certain kind of tenure-track job, the one that allows one to pursue research and writing while teaching upper-division and graduate-level courses in literature or cultural studies.

To O'Dair, the emergence of the star system suggests not the infusion into the profession of something evil or demeaning but rather that the profession has reached a crossroads. We have yet to acknowledge that higher education increasingly is taking on the task of educating people in basic skills, skills once taught in secondary schools. What seems to be occurring is that the profession is becoming bifurcated, with some Ph.D.'s destined to teach multiple sections of composition and others to do research and writing and the teaching of upper-division and graduate courses. For the next generation, one's potential to shine determines which destiny one will find.

Terry Caesar meditates on how the differing valences of travel have come to define the next generation's highly problematic professional future. The ability to travel for conferences and research has been, and still continues to be, the defining characteristic of academic professional success, and "The most luminous stars of any discipline are its frequent flyers" (consider the travel schedules of, say, Henry Louis Gates, Jacques Derrida, Stephen Greenblatt, or Gayatri Spivak). Yet for the next generation, Caesar argues, "nothing about their future experience . . . better represents its depleted prospects than the absent or marginalized opportunity to travel." Paradoxically, however, it is the definition of travel that has also changed, for where Derrida, Gates, and Greenblatt et al. travel as a sign of professional success, many of the next generation travel as a sign of professional marginalization, i.e. the part-time lecturer at three different institutions, the "freeway flyer," not the "frequent flyer." If the fictional narrative of the Big Theory generation is David Lodge's *Small World,* then the narrative for the next generation will be a narrative of nomads, of gypsy scholars. Yet, Caesar notes, "a more redemptive narrative is possible. It will not simply see [the gypsy scholar] lost in [the figure of Lodge's character, Kingfisher], any more than it will see the notion of a calling lost to market conditions, a career lost to jobs. . . . A liberating idea of travel—nomadic or not—may be all that is left to the next generation to deal with loss, including the loss of dignity."

Crystal Bartolovich analyzes the myth of the academic community in "To Boldly Go Where No MLA Has Gone Before," and she uses the strike at Yale by graduate students as her subject. Bartolovich points out that despite ample evidence to the contrary, the myth of academia as a serene grove characterized by "academic freedom" remains a potent one. Yet, as she writes, the myth of the "Academic Community" is one that "the next generation cannot afford to indulge uncritically." Bartolovich suggests that the anti-union stance of the Modern Language Association and many of Yale's senior faculty demonstrates that the union best represents the next generation's interests, rather than the profession's senior management, as it were. We need to "think about what 'academic community' as we wish to have it means in explicit terms," and we "cannot permit the MLA to give in to a fear of taking stands because powerful groups (such as the Yale administration) might be unhappy about it."

In "'It's a Beastly Rough Crowd I Run With': Theory and the 'New' University," Kalí Tal uses her experience at Arizona International Campus to speculate on the effects of the "new university" on the next generation and the future of the humanities. First, Tal suggests that our training (usually by '60s generation critics) in theory exacerbates generational strife because most of us will teach at nonelite institutions where Derrida, Foucault, and even Greenblatt and Fish remain opaque to many, if not most, of our older colleagues. Hence we "work in an environment in which [our] scholarship is not only incomprehensible to [our] peers, but regarded with suspicion and hostility." Given that high theory has also helped significantly diversify the humanities, the antitheory backlash (and the sense among many administrators that theoretical work is mere "foolishness") dovetails with the attenuation of the job market. Consequently, "The sense that the older generation has collaborated in pulling the temple down around its own ears is bolstered by the theory gap and the fact that this young generation of scholars is the most racially, ethnically, and gender-diverse cohort yet graduated by the U.S. university system." Third, the new emphasis on corporatizing the academy puts the next generation under siege, since theoretically engaged work does not produce revenue and is in general highly critical of such entities as Microsoft. Ultimately, however, Kal senses that the next generation, unlike the '60s generational, is in a transitional position, belonging to neither the old, relatively untroubled academy nor the new university, and what will result is not yet clear: "We stand at the division between an older university structure and some as-yet-undetermined new structure which, from all the signs, will not be any improvement."

Jesse Swan, in "Breaking the Monopoly: The Next Generation and the Corporate Academy," addresses the effects of the increasingly common public figurations of the academy as a corporation. After illustrating some of the ways corporate thinking currently shapes the university, Swan argues for active, and even hyperbolic, engagement of public discourses by the next generation. "When we do not counter these venal projects of corporate schemers," Swan explains, "we allow the academy to become another dehumanized site for playing out further fantasies of the free market." In addition to calling the next generation to public discourse, Swan proposes a series of commitments for the next generation in its scholarly as well as new public work. Most significantly, Swan urges his generation to propagate alternative figurations of the academy, which is essential so that "the academy will better its chances of vanquishing the corporate threats of exploitation and subservience it currently faces."

Jeffrey R. Di Leo, in "New Technology and the Dilemmas of the Posttheory Generation: On the Use and Abuse of Computer and Information Technology in Higher Education Today," offers a nuanced view of the relationship between the wired academy and the next generation. Di Leo argues that the new technological condition of the academy will affect the next generation in ways that will make difficult for them to either globally affirm or unconditionally denounce it. Some aspects of the technological revolution will clearly work to the benefit of the next generation, while others will clearly challenge their aims and ideals. The necessarily conflicted reaction that the next generation must have to this technology will make it very difficult for them not only to voice support for its increased intervention without contradicting a certain set of values that they hold, but that it will also be difficult for them to organize resistance to the rise of new technology within the academy without opposing another set of beliefs.

In "Theory after the 'Theorists'" Neil Larsen proposes that a legitimate disgust with an academic aristocracy of "theory" is in danger of ratifying inadvertently two of theory's most potent self-mystifications: the myth of its "sixties," insurgent genealogy and the presumption that theory is reducible to its own institutional conditions of reproduction. In partial exception to John Guillory's *Cultural Capital* and its exhaustive sociological case study of Paul de Man's theory machine, Larsen argues that theory in its formerly dominant, poststructuralist instance can only be linked to the social and ideological by reading it qua theory in a more rigorous sense—that is, by questioning whether it *is* theory. Larsen concludes by pointing out that, even in our own putatively posttheoretical moment, high theory's reification of "language" and "textuality" lives on in a more secular form in the case, for example, of "culture" as understood in a neopositivized, posttheoretical cultural studies. If theory is to be wrested from the academostars and the "techno-bureaucratic" elites, it must, in effect, first assume a nonreifying, fully critical stance vis-à-vis the sociohistorical totality.

David Galef's chapter takes a pragmatic approach to the issues facing the next generation. In the eighties, he writes, "Big Theory was at an all-time high . . . [and composition] programs were the unexciting workhorses of the industry, not flashy but dependable and necessary to the enterprise as a whole." For the next generation, however, the situation has changed radically. The "bull market" in theory jobs collapsed, and while the postwar generation's retirement proceeds apace, the projected expansion of job opportunities has not materialized, as the lines are either being closed down altogether or the classes are being filled with part-time lecturers rather than tenure-track professors. Galef, however, sees a further development, and that is the expansion of creative writing, rhetoric, and composition programs. First, the declining writing skills of incoming new students has sparked a significant increase in composition positions. And with this increase also came an increasing professionalization of composition studies: "Paradoxically, theory itself eventually gave composition its boost. For some time now, the way to legitimize a field in our profession has been to accord it serious study, to theorize it." Hence the growth of journals and conferences, indeed, entire departments, devoted to "rhet/comp." But also, the conditions of the profession itself, Galef notes, push us more and more into investigations of rhetoric and composition: "In a time of cutbacks in English departments, universities are nonetheless expanding and diversifying their writing programs." While the *MLA Job List* records fewer and fewer good tenure-track positions in old period categories, each issues boasts "scores of advertisements of posts in comp/rhet." Composition studies and creative writing (also a cash cow for the university, as Galef points out) are, in other words, growth industries, and like all growth industries they will attract more and more bodies who want to take advantage of its job prospects. The future for the next generation, in other words, may lie less in inventing a new theoretical paradigm, but in transforming service-oriented pedagogy into a theoretically sophisticated discipline in its own right.

Barbara Riebling also proposes that the next generation differs from their teachers in that we are drifting away from totalizing political claims and extreme antifoundationalism. Again, this is in good part a result of the collapsed job market. Rather than giving up, "the most characteristic response to this calamity by next generation scholars is to study their situation intently, using every hermeneutic tool at their command to analyze the forces that are crashing in upon them." To Riebling, the moral of Greenblatt's anecdote at the end of *Renaissance Self-Fashioning* about the father of the dying boy is the exact opposite of the one he draws: agency is *real,* and it is becoming an essential part of our criticism. At the same time, however, Riebling asserts that in the future, the next generation will be very careful about its battles: "Under siege from powerful forces, the next generation will be cautious about picking fights both inside and outside the discipline, and they will actively value peace and toleration." This position is not so much a retreat as a cold appraisal of the new realities, as the case of Kalí Tal amply demonstrates.

Susan Johnston worries about agency and its relationship to our ability to make ethical claims. The problem, according to Johnston, is that next generation critics "have inherited a kind of philosophy of despair, a radically nihilistic sense of resignation which goes by the name of postmodernism" which militates against making any kind of ethical argument because "any substantive ethical content perforce reflects and reifies the interests of one group at the expense of another," and she argues against the abandonment of all ethical claims in the wake of the poststructuralist discovery that all such claims are perforce "interested" and "situated." For Johnston, this is an intolerable situation, and she proposes that literary criticism "which explicitly appeals to shared ethical and moral bonds . . . cannot simply be understood as an attempt to reproduce hegemonic interests," adducing Habermas by way of creating an agenda for ethical criticism that builds on rather than repudiates the insights of the previous generation.

The volume concludes with a conversation between the editor and Gerald Graff, who argues that pedagogy constitutes the next generation's opportunity to remake the profession in its own image, and an epilogue by Michael Bérubé, who maps the recent history of criticism onto the recent history of rock and who enjoins the next generation to join various organizations, such as the AAUP or Scholars, Artists, and Writers for Social Justice (SAWSJ) so that next generation will not become the *Last Generation.*

To summarize, for most of the next generation, the job market and the general economic shifts in the North American economy figure as the seminal, shaping experience underlying our criticism, the unspoken warrant of what we choose to highlight about literature. In fact, it might not be exaggerating to say that, for most of us, getting a position will be the trauma that will haunt the rest of our professional lives for two reasons: the wretchedness of the process and, for the successful few (meaning those who have gotten tenure-track positions), the awareness that so many of our friends have not been so lucky.

Second, there is a growing impatience with the rhetorical excesses of the theory wars, perhaps exemplified by one eminent critic's (s/he shall remain anonymous) recent declaration: "Would that . . . we could all just be reasonable, fair-minded, objective. Too much water has passed under the bridge in this controversy for any such happy outcome. One side or the other is going to win out. The only real question, as the old union organizing song has it, is: Which side are you on?" In addition to the fact that the theory wars are not *our* wars,[36] many of us are hyperconscious of how such rhetoric, while perhaps playing well within a certain constituency, only serves to damage our credibility with administrators and those outside the academy as well as endangering our careers.

Third, many next generation critics suggest a return to agency for the professional and contextual reasons outlined above.[37] But at the same time, no one argues for doing away with the important insights of poststructuralist criticism. However, just as the deconstruction of agency and of bourgeois notions of individuality resulted from the manifold contexts of the '60s, the recuperation of agency results from our awareness of the ever-increasing exploitation of part-timers inside the academy and the exploitative labor practices of many multinational corporations outside the academy, just as our awareness of our own commodification reinforces the commitment toward doing politics both through traditional channels and, pedagogy, as well as though literary criticism.

Finally, there is widespread recognition that the next generation can no longer afford the luxury of concentrating exclusively upon scholarship; rather, whether we like it or not—and to be sure, many do not like it—we must combine our critical pursuits with what Swan calls "public work" in order to combat our highly negative public image and the ensuing damage to the institution we have committed our lives to. The next generation must, in other words, become more "public intellectuals" and less private scholars, tending our garden and working on yet another examination of (say) gender or class in our literature of choice. We must also strive, as Swan suggests, to become much more active in internal matters, such as university governance in order to effect change and provide alternatives to the corporatization of the academy, while at the same time continuing our political work outside the academy.

Although the tasks before us are clear, the shape of things to come is not. We are better (or at least I am better), it must be admitted, at diagnosing our situation than presenting a solution. Nonetheless, if the next generation (so far) lacks a blindingly original voice, a "founder of discursivity," as Foucault termed it, if we have yet to produce a Stanley Fish or a Stephen J. Greenblatt, our work elaborates, deepens, and pushes into new directions the previous work of literary criticism. Yet valuable as this work may seem, it might very well be that the task of the next generation lies more in ensuring the continued survival of the humanities. *Hoc opus, hic labor est.*

*Notes*

1. Eagleton, *Literary Theory: An Introduction* (Minneapolis: University of Minnesota Press, 1983), 47–53.

2. According to Michael Quinn, Gerald Gould's "Irony and Satire in *Henry V*" provides the "first full-length assault on the traditional reading of [*Henry V*]," and this article appeared in 1919 ("Introduction," *Shakespeare: Henry V: A Casebook,* ed. Quinn [London: Macmillan, 1989], 18).

3. One of the differences between the next generation and the '60s group is the less than

pervasive sense that the next generation even exists. Some, perhaps even many, do not regard themselves as belonging to a distinct group. My point, however, is that this by itself constitutes a significant difference between the next generation and the '60s critics, who very much regarded themselves as an entity unto themselves.

4. Which is not to say that the newer paradigms have not gone unchallenged, but such texts as Brian Vickers's *Appropriating Shakespeare: Contemporary Critical Quarrels* and Graham Bradshaw's *Misrepresentations: Shakespeare and the Materialists* argue for a return to pretheory days rather than providing a new alternative to, say, Dollimore and Sinfield's work on cultural materialism or Stephen Greenblatt's on cultural poetics. There is also a small but significant number of '90s generation critics who reject the '60s generation criticism as merely "fashionable," a view that would have more force if it were not for the inconvenient fact, brilliantly laid out by Gerald Graff in *Professing Literature: An Institutional History* (Chicago: University of Chicago Press, 198), that the New Criticism and positivist historicism were also once derided as "fashionable." One might call this movement the "new fuddy-duddyism."

5. While my examples here and elsewhere are drawn from early modern studies, since that is my primary area of specialization, they remain representative of more general developments within the field.

6. For example, Eric Mallin asserts that "Shakespeare's plays, which have *until fairly recently* been regarded as antiseptically literary, are in fact thoroughly touched . . . by the elements of the time" (*Inscribing the Time: Shakespeare and the End of Elizabethan England* [Berkeley: University of California Press, 1994], 16; my emphasis). Leaving alone whether or not early modern studies was ever as ahistorical as often thought, my point is that the New Historicism was at least fourteen years old by the time Mallin published this brilliant study. Yet Mallin is also echoing the rhetoric of embattled novelty that one continues to find in very recent theoretically inclined work. For example, in the introduction to her edition of *The First Part of King Henry the Fourth: Texts and Contexts* (Boston: Bedford, 1997), Barbara Hodgdon writes that "the six chapters of this volume . . . reflect both traditional and emergent critical perspectives" (5), by which she means attention to marginalized groups (including but not restricted to women) and to political dissent, neither of which can be fairly characterized as an "emergent"—as opposed to a thoroughly established—critical perspective in 1997.

7. Compare, for example, Waller's 1987 feminist critique of the New Historicism in her famous article, "Academic Tootsie: The Denial of Difference and the Difference It Makes" (*Diacritics* 17 [1987]: 2–20), with Laura Levine's comments in *Men in Women's Clothing: Antitheatricality and Effeminization 1579–1642* (Cambridge: Cambridge University Press, 1994), 8, 11. I am not criticizing Levine, whose work has influenced my own work on antipoetic sentiment, but merely suggesting that she is in this particular instance representative of a common phenomenon.

8. Cohen, "Political Criticism of Shakespeare," *Shakespeare Reproduced: The Text in History and Ideology,* eds. Jean E. Howard and Marion F. O'Connor (New York: Methuen, 1987), 18; Wayne, "Power, Politics, and the Shakespearean Text: Recent Criticism in England and the United States," *Shakespeare Reproduced,* 48.

9. Similarly, the ideas of the so-called conservative revolution of the 1994 elections, which

returned a Republican majority to both the House and the Senate, bear a remarkable resemblance to those bandied about by so-called 1960s radicals. See Lapham, "Reactionary Chic: How the Nineties Right Recycles the Bombast of the Sixties Left" (*Harper's* 290 [March, 1995]: 31–42).

10. As of this writing (December 1999), the decline has slowed somewhat, and the number of positions advertised since 1996–97 is actually somewhat higher (by about 2%) than the nadir of 1993–94. But Huber's conclusions are bleak indeed: "Although the 1995–96 figures suggest a short-term deterioration in the job market, they may also portend longer-term stability. But that stability would be at a low level; the total number of positions advertised in the 1995–96 issues of the *JIL* [the *Job Information List,* probably the most intensely studied text in all literary studies] remains lower than at any time during the late 1970s and early 1980s, when the academic job market was also depressed" ("1995–96 *Job Information List* Figures," *MLA Newsletter* 28.2 [1996]: 1). See also the special supplement, "The Modern Language Job Market: Available Positions and New Degree Recipients," *MLA Newsletter* 29.2 (1997).

11. When I got my Ph.D. in 1990, one was considered significantly lucky to go on the market with a few articles and a bunch of conference papers. Now people are graduating with multiple articles in the best journals and a book, occasionally even multiple books, in hand.

12. "Teaching against the Tradition," *Approaches to Teaching the Metaphysical Poets,* ed. Sidney Gottlieb (New York: MLA, 1990), 35. Patterson does not say whether she was offered the position.

13. Paul de Man, *Blindness and Insight: Essays in the Rhetoric of Contemporary Criticism,* intro. Wlad Godzich (2d ed., revised; Minneapolis: University of Minnesota Press, 1983), 102–103.

14. At the same time, however, the criticism can be unfair as most disciplines have their own language. Very few nonmathematicians could immediately apprehend a paper on differential calculus, and certainly business has developed its own linguistic tics. If "interrogating the phallocentric text" seems mysterious to some, "benchmarking" or "going through several process maps of various functional areas" is equally opaque to me.

15. In the liner notes to his 1994 CD, *Moodswing,* Joshua Redman asserts that he intends his music to combat jazz's stereotype as, to quote the acquaintance whom Redman says epitomizes jazz's bad public image, "complicated and weird. It's for those special types of people who like talking about stuff and figuring things out. Jazz is way too deep for me." Redman writes, "According to popular notion, jazz appears as an elite art form, reserved for a select group of sophisticated (and rather eccentric) intellegensia who rendezvous in secret, underground haunts (or inaccessible ivory towers) to play obselete records, debate absurd theories, smoke pipes and read liner notes. Most people assume that the appreciation of jazz is a long, arduous, and painfully serious cerebral undertaking. Jazz might be good for you, but it just isn't any fun." But rather than emphasizing that jazz forces you to think *and* feel, Redman defends jazz by making the intellectual element entirely secondary: "The intellectual aspects of jazz are ultimately only means to its emotional ends." Although one must sympathize with Redman's desire for a broader audience (i.e., for his desire to make a good living at playing the sax), his giving in to anti-intellectualism is depressing.

16. *MLA Newsletter* 29.2 (1997), 1. Of course, laudable as this effort is, there is still a sense of preaching to the converted in contributing to National Public Radio. Appearing on Oprah would probably reach a more crucial audience.

17. David Scott Kastan calls this movement "the New Boredom" ("Shakespeare after Theory," *Opening the Borders: Early Modern Studies and the New Inclusivism: Essays in Honor of James V. Mirollo,* ed. Peter C. Herman (Newark: University of Delaware Press 1999), 212.

18. In an interview with Peter Watrous, McBride makes explicit the assimilative, as opposed to innovative, nature of his music: "I might want to play some plucked bass the way Milt Hinton did it in Cab Calloway's band, and then turn around and play 'Bitches Brew,'" he said, referring to one of Miles Davis's albums from the '70s [which is credited with first combining rock with jazz]. "I just try [to] voice all the things I've learned in the jazz language, infuse the music with James Brown, but never let the music sound like plain funk" (Watrous, "Bassist Mixes the Virtues of Youth and Maturity," *The New York Times* (7 March 1995), B3.

19. It could be argued that this is also constitutive of postmodernism. The difference is that postmodernism tends to remain a collection of fragments, however artfully combined (e.g., John Zorn's music), whereas Marsalis and his followers play music that is unified and completely accessible.

20. *The Poetics of English Nationhood: 1590–1612* (Cambridge: Cambridge University Press, 1997). All references are given parenthetically.

21. See E. M. W. Tillyard *The Elizabethan World Picture: A Study of the Idea of Order in the Age of Shakepseare, Donne, and Milton* (Rpt. Harmondsworth: Penguin, 1963), first published in 1943; and C. S. Lewis, *English Literature in the Sixteenth Century, Excluding Drama* (Oxford: Oxford University Press, 1953). On Lewis's nostalgia, see Peter C. Herman, "Rethinking the Henrician Era," in *Rethinking the Henrician Era: Essays on Early Tudor Texts and Contexts* (Champaign: University of Illinois Press, 1994), 2–3, and on Tillyard, see Jonthan Dollimore, "Introduction: Shakespeare, Cultural Materialsim, and the New Historicism," *Political Shakespeare: New Essays in Cultural Materialism,* eds., Dollimore and Alan Sinfield (Ithaca: Cornell University Press, 1985), 4–7.

22. John Guillory, *Cultural Capital: The Problem of Literary Canon Formation* (Chicago: University of Chicago Press, 1993), 45.

23. *Los Angeles Times Magazine* 19 January 1997, 10. On the corporatization of the academy, see the brilliant treatment by the late Bill Readings, *The University in Ruins* (Cambridge, Mass.; Harvard University Press, 1996). Readings discusses how "the then-Chancellor, Melvin Eggers, repeatedly characterized Syracuse [University] as an aggresive institution that modeled itself on the corporation rather than clinging to ivy-covered walls" (10). Also, the position description for the chancellor of the CSU system asserts that "The Chancellor is the chief executive officer of the university system." Nor need the chancellor/CEO have an academic record, let alone a distinguished one. Instead, "The successful candidate should demonstrate an understanding of the teaching/learning process, scholarship, creative activities, and public service as these activities relate to the needs of a diverse student clientele." Excellence is restricted to "demonstrated success in management skills that relate to diverse constituencies and responsibilities."

24. Speech given at California Polytechnic, San Luis Obispo, 17 March 1999 (http://

www.calpoly.edu/~communic/news-releases/ltrs-speech.html; I have retained a hard copy should this link be erased).

25. For example, the CSU system recently attempted to "partner" with a number of technology firms (including Microsoft) in order to ensure that "every student, every faculty member and every staff member will have access to information technology in her or his CSU environment." The benefit for the private sector includes "access to a large number of prospective customers (who might also serve as a test population)" (these quotes are from a memo put out by the California State University's office of Integrated Technology Strategy [ITS]). Ex-chancellor Barry Munitz endorsed this project for the following reason: "When we put our 23 campuses together to partner with industry, we offer a third of a million students and their parents, 40,000 employees and two million alumni. . . . That's a larger collaborative package than any organization in the country can offer and it's very attractive to industry" (internal memo posted on Calfolk, 5/21/97; see the website at http://www.calstate.edu/its.sit/itp_sip.html). That students, let alone their parents, might not have considered being offered as a target audience for marketing campaigns as part of a university education does not seem to be an issue. Fortunately, in the face of considerable opposition from faculty and students as well as the corporations' unwillingness to shoulder a greater burden of the financial risk, the proposal has since been abandoned. Even so, it is unlikely that we have seen the end of such ventures. See also David F. Noble, "Digital Diploma Mills: The Automation of Higher Education," *Monthly Review* 49.9 (1998): 38–52.

26. This topic has generated its own bibliography. See, for example, Lydia Belatèche, "Temp Prof: Practicing the Profession off the Tenure Track," *Profession* (1994): 64–66; Katherine Kolb, "Adjuncts in Academe: No Place Called Home," *Profession* (1997): 93–103; and *Will Teach for Food: Academic Labor in Crisis,* ed. Cary Nelson (Minneapolis: University of Minnesota Press, 1997).

27. Reed renders this implication explicit when he said, concerning California's growing lack of primary and secondary school teachers, "We have to produce more teachers and we set a goal and it has a timeline and a number on it that by July 2000 we will increase our production of teachers by 3,000. We're currently producing 12,000 teachers annually, we're going to go to 15,000. When we get to 15,000 in July 2000, then I'm going to raise the bar again" (speech given at Cal Poly, San Luis Obispo).

28. Once more, according to Barry Munitz, "you simply don't have to build a traditional library these days," assuming that the Internet has "made the library as obsolete as the wooly mammoth" (quoted in *American Libraries* 26.10 [1995], 1016). As a result, there is a freeze on building new libraries in the California State University system. By way of contrast, there is no such freeze for the University of California.

29. Rothstein, "Technology: Gates's largesse stirs a discomfiting question: Is there indeed a computer literacy?" *The New York Times,* July 7, 1997, C3.

30. See David F. Noble, "Digital Diploma Mills, Part II: The Coming Battle over Online Instruction," forthcoming in *Sociological Perspectives* 41.4, also available at http://communication.ucsd.edu/dl/ddm2.html.

31. Rick Perlstein, "Desert Storm," *Lingua Franca* 7.8 (October, 1997): 11.

32. As evidence, here are two local examples that, I believe, are representative of this larger trend. In a memorandum dated Sept. 16, 1997, inviting nominations for the Performance Salary Step Increase (PSSI: pronounced—believe it or not and coined without any apparent irony—"pissy") committee, the Dean of the College of Arts and Letters at San Diego State University explains that "the criteria for awarding a PSSI are not a duplicate of the RTP [Research Tenure Promotion] process. Faculty whose outstanding or meritorious performance *has been in areas less traditionally recognized as valuable (such as community activity, advising, and development) will be given the same chance of being awarded a PSSI as those who are distinguished by excellent teaching and/or scholarship.* Accordingly, it may be the case that awards will be granted to some faculty who have not demonstrated as accomplished a record of professional growth as faculty who have applied but did not receive an award" (my emphasis). Also, in an op-ed, the president of California State University, San Marcos, asserts that "The role of the professoriate is changing—willingly or not—from the perspective of the faculty member to the demand of the student/customer. *This change will include teaching as a focus, not as a secondary activity adjunct to research. In addition, the rules for advancement within the profesion will also change*" (*San Diego Union-Tribune* 5 August 1998, B-5; my emphasis).

33. Quoted in *The Chronicle of Higher Education,* December 5, 1997, A41.

34. For example, in a letter to the editor on "Expanding Job Opportunities, " Jesse Swan, who identifies himself as "a third-year assistant professor of English at a state-supported liberal arts university," argues that we must argue against the increasing use of part-time faculty "using language that accomodates the requirements of public discourse" *MLA Newsletter* 29.2 (1997): 16.

35. "The further text of Proust's novel, for example responds perfectly to an extended application of this pattern. . . . The whole of literature would respond in similar fashion, although the techniques and the patterns would have to vary considerably, of course, from author to author. But there is absolutely no reason why analyses of the kind here suggested for Proust would not be applicable, with proper modifications of technique, to Milton or to Dante or to Hölderlin. This will in fact be the task of literary criticism in the coming years" (de Man, "Semiology and Rhetoric," *Allegories of Reading: Figural Language in Rousseau, Nietzsche, Rilke and Proust* [New Haven: Yale University Press, 1979], 16–17). Such pronounements were not restricted to deconstruction. Fredric Jameson, for example, begins *The Political Unconscious: Narrative as a Socially Symbolic Act* (Ithaca: Cornell University Press, 1981), with an even more forceful command: "Always historicize! This slogan—the one absolute and we may even say 'transhistorical' imperative of all dialectical thought—will unsurprisingly turn out to be the moral of *The Political Unconscious* as well" (9).

36. For example, when I took a seminar on the politics of sixteenth-century literature with Constance Jordan, she began the class by giving us all sorts of complicated essays by Quentin Skinner and others, arguing, essentially, that to understand the literature of the period we had to take history into account. After awhile I raised my hand and with great trepidation asked who had argued otherwise. I thought I was asking an idiotic question, but Prof. Jordan was amazed and pleased that what for her was still a highly controversial position, having done her graduate work at a place where historicized criticism was not encouraged, for the class consti-

tuted an assumed fact. For us, reading Renaissance literature without taking into account history would be like studying fish without noticing that they live in water.

37. As such, the reappearance of the individual subject may suggest a waning of the postmodernist moment, as described by Fredric Jameson in *Postmodernism; Or, the Cultural Logic of Late Capitalism* (Durham: Duke University Press, 1991), 10–17.

# ONE

# THE POSTTHEORY GENERATION

## *Jeffrey Williams*

### My Ge-Ge-Generation

We're in a strange place. We—that is, those in the postsixties but pre-Gen X generation, and who work in the profession of literature—find ourselves facing a confused and ambivalent scene of literary studies, defined for the most part by two looming factors: first, what seems to be the dispersion or breakdown of the paradigm of Theory;[1] and second, a drastically reconfigured job market, pinched in the vice of a restructured and downsizing university.[2] It is the interrelation of these two factors that distinctively marks what I'll call the "Posttheory Generation," the generation of intellectual workers who have entered the literary field and attained professional positions in the late 1980s and through the 1990s.[3]

I would normally relish this kind of manifesto for my generation, but, while heady, it taps into a series of stock tropes and clichés that do not quite accurately represent our situation. It carries with it associations of adolescent rebellion (à la James Dean or Jerry Rubin), providing a cheap shot of Oedipal displacement, clearing space to announce oneself and one's own place in the field. However, this change is not something that we have announced or precipitated, but something which has befallen us. Further, it invokes tropes of natural biological cycles that have questionable application to the institutional structures of intellectual work. And it also takes a glib note from advertising, promoting the new-and-improved way of doing things, the latest product on the shelf of literary study.

I use *generation* in an alternate sense, beyond simply an age label or product advertisement, and beyond staging a faux rebellion I'm fixed to win. I take it as an institutional demarcation, recording and diagnosing our institutional formation. Academic intellectuals are formed by similar, historically specific institutional circumstances and thus exhibit similar traits, which generate distinctive groupings that one might call "generations." Those circumstances encode professional modes, manners, discourses, concerns, and protocols as decisively as DNA. A generation might be fixed by general coordinates such as the extant critical conversation and time period, the state of the professional field, and the state of the university, as well as local coordinates such as institutional affiliation, professional connections, and mentors and teachers. Local generational markers—bluntly, who went where, when, and worked with whom—are usually consigned to trivial or peripheral status, circulated by gossip, gleaned in book acknowledgments or blurbs or picked up in anecdotes ("I played basketball with Stanley Fish, and he said . . ."), but in fact very literally distinguish those

academics and have distinctive force in constructing and disseminating specific methods and practices and in maintaining hierarchical relations.[4] They mark those coming into the profession with a set of filial resemblances and a particular lineage. More
general contextual factors such as the constitution of the professional field and the social function and value of the university also distinguish particular academic generations, defining the role of academic intellectuals—as teachers as opposed to researchers,
as bespectacled bookworms as opposed to "public intellectuals," or as men of letters
as opposed to new age, technocultural theorists. As Regis Debray points out, the role
of the intellectual has shifted significantly through the course of this century, from
teacher to writer to celebrity. Transposing Debray's formulation to the present American lit crit scene, one might say that the model of the literary intellectual has migrated
from teacher and scholar to master critic or theorist to culture critic and intellectual
celebrity—for instance, from R. S. Crane to Paul de Man to Andrew Ross or bell
hooks.[5] To put this another way, the apex of an academic-intellectual career has shifted
from teacher to researcher to star.

    In some ways, this sense of generation spins off Bourdieu's seminal concept,
the *habitus,* which he defines as "a system of dispositions common to all products of
the same conditionings" ("Structures" 59). What you learn in graduate school, perhaps more formatively than purported texts or canons of knowledge, is precisely this
system of dispositions, this code of appropriate professional behavior, expectation,
and evaluation. One might summarize it under the rubric of tenure—that is, the protocols and professional assumptions that circulate around the spectral image of tenure,
that enforce a certain standard of behavior, mode and choice of work, and mindset
for those employed in academic departments.[6] However, within the generative structure of the professional habitus, there occurs a range of differentiation of professional
position and purview. For instance, senior colleagues entering literature departments
post–World War II encountered and were formed by entirely different professional
pressures, expectations, and goals than those entering c. 1990. While that historically
particular grouping—for the most part those schooled under the GI Bill and landing
jobs during the mushrooming of state universities—shares the same habitus and professional field as more recent generations, their professional expectations and horizon
differ precipitously from those who entered the profession through the sixties and seventies, and further still from those who have entered the profession through the late
eighties and nineties. Given the exponential increase in research requirements, in the
sheer number of publications to get tenure or even to land a job, it hardly seems as if
that earlier generation is in the same profession from the standpoint of members of
the posttheory generation.

    I use the slightly ungainly term *posttheory* to define this generation to indicate
both its position in the history of critical practices—its seeming lateness on the scene,
coming after the monumental successes and ensuing establishment of the great Theories—and its position in the contemporary university, coming after the post-Fordist
reconfiguration of the university and in the midst of a job-traumatized field.[7] Thus
"posttheory" indicates the institutional position and prospect of this generation, both

as a by-now established practice and institutional form and as a shorthand for the historical coordinates of the late-twentieth-century profession of literature. Theory is not only a mode of discourse or the philosophical tenets of critical commentary, but designates what happened in and to the institution of literature roughly between 1970 and 1990. By extension, I suppose one could depict the sixties generation that came to the academy—so-called tenured radicals—as "the theory generation," since that generation marks the absorption of theory into the academy and the complex of changes signalled by the advent of theory.[8]

## The Way It Was

Once upon a time, in the halcyon days after World War II, it was a comfortable—one imagines pipe-smoking, tweed-wearing, sherry-drinking—profession. A beneficiary of the post–World War II welfare state, the profession stood witness to the PMC (the professional-managerial class) dream, an updated version of the good old American Dream. One could get a decent, federally subsidized education, bank a bit of cultural capital, and then be granted a genteel, manicured-lawn, middle-class life. Jobs were plentiful, and one only needed to be a live (white, male) body with basic motor functions to get an academic position through the '50s and '60s. Lest this seem too much of an exaggeration, George Levine recalls of his generation: "We were less troubled in the fifties at the very moment when English and higher education were experiencing their most rapid and rich expansions ever. When I got my degree from the University of Minnesota, *almost all my colleagues, no matter how dumb they were, got at least three job offers*" (my italics; 43). The university was a booming business, both ideologically and materially, fuelling the Fordist dream as a subsidiary venture of the military-industrial complex.

Wayne Booth, in a reminiscence of his several decades in the profession featured in *PMLA,* gives another revealing view of what it was like to work in that halcyon once-upon-a-time. He tells a remarkable story about his job search, which prompted him to move from an untenured job at Haverford to a tenured one at Earlham:

> When I talked with the president of Earlham about becoming head of the English department [after three years at Haverford], I said, "I assume this will include tenure?"
>
> "Of course," he replied, and the subject left my mind for several years. . . . Would that all young teachers could have the gift of those "several years"—I honestly cannot remember how many—to settle in, relax, think, plan without pressure, and then, if and only if they really want to, produce a repeatedly revised and rethought book, as I released The Rhetoric of Fiction at age forty. I chose to write that book, taking seven years to make all the choices it entailed—not counting the years that went into the dissertation, fragments of which survived in the book. (946)

In light of the current job crisis and the meaner-leaner years of the retraction of the welfare state, this story now seems vaguely fantastical, but it succinctly characterizes the experience of the earlier generation. Due to the expansion of universities—state universities, such as the State University of New York or California system, as well as private universities, which also benefitted greatly during this period—through the massive infusion of research and development money in the wake of wartime industrial expansion and the carryover into Cold War growth, there was an extraordinarily high demand for new Ph.D.'s, and there was a disproportionately high number of jobs for prospective candidates. Booth, to his credit, tells this story not as a nostalgic reminiscence but as an occasion to launch a series of proposals to remedy the fallout from present academic speed-up and the draconian pressure to publish.

Beyond what it tells about the job market, what is also revealing about this story is the effect it had on his research, or rather the model of research that is promulgated by the institutional conditions he describes. First, there is no dire necessity to publish; Booth's project is not regulated by the timeline of tenure, but the result of leisurely reflection. In other words, it is relatively disinterested since it is detached from the exigencies of employment—in blunt terms, from fear of losing a job. Further, the kind of big book that Booth wrote—which was a large-scale, comprehensive statement on novels, holding a certain provenance over the field and staying in print for nearly thirty years—is hardly feasible or practicable under current professional conditions, particularly not for junior faculty. The elite model in literary research was this kind of big book that made a comprehensive statement on a genre, or on a literary period, or on a literary problem, and that assumed an encyclopedic range of literary reference and a definitive span of investigation. Think of the various influential critical books of the period—M. H. Abrams's *The Mirror and the Lamp,* Angus Fletcher's *Allegory,* D. W. Robertson's *Preface to Chaucer,* and so on—which stood as standardbearers for decades.

Under current conditions of productivity, it goes almost without saying that someone from the posttheory generation could never take ten or fifteen years to finish a book, particularly a first book, and expect to keep his or her job. Rather, the commonplace rule of the game is that one needs at least one book (and frequently a second on the way) to get tenure, as well as articles, conference presentations, and other recognizable if token markers of professional accreditation. My point here is that the exigencies of the job market influence, if not determine, the nature of legitimate and appropriate research (to more obviously sexy, which is to say marketable, topics, such as crossdressing rather than Chaucer's sources) and the scope and depth of a research project (now the typical book is usually a compendium of essays, rather than a monograph on, say, Herbert). This accelerated cycle of production ups the ante on publications and reputation, again particularly for the untenured but also applying to those with it, since you need to maintain a certain level of "visibility"—one's name frequently and prominently attached to articles and books—to maintain standing.

Further, given the current cycle of intense competition and by extension overproduction of scholarship, there is a parallel speed-up of reception and effect—of intellectual shelf life and durability. Contemporary literary scholarship hardly exists for the ages but is extraordinarily transitory and impermanent, with an average life expectancy or relevance of only a few years. This in turn influences the cycling of critical approaches and theoretical models, which move through the scene within a few years (for instance, whatever happened to reader response? and even now, one hears of "post-Butler" work). In a certain determinative sense, these changes are linked to the increasing capitalization of academic publishing; as financially pinched universities cut subsidies and other forms of support (such as office space), university presses are under a great deal more pressure to publish profit-making titles in place of the traditional scholarly staple, the (subsidized) monograph. They take their model from commercial presses, emulating the early nineties zenith of Routledge with its array of sexily jacketed, trendsetting, and profitmaking books in theory and cultural studies, books that might not stay in print for more than three or four years, after their returns fall below margin. Disposability has become the rule rather than the exception, spurred by structural changes in publishing, such as recent changes in tax depreciation laws, so that presses rarely keep books in print longer than a few years, if that.[9]

## THE DESCENT OF THEORY

The posttheory generation is paradoxically positioned, intensely theoretical, and versed in theoretical concerns, while at the same time comprising the generation *after* theory, that is, after the theoretical debates and wars of the 1970s among deconstructive, marxist, feminist, reader-response, psychoanalytic, and structuralist camps that dominated the field and transformed normal practice in literary studies. They pitted themselves against the bogeyman of the new criticism and more staid "traditional" scholarly methods and approaches. To construct a sort of genealogy, the teachers of those in the posttheory generation most likely served in the theory wars, so for the posttheory generation that war loomed in the background like pictures in a scrapbook, bespeaking excitement and passion but no longer carrying a sense of immediate action or danger.

   Those in the posttheory generation might have been students of the theory gods and gurus, of the major figures of the advent of the epoch of theory—people like Stanley Fish, Hillis Miller, Paul de Man, Edward Said, Elaine Showalter, or Fredric Jameson, all of whom have taught a number of identifiable students—or students of their students—say, of Eve Sedgwick or many other less established figures who had bitten the theory bullet[10]—or finally students of those who simply recognized the professional dominance and exigent force of theory, cynically or conscientiously, so that it became a tacit requirement for a dissertation or an article that it take a theoretical label, naming its theory in the first chapter. In short, the posttheory generation was taught to *take theory*—not traditional scholarly methods, not normal practical criticism—*for granted,* and theory in turn provided a threshold stamp of professional value.[11]

In part because of the institutional position and relative symbolic capital of those who espoused the turn to theory, and because of the institutional needs that theory fulfilled, within a number of years theory and its terms, discourses, moves, and mannerisms became established and part of the expected terrain of graduate school training. You learned to talk the theoretical talk to walk the professional walk. By the late eighties, theory was readily dispensed, if not on street corners, in the spate of theory anthologies, primers, book series, ad infinitum (see Williams, "Packaging"). Theory went from rags to riches, from scratching at the window to owner of the mansion; it went from being a technical pursuit like bibliographical theory that only a few people did to attaining canonical status as a graduate school litmus test and as a minimum stamp of acceptability for publication. In short, it became the measure for professional accreditation.

Until about 1940 the dominant professional justification of the field was scholarship—literary history, the residual effects of philology, and so on.[12] The programmatic turn represented by the new critics and the Chicago critics occurred precisely in the face of the methods and concerns of the then-normal method—in the sense that Thomas Kuhn uses when he speaks of "normal science"—of historical scholarship. The twin documents, R. S. Crane's polemic for the importance of criticism, "History vs. Criticism in the Study of Literature," and John Crowe Ransom's manifesto for the professional priority of criticism, "Criticism, Inc.," argue explicitly to displace scholarship and announce the epoch of criticism and the practice of close reading. Criticism, in this moment, was envalued as the prestige and "natural" practice of literary studies—rather than history, textual scholarship, literary history, biography, or appreciation.

Following on this, one way to see Paul de Man's more programmatic statements on theory are not as arguments about theoretical issues such as interpretation, allegory, or literariness, but as polemics competing for presitge in and provenance over the literary field. For instance, "The Resistance to Theory" not only argues for the inherent inconsistencies of theoretical practices but rhetorically casts the entrenchment of theory as inevitable and competing pursuits as neurotic symptoms. Its polemic is directed at displacing the previously established practice of close reading for the sake of theory, as well as to elevate deconstruction among the menu of choices of extant theories, particularly history. The early texts of the theory years—by Derrida, Cixous, Fish, Kolodny, Jameson, and so on—frequently invoke this polemic for the new moment and project of theory, as well as their particular versions of theory, announcing the grand sweep of their revisions of Western metaphysics, patriarchy, interpretation, the sexist canon, class, and so on. To borrow a term from science referring to largescale projects like the Supercollider as "big science" (see Weinberg), I would call this the moment of "big theory," to connote not only the ambitousness of its conceptual sweep, but also the prominence of its institutional placement.

To invoke another sense of generation—analogous to computer generations, to stages of product development rather than biological supercession—the posttheory generation registers a shift in mainstream lit crit, from the armature of dense theoretical machinery and formulations to more flexible and streamlined second- and third-generation theoretical elaborations. More recently, the aggregate practices of cultural studies, lesbigay studies, race studies, and so forth, mark a new moment for the critical field, a shift in normal scholarly or critical work to the various and microspecified configurations of "studies" areas, in general from big theory to little theories.

Typically, the history of theory is drawn on the lines of the history of philosophy or of ideas, as a grand and usually victorious parade of ideas and discoveries transacted somewhere in the metaphysical ether and concretized in anthologies, primers, and introductory histories as a disembodied series of texts and arguments. However, this other sense of theory underscores its shifting professional-institutional uses and functions. Institutionally, the move to "criticism" and the methods of close reading offered a transferrable technique for the newly expanded, post–World War II university, a technique that was far more amenable and adaptable pedagogically than the older, more cumbersome memory and fact-based model of historical scholarship and philology. Gerald Graff explains in his account of the institution, *Professing Literature:* "As the university increased in size, the need arose for a simplified pedagogy, encouraging the detachment of 'close reading' from . . . cultural purposes . . . [placing] a premium on methods that . . . could easily be replicated" (145). Formalism provided a model of technological efficiency and fulfilled a new institutional need. Its success and entrenchment, in other words, derived from its socioinstitutional situation.

From the late 1960s through the 1970s, in the era of fattened research dollars, theory provided literature departments with a high-tech research agenda (see Guillory). Rather than the pedagogical need spurred by the massive infusion of new students into the post–World War II university, Theory responded to the research need of what Clark Kerr called the "multiversity." In the contest of the faculties within the university, a contest not only over the philosophical bases of disciplines but over funding, theory issued a revamped rationale for the humanities beyond the appreciative and essentially belletristic rationales of previous modes. (Whatever its technical mastery, the new criticism was based finally on the apostrophic appreciation of poetry). In the heyday of structuralism, it reconfigured the humanities as part of the "human sciences" (to recall a common phrase of the time that we don't hear anymore), and thus reassured the intrainstitutional prestige of literature departments, particularly in the face of the growing predominance of the social sciences, which adopted largely quantitative and quasi-scientific methods.[13] Literature departments took the position that philosophy historically held as a master discipline, spearheading the "human sciences" in the United States and exporting methods and knowledges to other disciplines.

To bring the theory story up to date, the recent turn from high theory to cultural criticism, and from characterizing ourselves as theorists to public intellectuals, indicates not so much the "exhaustion" of theory or a revival of social conscience; rather, it responds to a shift in the role of the university, to the defunding of welfare state entitlements such as education, and to imperatives for "accountability" of public institutions. Supplanting the internal rationale that theory provided when the university's public position was relatively assured, cultural criticism projects a more public rationale, putatively shedding the obscurity and internecine interest of theory. The stakes of this shift are the topic of the last section of this chapter.

The foregoing narrative of the contemporary critical field is admittedly schematic; to be accurate, different modes of critical practice are ongoing at the same time, some scholars still doing traditional historical research, some bibliographies, some close readings of literary texts, some high theory, and some have been doing "public" criticism all along. Still, the dominance of one particular model over others registers our professional position and its institutional warrants. As Bruce Robbins puts it: "Criticism is our work and its history is in a sense our collective professional autobiography" (780). The dominant image of inquiry and practice offers a self-justifying rationale for the profession and discipline, for its existence and value, and legitimates preferred research agendas—like preferred stock—that fulfill its institutional mandate. Philology now yields low residuals, but cultural criticism and its claims for public relevance yields high.

## TRICKLE-DOWN THEORY

Theory sometimes gets a bad rap, as obfuscatory, hyperspecialized, and elitist. In this view, it overwhelms if not ruins literary studies with an obscure, jargon-ridden langauge that hardly anyone can understand. It is taken as a fall away from public accessibility or relevance, not to say from sheer communicability. Ironically, however, there is a different way to see theory: in a certain sense, through the 1970s and 1980s it served as the lingua franca of literature programs. Its establishment provided a common language, a common component of education, and a common filter through which to frame discussions in literary studies, so that people divided by the fences of their particular fields of specialization could communicate, particularly in the expanded university that fostered the splitting off and compartmentalization of subfields.[14] One became a hyperspecialized medievalist or Romanticist, most likely dealing with a few figures and from a particular angle (women in Old English poems or the new historical background of Wordsworth poems), rather than a generalist. Theory provided a kind of new generalism, supplanting what had once been the literature curriculum (see Guillory), a bridge over which specialists could communicate across fields. No doubt this common language is a decidedly professional one that functions as a threshold or credentializing device for legitimate critical work—you cannot publish a critical essay without cognizance of theory and the extant "critical conversation," as it is called—but, within its institutional precincts, theory comprised a common channel of communication that hip scholars tuned in to.

Circa 1970 or thereabouts, Theory carried a revolutionary vista, to retool the previous mode and manner of criticial practice, to recast the canon, to reconfigure literature programs and university structures, and more generally to transform the retrograde institution of what had been known as Western civilization. As I mentioned earlier, its stated aims, depending on the theoretical camp one joined, were to subvert Western metaphysics, as Derrida rather grandly put it, and its attendant ideologies, such as Enlightenment rationalism, capitalism, and patriarchy. The "big theory" projects of those years—the litany again, deconstruction, feminism, marxism, reader response, etc.—were polemical nodal points, aligning those in literary studies in various camps with loyalty to specific theoretical critiques—of epistemology, of sexist oppression, of class oppression, of interpretation, and so on. As Terry Eagleton puts it, "I think that back in the seventies we used to suffer from a certain fetishism of method; we used to think that we have to get a certain kind of systematic method right, and this would be *the* way of proceeding" (*Significance of Theory* 76).

If big theory functioned as manifesto and declaration of theoretical commitment and a vehicle of contest, as an oppositional device for the theory generation to displace previous modes of criticism, the clichéd tenets of philosophy, and the humanistic rationale of the university, for the posttheory generation it serves a different purpose, more as an already accepted background, a language that has been assimilated and imbricated in not only the discourse but the possibilities and ways issues are framed in literary studies. The broad commitments entailed by particular theoretical camps and affiliations (say, to the redistribution of wealth or the overthrow of patriarchy) have dispersed to provisional, localized, pragamatic interventions, rather than building to or drawing from a systematic critique. Posttheory, as represented in the broad range of cultural studies and organized by various modalities of identity, and as represented in the array of what Mas'ud Zavarzadeh calls "post-alities," such as postmarxism or postfeminism, represents the balkanization of the prospects of theory.

Recent critical work recombines and reworks older theoretical positions, developing less exclusionary, more eclectic and flexible hybrids. For instance, the deconstructive critique of center and margin underwrites the general project of postcolonialism—impossible to think of without the conceptual mediation of the "Other"—at the same time that it also draws on the marxist critique of power and imperialism. And postcolonial studies are frequently rooted in specific historical instances and places, in local situations rather than global ones. Or the feminist distinction of sex and gender combined with the poststructural battle cry of antiessentialism has morphed to gender studies and underwrites lesbigay studies. Rather than being unified by a single-minded front and a common cause, the project of feminism, as some senior feminists have lamented, has fractured to multiple feminisms.[15]

In a sense, to paraphrase a Rortian phrase, the current moment registers the breakdown of the "dream of theory," that theory form a consistent system through which to describe the world. And there is a way in which these current modes of critical practice mark the end or "death" of theory, as has been proclaimed in a number of places.[16] However, more subtly and deeply, the moves and gestures of theory nonetheless permeate and spectrally inform practice. As Derrida himself puts it in a recent interview, to say deconstruction is dead is akin to saying that Freudian psychoanalysis is dead. As Derrida explains, there is a way in which deconstruction, as an academic fashion, has waned, but "psychoanalysis has taught that the dead—a dead parent, for example—can be more alive for us, more powerful . . . than the living" (qtd. in Stephens 23–24).

Rather than being based on the paradigm of an overruling concept or structure of thought (sex, class, epistemology, and so on), posttheory takes a more adaptive and less contestatory tenor, borrowing from various theoretical camps in a way that previously would have been inconceivable. On the one hand, it is conceptually less dogmatic, but on the other hand, more amorphous than big theory. For instance, it seems to have trickled down to the loosely allied focuses of study affiliated with or defined by identity politics, the prolific and active individual critical practices of what I'll call identity studies. I would provisionally characterize identity studies along the lines of three axes: (1) sex, those researches defined by sex, by sexual orientation or gender, which encompasses women's studies, gay and lesbian studies, the new and seemingly reactive men's or masculine studies, the more neutral gender studies, transsexual studies and work on cross-dressing (sometimes called genderfuck), pornography studies, and so on, as well as versions of feminism; (2) race, those researches defined by race or ethnicity, such as African American studies, Asian American studies, Chicano studies, Native American studies, the more general ethnic studies, Jewish studies (and attendant substudy areas, such as Holocaust studies), of late whiteness studies or what is sometimes called "the new abolitionism," and so on; and (3) place, those researches determined by location or national affiliation, such as Caribbean studies, New Zealand studies, Canadian studies, Pacific Rim studies, and old standbys such as American studies, as well as the more generic postcolonial or subaltern studies.

In this sorting to the various subfields of identity studies, the project of posttheory seems to have shifted to localized units of production, similar to microbreweries, away from large-scale, totalizing concepts such as class, or race or sex for that matter. This shift might be located within the context of larger historical forces (say, the end of communism, claimed by some to consign Marxism to the ash heap) and parallels the rise of contemporary identity politics, which seems to have balkanized the Left and any sort of large-scale Left project. However, for the most part the move to posttheory and microspecified uses of theory bespeaks hyperspecialization and differentiation, which mirrors contemporary corporate employment alignments that are "flat" or horizontal rather than vertical. In the way that the workplace has been further cellularized and winnowed out, theory has been flattened and diffused along these axes rather than clustered around an organizing focus. Each interest takes a microtheory of its own, rather than feeding to a larger totality.

There is also an alternative sense in which theory has trickled down or been diffused: because of the intense overproduction of Ph.D.s, those highly trained in elite graduate programs have gotten jobs at places like East Podunk University or West Jesus State College and therefore carry their professional formation and makeup to schools formerly without significant access to elite professional operations. Academic institutions are organized on a kind of stepladder hierarchy that might be divided into five stages: high elite institutions (Harvard and the rest of the Ivies, Stanford, Chicago, Duke, etc.); elite (eminent programs not quite up to the first rank, such as Emory, or distinguished state universities, such as University of Wisconsin or Rutgers); semielite (somewhat distinguished state universities such as SUNY–Binghamton); common (most likely state universities like Northern Illinois University, as opposed to Illinois proper); and refugee (the Podunk schools).[17] Most often, hiring is done on a kind of status formula, whereby the candidate would most likely be hired at a level lower than where s/he was trained. In other words, someone from Yale might get a job at Michigan, but it almost never works the other way around. In the current job market, those in the posttheory generation have frequently placed several levels lower in the hierarchy, if they have managed to land a full-time job at all. On the one hand, this has destabilized the system of institutional status and reward, belying its tacit premise of merit. On the other hand, it has intensified the system of institutional status—a kind of dustbowl effect—putting a premium on any sort of insitutional purchase. The fallout from this has the strange side effect of professionalizing the provinces, those places that otherwise would have never seen the likes of hotshots from Duke nor heard much about the posttheoretical baggage they carry with them in the previous job market. This has not only served to spread theory throughout the land, but it also serves paradoxically to level the class function of theory as a hieratic language. It has reconfigured theory from being an elite professional marker to becoming commonplace, an expected horizon and mode of discourse in the canon of the literature department.

## PUBLIC MAKEOVER

The institutional purpose that theory once served, to legitimate the field of literary studies largely within the post-Sputnik, boomer university and upgrade its professional status, is no longer as necessary or urgent as it had once been. That is, theory delivers different goods in the present socioinstitutional milieu. As mentioned earlier big theory provided a hyperprofessionalist rationale for the importance of literary studies or, more exactly, literature *departments,* shoring their relative position within the context of the university; now, however, the advertised preferred stock of cultural criticism and particularly public criticism—underwritten by the developments of theory but broached in more accessible terms and geared to a more general, educated if not belletristic audience—answers a demand for an overt public rationale, as a channel to justify literature departments to a public at large in a time of budget cuts, questions of accountability, and doubts about the relevance, cost effectiveness, and value of higher education. The PC debates of the early 1990s registered a crisis of legitimacy for the university and its social role, and especially for the humanities, a crisis that public, cultural criticism answers in a way that theory couldn't.[18]

The work of Michael Bérubé stands as a prominent example of the public turn in criticism in the 1990s, in both his persistent call for more public accessibility for criticism in the essays collected in the aptly named *Public Access,* and the example of his various pieces in wide circulation journals such as *The New Yorker, Village Voice, Harper's,* and the like.[19] It's no accident that Bérubé first made his name with his essays on the PC controversy rather than, say, his more scholarly work on reception theory; Bérubé's semijournalistic, hip-toned, and theoretically informed writing filled a particular space, as an academic crossover, to represent narrowly academic disourses in official channels of PMC culture, like *The New Yorker.*

The model that Bérubé proposes to counter threats to the humanities is "bite-sizing" theory, making our research more popular, easier to digest, and more marketable to a broader audience (161–78). Bérubé exhorts those of us in the humanities: "The PC wars should have taught us one lesson—namely, that if we don't popularize academic work it will be popularized for us" (163). Thus, we should restate and summarize extant work for a general audience (167). Bérubé's prescription carries a kind of Henry Ford no-nonsense sensibility that is hard to argue with; it would no doubt be a good thing if our writing were better, and if we got the word out about what we do, especially to dispel what seem caricatural misunderstandings of our work.

However, in a different sense, Bérubé's argument also works as a professionalist jeremiad (it's last line is "Profession, revise thyself"), disabusing the excesses of previous practice (the obscurity of theory), not to disband the project but to reaffirm the faith of the professional congregation through its call for a new mode of criticism. Thus it stands in the line of Ransom's "Criticism, Inc." and de Man's "Resistance to Theory" to recast the function of criticism in response to an institutional need. In other words, while beckoning to a larger world, it also presents a hyperprofessionalist rationale (it addresses those in the profession, not outside) and reasserts the status of the profession. This projection of a larger world relevance, at the same time reassuring the status and autonomy of the profession, is a contradiction typical of professionalism, as Bruce Robbins shows in *Secular Vocations.* In this sense, rather than being revolutionary, Bérubé's call is paradoxically conservative, in that it leaves the profession essentially intact; we need to revise our self-presentation, our advertising and public image, rather than, say, our politics.[20]

Even on its own terms, the prescription for public access is not necessarily as salutary as it might seem. For one thing, people like Frederick Crews, Harold Bloom, Roger Shattuck, and Camille Paglia already fit the bill for "public access," speaking to large public audiences, although I doubt Bérubé, who espouses a left politics, has these folks in mind to represent the values and virtues of our work. Public access per se is thus an empty category, or finally a marketing category, applying to anyone who appears in public rather than strictly academic media. For another thing, as I've mentioned, public access largely applies to mainstream, PMC venues, such as *The New Yorker* or *Harper's.* While these certainly reach larger audiences than standard academic fare, they are still limited to a narrow slice of the public sphere and don't speak to the large mass of people who do most of the work in this country. Public access, then, must be linked with a concept of the public good; it requires a politics to be worth it, otherwise it merely yields a *public relations* for the humanities, to justify what we're doing in literature departments, rather than a political vision of what literary and critical education should do or a theoretical argument about the sociocultural function of the humanities.

Bérubé is not by any means the only one to push toward a more popular zone of writing, from the formerly insulated zone of academia to a more general (educated, largely white, middle-class) audience. The past several years have witnessed a great deal of such academic crossover work in the humanities, most prominently perhaps in the recent work of former theory gurus, such as Jane Tompkins's *West of Everything,* Henry Louis Gates, Jr.'s *Loose Canons,* and Cornel West's *Race Matters,* as well as in the turn from elite criticism to personal criticism and autobiography, exemplified by Alice Kaplan's *French Lessons,* Frank Lentricchia's *The Edge of Night,* Gates's *Colored People* and Tompkins's *A Life in School,* among many others. This turn, I believe, indicates not simply the exhaustion of theory but speaks to a renewed rationale for literature departments; the return to literature and to belletristic modes represents a retrenchment of our presumed disciplinary object, to justify our discipline in the face of public questions of accountability. Our old standby, literature, projects a more comprehensible public justification than undoing binaries or subverting Western institutions.

While the call for public relevance holds out a salutary vista, the biting reality is that it occurs at precisely the same time that the workforce becomes less democratic, more ruthlessly pared down, and less open to those from nonprestige positions, as state universities close down or become prohibitively expensive and less accessible to a broad social spectrum of people. In this, despite its altruism, public access might perversely serve an antipublic function by solidifying the position of those privileged enough and institutionally empowered to speak to the public, presumably for the rest of the humanities. It celebrates those who might write for the glossy mags, presenting them as the exemplars of professional success, in other words evacuating a less glamorous scholarly model for the model of the entrepeneurial crossover, the journalistic, media consultant professor. By the same token, it also carries a convenient and blatantly ideological rationale for hideous employment practices that in effect blames the victims of university downsizing: it's our fault, we haven't been out there selling our wares to a popular audience, so we deserve what we get if we don't get with the program.

A possible consequence of public access—while *material* access to the university and to the professional field becomes more and more rarefied—is to promulgate a model of academic celebrity, hypostasizing the model of intellectual star, with broad public appeal and name recognition, as an ideological carrot—a kind of intellectual Horatio Alger story—for those struggling with the blunt exigencies of employment, for those unemployed and "underemployed" to dream and strive for, at the same time that socioinstitutional conditions make that dream more and more fantastical. This negative vista of public access goes a long way to explaining the recent proclivity for academic-intellectual autobiography, to augment the star function of what James Sosnoski calls Master Critics, presenting details of the life to the paparazzi.[21] In its worst light, public access carries a careerist logic and desire, that the profession of literature might be recast in terms of media success stories, putting a more glamorous face on the otherwise disintegrating situation of public access to education.[22]

The crucial question that must precede the call for a better public image and spin on the humanities is that of the institutional conditions and channels that permit or deny access—in other words, public access not for *us*, but for those wishing to take their entitlement to a public education. It is not quite true that left intellectuals have buried their heads in the sand and escehewed public visibility; however, actual access to the accredited institutions of media, of publishing, and of the academy are far from open and at best only allow limited forays from those outside the circuit of institutional privilege. The question of access, then, is a question of reforming and opening those institutional channels rather than simply recalibrating writing style. The pressing task of criticism in the current moment—indeed, the obligation of critics—is to reinvent the institution of literature in ways that truly permit public access, reconfiguring the jobs and employment conditions of those who work in that institution more equitably and humanely, and restructuring the university as a place of education and opportunity for all rather than as a darwinist finishing school for the nascent professional-managerial and ruling classes.

*Notes*

1. Or what Quentin Skinner, taking a note from C. Wright Mills, calls "Grand Theory," which he defines as systematic, "abstract and normative theories of human nature and conduct" (3). See his introduction to *The Return of Grand Theory in the Human Sciences,* which gathers a series of essays on major figures of the moment of theory, including Derrida, Foucault, Habermas, Althusser, and Lévi-Strauss.

2. For the interrelation of larger historical factors and what has happened to universities—the downsizing and the evisceration of the labor force—see Ohmann. For the general characteristics of post-Fordism in which the restructured university participates, see Harvey. For more detail about the winnowing of jobs, see note 7 below.

3. See Huber's series of MLA reports on the job market in literature and languages. There was a notable upswing in the number of jobs advertised, beginning around 1986, peaking in 1987, 1988, and 1989, slipping a little in 1990, down to the trough of the present, when less than nine hundred jobs were advertised. These statistics give an indication of some of the causes of the formation of the present academic (sub)generation, since the years 1986 to 1990 represented a brief hiring peak, with over nine thousand job positions advertised. In short, this infusion served to fix the generation by simple arithmetic.

4. Pierre Bourdieu, in his influential sociological work, deciphers how social distinctions operate in French culture. For my purposes, I draw on Bourdieu's concept of distinction to examine the construction of academic hierarchies and social relations particular to literary studies on the American scene. Despite our powerful theoretical tools, we have largely left unexamined our own system of social distinction.

5. On "master critics," see Sosnoski. Debray deals specifically with the French intellectual scene, but his basic point—that the social role and influence of intellectuals has shifted through the century, or, put another way, the role of intellectuals is socially defined—carries over to the American scene. In Debray's scheme, intellectuals have been defined as or derived their influence from being teachers roughly in the time period before World War II, from being writers in the postwar years up through the sixties (Sartre is a central example), and from being media celebrities thence (figures like Foucault and Lacan drew hundreds to public lectures and appeared on TV, in gossip columns, etc.). For the current apotheosis of the academic as public celebrity, see the *New York Magazine* feature on Andrew Ross, "Yo, Professor" (Mead), as well as the spate of articles announcing the new public intellectuals, such as Cornel West, Henry Louis Gates, Jr., or Camille Paglia.

6. See my "The Life of the Mind and the Academic Situation" on the disciplinary rather than altruistic dimension of tenure.

7. As Richard Ohmann points out, "in the mid-1960s over 90 percent of new humanities Ph.D.'s had full-time tenure-track appointments; in recent years the figure has hovered around 40 percent" (231). It is hard to express the real effect, in human terms, of this shift from stable and ready employment to constant and pervasive job *in*security. Not that the immediately previous generation had it easy; as Orr indicates, the contemporary job crisis began about 1970. But, as Brodie notes, jobs are still fewer in real terms than was the case in 1975 (15).

8. For a post hoc declaration of the theory generation and its difference from older formalists, see Sprinker. As he puts it, "Let them have *PMLA*, if they want it. We've got *Cultural Critique, Signs, Feminist Studies . . . diacritics, boundary 2 . . . Critical Inquiry . . .*" (127). Note that almost all of these journals were founded around 1970, and definitely mark that generation. To the posttheory generation, most of these journals represent closed shops; rather, from our standpoint, we have a new bloc of journals, such as *Postmodern Culture, minnesota review, Journal X, differences, Symplokē,* the revived *College Literature,* and so on.

As it is frequently depicted, the turn to theory in the sixties represented "politics by other means." Contrary to this usual view, though, Terry Eagleton points out that many of the figures affiliated with the advent of theory—Fish, Gadamer, Kristeva, Bloom, Iser, and so on—were hardly revolutionaries, or for that matter on the left. And as Eagleton also points out, there can be a way of seeing the refuge in the academy as a *displacement* of politics, to "signifiers and sexuality" (3). My point here is that the situation is no doubt complicated and the ascription of theory as a sixties or boomer phenomenon is only qualifiedly true, though I would maintain its *absorption* occurred under the auspices of the coming to age of the boomer generation.

9. For a report on recent changes in publishing, particularly on how quickly even academic books are remaindered and go out of print, see Allen.

10. Hillis Miller was Sedgwick's dissertation director. This is Miller's list of those whom he dubs promising younger scholars engaged in the project of theory, particularly in the negotiation of the chasm between language and history, in his 1986 MLA presidential address:

> Among those engaged in this work from one position or another, perhaps in the end from wholly incompatible positions, from one side of the canyon or down in its depths (but the more points of entry to this question the better), I name, in no partic-

ular order, not only [Andrew] Parker and [Gregory] Jay but also Michael Sprinker, Deborah Esch, Thomas Keenan, Cynthia Chase, John Rowe, Jonathan Arac, Michael Ryan, Ned Lukacher, Gayatri Spivak, Andrzej Warminski, David Carroll, Suzanne Gearhart, Jean-Luc Nancy, and Philippe Lacoue-Labarthe. (291)

One could of course construct a number of other lists and theoretical family trees.

11. See John Guillory's arguments for the use of theory to provide a research program for the humanities, in effect replacing the function of the literature canon, in *Cultural Capital.*

12. To cast further back, see Warner for his discussion of the way in which the professional object of the field was reformed at the turn of the century, largely from germanic philology to literary appreciation and interpretation.

13. There's a commonplace view that the humanities competed with the fattened role of the sciences in the post–World War II university. However, Elizabeth Wilson shows that literature competed more directly with the social sciences rather than the sciences in their mutual tasks of studying the social world rather than the natural world.

14. See Graff on the "field-coverage principle" (207–208). Relevant to this positive redescription of theory, Richard Rorty depicts theory as a new mode of writing somewhere between philosophy, literature, and scholarship, rather than simply a derivative or "service" language to literature proper (66).

15. In "The Feminism Which Is Not One," Devoney Looser discusses the present shifting moment of feminism to a third or fourth generation and the question of loyalty to an earlier, singularly minded feminism. See also Eve Sedgwick's comments on the relation of gay studies to feminism in "Sedgwick Unplugged" (60–61).

16. Barbara Johnson deals with this death trope in *The Wake of Deconstruction.* A number of recent titles testify to the tenuous position of (poststructural) theory at present, such as *After Poststructuralism* (Easterlin and Riebling) or the early polemic for cultural studies, "After Theory," a special issue of *Dalhousie Review* (Smith). These reports, which might bespeak a *desire* of the field as much as the reality of it, are not unique. For a fuller discussion of these projections of a rupture in theory, see also my "The Death of Deconstruction, the End of Theory, and Other Rumors."

17. See Terry Caesar's "On Teaching at a Second-Rate University" for a relevant discussion of academic hierarchies. I differ here from Caesar, who sorts universities on a single axis, elite and nonelite, first and second rate.

18. See Lauter for a particularly cogent analysis of the PC wars, explicitly making this connection between the scaling down of the university and PC-baiting.

19. It's worth noting that Bérubé locates himself explicitly as a member of the posttheory generation, recounting the story of his coming to theory during graduate school in "Discipline and Theory" (43–58).

20. To be fair, Bérubé has consistently advocated a liberal-left politics, and has been especially active on behalf of graduate student unions and to reform the academic job market. My point is to examine the professional-institutional uses to which criticism (theory, public, etc.) is put, frequently in spite of our prescriptions and what we say we are doing.

21. See David Shumway's discussion of the star system and speculation about the recent prepoderance of autobiographies of well-known theorists.

22. There is a certain way in which one can read Bérubé's text as this kind of celebratory success story. See particularly his account of his publishing in places like the *VLS* in "Bite-Size Theory" (171). This is not to single out Bérubé unduly; rather, I take his case as exemplary of a current trend. However, it is to register adamant reservations about this kind of prescription in light of the present job crisis, making me fear that such a celebratory prescription is like fiddling while universities and educational enfranchisement for the mass of people in this country burn.

*Works Cited*

Allen, Charlotte. "Indecent Disposal: Where Academic Books Go When They Die." *Lingua Franca* (May 1995): 44–53.

Bérubé, Michael. *Public Access: Literary Theory and American Cultural Politics.* New York: Verso, 1994.

Booth, Wayne. "Where Have I Been, and Where Are 'We' Now, in This Profession?" *PMLA* 109 (1994): 941–50.

Bourdieu, Pierre. *Distinction: A Social Critique of the Judgement of Taste.* Trans. Richard Nice. London: Routledge, 1989.

———. "Structures, *Habitus,* Practices." *The Logic of Practice.* Trans. Richard Nice. Stanford: Stanford University Press, 1990, 52–65.

Brodie, James Michael. "Whatever Happened to the Job Boom?" *Academe* (Jan./Feb. 1995): 12–15.

Caesar, Terry. "On Teaching at a Second-Rate University." *Conspiring with Forms: Life in Academic Texts.* Athens: University of Georgia Press, 1992, 145–65.

Crane, R. S. "History vs. Criticism in the Study of Literature." *The Idea of the Humanities and Other Essays Critical and Historical.* Vol. 2 Chicago: University of Chicago Press, 1967, 3–31.

Debray, Regis. *Teachers, Writers, Celebrities: The Intellectuals of Modern France.* Trans. David Macey. London: New Left Books, 1981.

de Man, Paul. "The Resistance to Theory." *The Resistance to Theory.* Minneapolis: University of Minnesota Press, 1986. 3–20.

Eagleton, Terry. "Discourse and Discos: Theory in the Space between Culture and Capitalism." *TLS* 15 (July 1994): 3–4.

———. *The Significance of Theory.* Oxford: Blackwell, 1990.

Easterlin, Nancy, and Barbara Riebling, eds. *After Poststructuralism: Interdisciplinarity and Literary Theory.* Evanston: Northwestern University Press, 1993.

Giroux, Henry, David Shumway, Paul Smith, and James Sosnoski. "The Need for Cultural Studies." Smith, 472–86.

Graff, Gerald. *Professing Literature: An Institutional History.* Chicago: University of Chicago Press, 1987.

Guillory, John. *Cultural Capital: The Problem of Literary Canon Formation*. Chicago: University of Chicago Press, 1993.

Harvey, David. *The Condition of Postmodernity: An Inquiry into the Origins of Cultural Change*. Oxford: Basil Blackwell, 1989.

Huber, Bettina J. "The Changing Job Market." *Profession* 92 (1992): 59–73.

———. "Recent Trends in the Modern Language Job Market." *Profession* 94 (1994): 87–105.

Johnson, Barbara. *The Wake of Deconstruction*. Cambridge, Mass.: Blackwell, 1994.

Lauter, Paul. "'Political Correctness' and the Attack on American Colleges." *Higher Education under Fire: Politics, Economics, and the Crisis of the Humanities*. Ed. Michael Bérubé and Cary Nelson. New York: Routledge, 1995, 73–90.

Levine, George. "The Real Trouble." *Profession* 93 (1993): 43–45.

Looser, Devoney. "This Feminism Which Is Not One: Women, Generations, Institutions." *minnesota review* n.s. 41–42 (1994): 108–17.

Mead, Rebecca. "Yo, Professor." *New York Magazine* (14 Nov. 1994): 48–53.

Miller, J. Hillis. "The Triumph of Theory, the Resistance to Reading, and the Question of the Material Base." *PMLA* 102 (1987): 981–91.

Ohmann, Richard. "English after the USSR." *After Political Correctness: The Humanities and Society in the 1990s*. Ed. Christopher Newfield and Ronald Strickland. Boulder, Colo.: Westview, 1995, 226–37.

Orr, David. "The Job Market in English and Foreign Languages." *PMLA* 85 (1970): 1185–98.

Ransom, John Crowe. "Criticism, Inc." *The World's Body*. Baton Rouge: Louisiana State University Press, 1968 [1938], 327–50.

Robbins, Bruce. "The History of Literary Theory: Starting Over." *Poetics Today* 9 (1988): 767–81.

———. *Secular Vocations: Intellectuals, Professionalism, Culture*. New York: Verso, 1993.

Rorty, Richard. "Professionalized Philosophy and Transcendentalist Culture." *Consequences of Pragmatism (Essays: 1972–1980)*. Minneapolis: University of Minnesota Press, 1982, 60–71.

Sedgwick, Eve Kosofsky. "Sedgwick Unplugged (An Interview with Eve Kosofsky Sedgwick)." With Jeffrey Williams. *minnesota review* n.s. 40 (1993): 52–64.

Shumway, David. "The Star System in Literary Studies." *PMLA* 112, 1 (1997): 85–100.

Skinner, Quentin, ed. *The Return of Grand Theory in the Human Sciences*. Cambridge: Cambridge University Press, 1985.

Smith, Paul, ed. "After Theory." Special issue, *Dalhousie Review* 64, 2 (1984).

Sosnoski, James. *Token Professionals and Master Critics: A Critique of Orthodoxy in Literary Studies*. Albany: State University of New York Press, 1994.

Sprinker, Michael. "Commentary: 'You've Got a Lot of Nerve.'" *Shakespeare Left and Right*. Ed. Ivo Kamps. New York: Routledge, 1991, 115–28.

Stephens, Mitchell. "Jacques Derrida." *New York Times Magazine* (23 Jan. 1994): 22–25.

Warner, Michael. "Professionalization and the Rewards of Literature: 1875–1900." *Criticism* 27 (1985): 1–28.

Weinberg, Alvin M. "Impact of Large-Scale Science on the United States." *Science* (July 1961): 161–64.

Williams, Jeffrey. "The Death of Deconstruction, the End of Theory, and Other Ominous Rumors." *Narrative* 4, 1 (1996): 17–35.

———. "The Life of the Mind and the Academic Situation." *College Literature* 23, 3 (1996): 128–46.

———. "Packaging Theory." *College English* 56 (1994): 280–99.

Wilson, Elizabeth. "A Short History of a Border War: Social Science, School Reform, and the Study of Literature." *Poetics Today* 9 (1988): 711–35.

Zavarzadeh, Mas'ud. "Post-Ality: The (Dis)Simulations of Cybercapitalism." *Transformation* 1, 1 (1995): 1–75.

# Two

# Stars, Tenure, and the Death of Ambition

## *Sharon O'Dair*

Star systems aren't unusual; they structure several fields of human endeavor, including sports, entertainment, and highbrow creative activity like painting, fiction writing, or opera singing. What these fields have in common is the privileging of unique individual resources, as the economics textbooks put it, which results in both the difficulty, one might say the impossibility of becoming a star, and the alluring, almost unimaginable constellation of rewards that go to the few who become stars. Those rewards—$2 million to write a novel or an exposé, $10 million to act in a film, $3 million to put a ball in a hoop, not to mention fame, adulation, pampering, authority, and power—create a dynamic pull on the thousands, even millions of people who start out to be a star. *That* is why people start out to be stars; that is why they take the risk in the first place. The rewards are enormous, even disturbing, and must be, because the odds are so slim that anyone will catch the gold ring.

*Hoop Dreams* is symptomatic, and the film should not surprise its audiences. Twenty-five years ago, when I was in high school, I remember the small tough boys lingering at the field, longing to play college football and even, maybe, professional football; but they knew, even then, that one in seventy high school players play in college and that one in seventy college players play in the pros. Thirty years ago, I watched a boy, a very big boy he seemed to me, emerge from my street, from just a couple of houses down, to play on the offensive line of the New York Jets. He blocked for Joe Namath, who, when in college, quarterbacked the team at the university where I now work. It was goofy, it was *miraculous,* to see on television the brother of one of my playmates, crouched in a three-point stance, butt raised in the air, poised to counter the moves put on him by someone like Deacon Jones. Who, him? The guy down the street? Why? Yet I dare say that if you saw me in that neighborhood thirty years ago—blazing with energy and smart as the dickens but kind of scruffy and loud—you might wonder how it came to be that I now walk around the University of Alabama with a certain professorial and professional authority. You might say, who, her? Why?

The boys' hoop dreams are absurd; they've committed themselves to an impossible goal, not the one on the court in their playground or gym, for they can indeed learn to shoot a basketball very well; the impossible goal they've committed to is the NBA. And yet, without such commitment, neither boy would know if he might be the next big thing, would he? And that commitment, working, working, working day and night to perfect the skills that get you noticed, is, we all know, good for you;

it's a discipline whose benefits can be transferred to other settings, to the classroom or the office, as the boys in *Hoop Dreams* discover when all is said and done. But one question the film poses and does not answer is this: How do you know when your commitment becomes a sign not of your ambition but of your delusion? How do you know when to begin to apply your skills elsewhere?

Such a question, I suspect, cannot be answered: there is no decision calculus for it that is effective or convincing. Each individual answers the question differently, and yet for most people, thankfully, answering that question is relatively easy. I figured out in high school that I would never be a successful athlete: despite some attributes in my favor—energy, quickness, intelligence, and better than 20–20 vision—my body just wasn't big enough or strong enough or fast enough to get me onto the U.S. Olympic team in women's volleyball. (I discovered even earlier that I would never become a world-class middle-distance runner; at age twelve, my routine was to find myself easily beaten in a 440-yard run by nine-year-old Mary Decker.) A poet I know turned away from the study of music when, in high school, she realized that her hands were too small to play the piano and her memory not good enough to master scores. But some people find their ambition much more difficult to let go, and discover their delusion only after spending four years or eight playing basketball in Japan or Australia or in semipro leagues in the Midwest. Some people never discover their delusion, and continue to blow a sax in a bar band for decades, not for fun or the love of music, but in anticipation of the big break that will make them stars.

And other people, some of whom were our students or our graduate school peers, discover their delusion only when they spend four years or eight driving the freeways of Los Angeles or New Jersey teaching composition classes for a small paycheck and little else—no recognition, no respect, no possibility of advancement.

Nowadays, the star system structures—or partly structures—the academy, or at least English departments, *because* there are so few tenure-track jobs. We can haggle incessantly over how and whether "it was better" in the 1950s and 1960s, but we do know that in the '50s and '60s life was far less rigorous and competitive for graduate students and junior faculty, as George Levine points out: "When I got my degree from the University of Minnesota, almost all my colleagues, no matter how dumb they were, got at least three job offers."[1] Levine's admission is rapidly becoming famous, achieving for those whom Jeffrey Williams calls the posttheory generation the fame of the scandalous, of a small blade of truth among so many tall tales. Another fact we know is that when even the dumb can choose between several offers, no one will be courted as a star because no one will even be required to publish; when even the dumb get jobs, publishing can be "relatively disinterested and detached from the exigencies of employment—in blunt terms, from fear of losing a job," as Williams points out in commenting on another reminiscence of the way we were, by Wayne Booth.[2]

Stars are born in the academy out of the necessity to publish and the necessity to publish is born out of a contracting job market, worsened by the effects of tenure and the (wasteful and immoral) overproduction of Ph.D.'s. Publications become for us the commodities we can sell and that can sell us as stars or stars-to-be. No one pays star salaries to those who think and read in order to teach. No one does now, and no one did in the 1950s or the 1960s.

In making these assertions I am, it should be noted, positing causal relationships: the necessity to publish creates stars, and the contracting job market (worsened by tenure and overproduction of Ph.D.'s) creates the necessity to publish. Positing causal relationships is not, I realize, fashionable in contemporary literary or cultural criticism. What's fashionable is to suggest that the situation, any situation, is overdetermined in its complexity, an overdetermination that subverts the attempt to assess the importance of various factors contributing to that situation, and therefore allows the privileging of any factor as (suggestively) causal. Thus, in an essay on "The Star System in Literary Studies," one that places you and me in a relationship with Jacques Derrida that resembles a fifteen-year-old girl's relationship with Leonardo DiCaprio or Keanu Reeves, David Shumway does not argue that "movie stardom is a direct historical cause of the star system in literary studies" but that "celebrity in its many forms, including stardom, helps account for the rise of the academic star system."[3] And in commenting on the explosion in publishing, and particularly on the turn from literary analysis to cultural analysis, Michael Bérubé writes:

> I would have no difficulty with this profusion of material for study . . . if it were not *coincident* with the collapse of the job market. It's not that I believe the job market would improve if we would all agree to stick to reading *Piers Plowman* and leave the hip-hop to writers for glossy magazines; the market works by variables that have nothing to do with the profession's intellectual interests. . . . And that's the problem, particularly for our graduate students: the discipline thinks it's going from literature to culture, and the market tells us we're going from literature to technical writing.[4]

In this case, if Bérubé is correct, and I have no reason to think he is not, we are not listening to what the market is saying, and neither are our graduate students. For if we were, more of our graduate students would be doing dissertations in rhetoric and composition, or in other ways preparing to obtain tenurable positions in the teaching of composition or of writing more generally: the market surely won't improve by sticking to *Piers Plowman,* but it likely would improve by sticking to technical writing. Indeed, Bérubé seems to suggest that the "collapse of the job market" in English is a certain kind of collapse, not just in full-time, tenure-track jobs, but most especially in full-time, tenure-track jobs to teach upper-division and graduate level courses in literature, and in some cases, cultural studies.

Evidence for this point is difficult to come by, but I will try here to make a case for it. It seems to me that to understand "the collapse," one must consider, at a minimum,[5] three pieces of data and preferably, as I shall point out, for as many years as possible: (1) numbers of positions available—and ideally, numbers of tenurable positions; (2) numbers of Ph.D.'s awarded; and (3) the kinds of positions available, for example, whether in literature or composition, and even in what subfields. For example, Bettina Huber's charts and figures and tables derived from MLA joblists clearly demonstrate that the number of positions advertised in 1991 was less by some two hundred than the number advertised in 1975, a fact that is cited widely enough, and sometimes, I'm afraid, to suggest that "the collapse" is something new—a horrific drop-off from the glory days of 1989—or at least something worse than ever before, as graduate student Erik D. Curren does in an essay published in the same issue of *Profession* that contains Huber's analysis.[6] For Curren, the story of the job market begins in 1975, and it is a "story of dramatic boom followed by even more dramatic bust": he focuses on the "large increase in the number of jobs advertised beginning in 1983–84," which peaks in 1988–89 at over two thousasnd positions and then falls over the course of five years to just over one thousand.[7]

But this story doesn't have a determinable origin, or if it does, it isn't in 1983 or even in 1975. Consider first the demand side of the issue—numbers of positions advertised—which for Curren begins in 1983. If you take a longer view—say the years Curren cites (1975–76 through 1993–94)[8] but doesn't emphasize—it is arguable that the "boom" years are as much of an aberration as are the "bust" years: that is, an approximate average number of positions advertised over that nineteen-year period is fifteen hundred per year. Twelve years record total number of positions at between twelve hundred and fifteen hundred; and only two years—1992–93 and 1993–94 —record total number of positions at less than twelve hundred.

The limitations of Curren's "short view" are even more significant, I think, when considering the supply side of the issue, that is, annual numbers of Ph.D.'s granted. Curren implies that a person looking for a job in the early 1990s faced a tougher market than did a person looking for a job at any time since 1975. But to do so he must cite the backlog of Ph.D.'s granted in the late 1980s to darken the statistics: only then does "the ratio of jobs to applicants" for him and his peers become "considerably worse" than "better than one-to-one."[9] Yet in making this implied comparison, Curren fails to consider the effects of backlog for the applicants in 1975 (or any other year), perhaps because, for example, Huber makes clear that the number of Ph.D.'s granted in the five years *before* 1975 averaged approximately thirteen hundred per year, while the number of Ph.D.'s granted in the five years *before* 1991 averaged approximately eight hundred per year. Whatever backlog his generation faced or faces *must* be smaller than that faced by the group in 1975, since the ratio of jobs to applicants during those five years before 1991 was greater than two-to-one, whereas for the group in 1975, the ratio was just slightly above one-to-one. (This last figure is a guess, since like Curren, I do not have figures for the numbers of positions in years before 1975–76.) Many, if not most of the job seekers who received their Ph.D.'s in the late 1980s, like myself, must have gotten jobs.

Defending the claim of the early 1970s Ph.D.'s to the title "Group to Hit the Worst Job Market" is not my intention here. Further, I am aware that from the perspective of a job hunter in 1994, the drop-off in available positions seemed and was astonishing. Trying to negotiate the job hunt in the early nineties felt like hell; of this I am convinced. But I do think it poor argumentation (as well as history) to try to assess job market collapse, as Curren does, by taking the short view, as, for example, in pointing to an upswing in Ph.D.'s awarded—"from a recent low of about 650 in 1987 to about 850 in 1991"[10]—without acknowledging or factoring in the second most recent upswing in Ph.D.'s awarded, from just over 300 in 1957–58 to 1350 in 1973–74, as if this second most recent upswing had no effect on the conditions Curren is trying to analyze. For Curren, the huge number of Ph.D.'s awarded in 1974, that huge number from which even the number in 1976 is a decline, simply does not exist. And the slightly smaller number in 1976, from which, thankfully, we have continued to decline, seems to be a given or something that just appears on a chart. It is not; that huge number has a history.

In fact, however, Curren needn't rely on bad history to make his claim. I do think Curren and his peers face a more difficult job market than did the group in the early 1970s. But the job market is made more difficult not just because of numbers of jobs, which currently are not that far below historical norms; not just because of the numbers of Ph.D.'s awarded, which currently are just about or slightly below average, depending on which date you begin with (say, 1957–58, 1973–74, or 1975–76); and not just because of the effects of the two factors working together. The job market is worse now than it was because, in addition to the usual stiff competition for available positions, these positions are, I suspect, actually different from the positions available in the 1970s or certainly in the 1960s.

The crucial variable here is the third one I cited above: the *kinds* of jobs that are available to Ph.D.'s. Are these jobs in literature? and in what subfields? Are these jobs in writing? Are they tenure track? And if so, are they junior or senior appointments? Data about this is especially difficult to come by, and more data is necessary before one could argue this point conclusively, but Huber's analyses do lend some support to the hypothesis that the job market collapse is perhaps more accurately to be described as the collapse of a certain kind of job. The question for people like Bérubé or me or our students might be phrased, therefore, like this: Is some sort of pressure being placed on the numbers of tenure-track positions in literature?

Huber's data and analyses suggest two points of pressure. First, the growth in positions in minority literatures, especially African American literature. According to Huber, this category "accounted for 1% of all positions advertised in 1982 but increased to 7% in 1993."[11] In a doubtless somewhat inaccurate survey of the October 1996 joblist, I found that 14.9 percent of all tenure-track positions were in this category.[12] In itself, such growth, even explosive growth like 1500 percent since 1982, would not imply a constricting of the market for Ph.D. literary critics; it would simply imply a shift in literary interests. But to the extent that a position in African American literature requires a scholar who is an African American, then that growth does imply a constricting of the market for Ph.D. literary critics. I have no idea of the extent of such linkages, but I am surely not the only person who has heard Henry Louis Gates speak of a brilliant graduate student who could not find a job in his field of expertise, African American literature, because he was white. In the extreme case, then, where all such jobs require such a scholar, 12 to 15 percent of all tenure-track jobs are open only to, say, 1 to 2 percent of the applicant pool. Such a situation is a significant mismatch of supply and demand; and its effect is significant not just on the prospects of African American graduate students but also on the prospects of others, which in some cases do not exist, since in an era of limited financial resources and indeed of downsizing, institutions' demand for scholars in medieval or eighteenth-century literature must be weakened. In passing, I might note the irony that this kind of hiring pattern is imposed on the profession and on graduate students in particular largely by professors tenured in the 1960s and 1970s who faced a market in which less than 1 percent of positions called for expertise in this specialty.

A second significant point of pressure on numbers of tenure-track jobs in literature is the growth in composition and rhetoric. Holding steady throughout much of the 1980s and early 1990s was the percentage of jobs available in the teaching of writing—at about 21 percent, despite a fall-off of about 7.5 percent which occurred around 1990. Huber notes a significant fact about these jobs in writing: increasingly throughout this time period, institutions have opted to make such appointments tenurable: "Since 1989 two-thirds or more of the positions in writing have been tenure-track, compared with 44 percent in 1982," and in 1993, the figure was 82 percent.[13] During this same period, it should be noted, a shift toward tenure-granting positions has characterized the profession as a whole, from 62 percent in 1982 to 85 percent in 1993.[14] Still, it seems a reasonable inference that a higher percentage of tenure-track jobs are to be found in rhetoric and composition, technical writing, developmental English, English education, and the like, than ever before. And indeed, based on my calculations of the data on October joblists in Huber, as well as my own tallying of the jobs offered in the October 1996 joblist, the percentage of tenure-track jobs that require specialization in composition has increased, from 21.8 percent in 1982 to 26.5 percent in 1993 to 29.1 percent in 1996.[15]

To be sure, data from just three years do not conclusively indicate a trend; often, in our profession, numbers and percentages oscillate. But these data do *suggest* a trend, and they suggest that pressure is indeed being placed on the number of tenure-track positions in literature: in 1982, 22.8 percent of all tenure-track positions were in composition or minority literatures, while today that figure has just about doubled, to almost 45 percent, which means that for every thousand tenure-track jobs, over two hundred that were available in 1982 to most graduate students in literature are no longer available to them.

But if our graduate students responded to that pressure by doing dissertations in composition—the only logical market response, since there is little most of them can do to compete for the positions in minority literatures—then it follows that we literary and cultural critics would have fewer graduate students to work with and to supervise, or even to take our classes. We might find ourselves, occasionally, teaching composition. Instead of accepting that horrifying situation, most of us—professors and graduate students alike—would rather call the situation a "conundrum," as Bérubé does; we would rather up the ante and *take the risk* of grabbing the gold ring, of getting a tenure-track position teaching literature. If I were faced with the choice of doing a dissertation on slasher films, or even on slacker films, which might qualify me for one or two positions in the country, or doing a dissertation on pedagogy in the composition classroom, which might qualify me for dozens or even hundreds, I know which choice I would make. I'd be watching lots of movies; or, if I didn't like the odds that my slacker dissertation would be better than the others produced that year *and* that I would have also published whatever number of essays is the currently necessary benchmark,[16] I'd make moves to change my career, to apply my Ph.D. outside the academy, perhaps, or to get into a professional school.

And why would I choose business school or law school over a job teaching composition? As if the answer weren't obvious: teaching composition isn't fun or challenging or respected or rewarded. (After all, even our colleagues who specialize in rhetoric and composition rarely teach it; mostly they supervise others who teach it.) Or at least nowadays it isn't any of those things. In the 1950s and 1960s, life *was* better for those dumb professors with three job offers, and not just because they could choose among offers and did not have to publish. Life was better because their students were closer to them in intellectual development and achievement. Sometimes, the teaching of composition was done in the context of a humanities class, an early form, perhaps, of "writing across the curriculum." But even when done within the context of the traditional composition classroom, students arrived in college with the ability to compose essays—or at least sentences and paragraphs. In that context, the difference in development and achievement is small between an assistant professor and her students, and teaching composition is a matter of refining skills and extending them—not just the students' but the professor's own. Today, an enormous gap has opened between the assistant professor and her students. The situation is such that, to get a job, the assistant professor must have already published widely, two or three articles at least, and in some cases, perhaps, a book; yet to get into freshman composition, the students have had to do very little—remediation is almost the norm, and often they cannot construct a coherent sentence. (Of course, I exaggerate, but perhaps not by much. William Galston, a professor at the University of Maryland's School of Public Affairs, notes that "almost half of the students entering the California State University system need remedial instruction in either reading or mathematics.")[17] In this context, teaching composition is—or should be—a matter of rudimentary drill, dull and dulling, although necessary and important.

Ironically, our situation—the emergence of a star system—is the result of (or as Bérubé might say, *coincident with*) the expansion of higher education since the end of World War II; it is also the result of—or coincident with—the collapse of effective teaching in secondary schools during that same period. Data suggest that "in 1945 there were enough slots in postsecondary education for only one of five Americans aged eighteen to twenty-two. By 1992 the number had grown to about *four* for every five."[18] Such enormous structural change was bound to affect the ways institutions attract and reward their employees; most immediately, thousands and thousands of composition courses needed to be staffed. That universities chose to staff these courses with graduate students, however, was not inevitable, nor is it inevitable that we continue to staff these courses in this way. Yet it must be acknowledged that delegating composition to graduate students served not just university administrations but also departments and, let us not forget, tenured and tenure-track professors as well, who received thereby not only the opportunity to teach graduate students but also the release time from teaching necessary in order to do research or to write. Graduate students enabled stars to become stars, and all of us needed stars to induce graduate students to take a crack at stardom, a crack that might last three or four years or more and, therefore, allow us to staff all those sections of composition.[19]

Our job market has become split or segmented, a split masked for decades by the delegation of composition to graduate students but one which looks to become institutionalized as, facing a moral imperative, we reduce the size of Ph.D. programs but face a continuing need to staff freshman- and sophomore-level courses, a need that may increase if Bill Clinton is successful in making the first two years of college universal or mandatory. Indeed, the "new kind of job" Bérubé derides—"a 4/4 instructorship leading (for the worthy candidate) to tenure *without* promotion"—which is offered to one of Bérubé's students by a "nearby college,"[20] has already been promoted as a useful way to manage human resources by the past vice-president for academic affairs at my *university.* One of the benefits of this proposal, said the vice president, is that it allows productive, tenured scholars to concentrate on their research; another is that it offers currently underemployed Ph.D.'s secure employment, if not advancement. If Bérubé's "new kind of job" does signal an institutionalization of the star system, of a bifurcated market, in which students can more accurately predict the odds of landing a certain kind of job, it is arguable that this would be an improvement—though still not the best solution, in my opinion—over the situation that has obtained in recent decades, in which graduate students assume that their days of teaching composition are limited (that they, too—all of them—will be like Mike, stars who teach undergraduate majors and graduate students, but mostly work on their writing and their research), when the far more likely scenario for them is to become just like an increasing number of America's workers—holding down three or four part-time jobs.

What has happened, historically, is that a star system has been superimposed on a model of recruitment and compensation based on lifetime tenure and service that, even in this century and despite a good degree of professionalization, largely resembled that of the clergy. As Gerald Graff has pointed out, in our profession there remain many traces of the "quasi-monastic" origins of college teaching.[21] Currently, therefore, a gap exists between the realities of our market situation and the ways we think about ourselves and our roles in higher education and in society. Much of the talking and writing we do now, and in particular "metaprofessional" discourse like this chapter, is an attempt to work through this change, to understand its implications for our roles and for our institutions; in this sense, such metaprofessional discourse is essential work, morally necessary.

Adjustment to these new conditions, to the changes in our status, will take some time and effort. Acting like stars, we continue to think like quasi-monastic teachers, and such mental dissonance causes problems. We like some of the rewards associated with the star system—visibility, celebrity, mobility, and enhanced salaries; and we like some of the rewards associated with the tenure system, particularly academic "freedom," and of course, the virtual impossibility of losing your job. What we haven't faced up to is the possibility that the two reward systems are incompatible; right now, the two seem to coexist reasonably well, if uneasily. That the two are incompatible may become inescapable as a bifurcated system of employment becomes institutionalized, resulting in the (morally) dubious situation that some tenured instructors, teaching 4/4 loads, will have published and no doubt will continue to publish more and better work than some tenured professors, teaching considerably less.

Because we continue to think like quasi-monastic teachers, assuming lifetime tenure is sacrosanct, many of us see the emergence of the star system as cause for alarm, for fretting and worrying, or for attacks on a larger culprit, such as, in Shumway's case, "the importance in contemporary America of celebrity in its many forms" or, in Laurie Langbauer's case, "the customary economy of marketing under capitalism"[22]—whatever that *means,* presumably the absurd notion that (commodity) capitalism is nothing but a star system. Because we continue to think like quasi-monastic teachers, assuming as a bottom line the benefits of lifetime tenure, we do not accept our star system for what it is: not evil or demeaning, but risky business, with potentially huge rewards, that is played successfully only by those with unique talents who are—additionally—both positioned to perform and able to maintain their performance over many, many years. Because we continue to think like quasi-monastic teachers, even critics as astute as Shumway or Bérubé, who genuinely seem to care for their underemployed students, cannot bring themselves to call for the abolition of lifetime tenure.[23] Rather than call for such structural change in the profession, Shumway calls for a change of heart, a change in attitude: "The star system depends on fans, an impoverished community focused on individuals who are not part of the community. It would be better for literary scholars, teachers, and students to stop being fans and to recognize that they can authorize knowledge without the name of a father or mother."[24] And Bérubé, though he discourses long and hard about value and aesthetics, merely bemoans the fact that nowadays "junior faculty and Ph.D. candidates [publish and teach] more just to get a job than most senior faculty [did] to earn lifetime tenure thirty years ago."[25]

If tenure did not exist, or existed in a form different from that institutionalized today, Bérubé's student, with two articles, great teaching evaluations, and a completed book manuscript, wouldn't be competing with other recent Ph.D.'s, under a bifurcated system, for a 4/4 instructorship; he or she would be competing for a professorship, and competing not just with my colleague, Professor Deadwood, who hasn't published a word in two decades, but with me, and even with Bérubé himself. Such a situation is one, I suspect, that even the biggest stars among us find just a bit disconcerting: tenure may be our "reserve clause," keeping our salaries low and effectively tying most of us for an entire career to just one institution; but, unlike baseball players who sued repeatedly for freedom from it, most of us like being tied down.

Most academic stars, I think, do merit their stardom; at the same time, others do not. But merit is a tricky concept, as all of us should know by now, and our crisis over value—and merit—will not be settled easily. We cannot appeal to objective criteria, like the ability to hit a fastball safely three out of every ten times or the ability to hit high C safely all of the time. And even if we could appeal to objective criteria, judgments of merit would be placed on only slightly firmer ground, as I shall suggest in discussing the following argument made by Harriet Hawkins in her book, *Classics and Trash.* Hawkins asserts that

> Like sports, all arts can be seen as democratic in so far as artistic ability, like athletic ability, knows no class distinctions. On the other hand, sports and arts alike can be seen as profoundly elitist, as genetically determined, and thus in one sense hereditary aristocracies, since some people are born with great natural talent or ability and others are not. No amount of effort or training or wealth could make Florence Foster Jenkins sing like Kiri Te Kanawa.[26]

With all due respect to Hawkins, who (wo)manfully tries to argue a moderate position on canonization, this particular argument strikes me as naive or, possibly, disingenuous. The happy assertion that talent will win out over class advantage, that money cannot make Jenkins sing like Te Kanawa or that money cannot make me (despite my considerable jock credentials) play basketball like Sheryl Swoopes, ignores the fact that without (someone's) money, Te Kanawa won't sing like Te Kanawa, and Swoopes won't shoot like Swoopes.

The road to stardom is an arduous one to travel, requiring not just talent but luck and more importantly financial and institutional supports of various kinds. As Michèle Lamont reminds us in "How to Become a Dominant French Philosopher: The Case of Jacques Derrida," intellectual legitimation depends on "institutional supports, [and] the access to institutional supports depends on intellectual collaboration, and . . . cultural capital has an important role in either blocking or facilitating access to intellectual circles and institutions that affect the institutionalization process."[27] Like the boys in *Hoop Dreams,* the budding intellectual jumps at the chance to attend the school that will allow her to hone her mind and make the connections that will get her admitted into the college that will allow her to hone her mind and make the connections that will get her admitted into the graduate school that will allow her to hone her mind and make the connections that will get her an appointment as an assistant professor in the kind of university that will give her visibility and voice within the profession. But like the boys in *Hoop Dreams,* she faces the possibility that at any point in that sequence, even as early as high school at St. Joe's where Isiah Thomas looms large like Stephen Greenblatt, she could blow out a knee. That is to say, she could blow out a metaphorical knee: she could become cynical, angry, bored, frustrated; she could make a mistake, fall in with the wrong crowd, get into formalism or Marxism; and either leave the profession entirely or decide to settle for less than visibility and voice, which is exactly the settlement most all of us must take, or make.

Talent doesn't just win out over money or class advantage; it might, or might not, and most often, I suspect, talent withers or dies in the long process of pursuing expensive training. In sports, in entertainment, and in the academy, the stars we get are the ones who survive. And in the academy, survival is so much easier if, to quote Lamont once more, you have "access to intellectual circles and institutions that affect the institutionalization process" (587)—if you get into an elite graduate program, if you work with a star who promotes your work, if you become an assistant professor at a high-prestige institution, and if you play the professional game by the unwritten and unpromulgated rules, only rocking the boat gently, if at all.[28]

There may be, as the clown concludes in *As You Like It,* "Much virtue in If." But there is also, as the structure of our profession reveals, Much anxiety in If.


I have suggested that the profession is characterized nowadays by two reward systems, an older system based in lifetime tenure and an aversion to risk, and another, newer system based—theoretically—entirely on risk. Given the enduring appeal of the tenure system, particularly to those who are tenured, but also to those who are not, I see little chance in the short run that tenure will be eliminated and all positions filled competitively, a situation that would result in higher salaries and more mobility for those who are competitive and successful in the market. In the short run—assuming, of course, that external conditions having to do with funding remain the same, that is to say, dismal—I suspect that a bifurcated system will be institutionalized and that the great prize of the profession's weakly realized star system will be obtaining a tenurable position that allows one to focus on research and writing, particularly liter-ary and cultural criticism. Competition for these positions will be fierce, and proba-bly fiercer than ever, for reasons I have outlined above (that is, the increasing per-centage of tenure-track jobs calling for specialization in minority literatures or in composition); and therefore "places like East Podunk University or West Jesus State College," as Williams so nicely puts it,[29] will continue to be able to attract and em-ploy Ph.D.'s trained at elite institutions. The professionalization of the provinces will continue.

As I conclude this chapter, I would like to tease out some of the effects of this situation on the individual professor. How do you, how does anyone, respond when the hot-shot pleasures of Berkeley or Durham are left behind for the gold ring, tenure-track position at East Podunk? What attitude do you adopt toward the possibilities for further and greater stardom—for higher salaries, for mobility, for a bigger, flashier ring—once you take up your duties at West Jesus State or, even, as in my case, at the University of Alabama?[30] I suggest there are several logical responses to the conditions in which we work, and these responses, in turn, affect the ways we work, the kinds of work we do. These are not mutually exclusive types of response, but rather, dimen-sions of response. At the same time, however, I suspect that a given individual tends to hold largely to one response or another, even as he or she might pass through one or another of them.

First is the "liberal optimistic" response. Liberal optimism often drips from the mouths of those *not* in the hinterlands and not in the posttheory generation, say, one's ex-professor at Yale or Johns Hopkins. It can also drip from the mouths of your peers in graduate school whose jobs did not land them in the hinterlands. But liberal optimism isn't just condescending sneer, or even sympathetic encouragement, sincere or not; it characterizes most young professors when they hit the hinterlands because liberal optimism is a sign of ambition. Wherever they are to be found, liberal optimists insist that important work can be done and is found anywhere nowadays. At its extreme, liberal optimists go so far as to suggest that such diffusion is one of the benefits of the shrunken job market. Liberal optimists conclude that those in the hinterlands who are producing important work are in fact capable of big-time stardom in the academy; the academy will recognize that work when it is produced. Liberal optimists conclude that if you publish enough, producing work of consistent quality at an appropriate rate in one or more recognizable areas of scholarship, you will be recognized for the merit of your work, and you will become a star, or a bigger star than you were. For liberal optimists, the hinterlands do offer "access to intellectual circles and institutions that affect the institutionalization process": the periphery is the center, and you will be able to move from the hinterlands.

Second is the bitter, cynical response. The bitter cynic thinks the liberal optimist is naive. The bitter cynic is born at a certain moment, a moment when an assistant professor in the posttheory generation who teaches at West Jesus State concludes that, especially once she is tenured, she is never going anywhere else, no matter how often and how well she publishes. Never. Going. Anywhere. Else. She looks at the MLA joblist and sees that annually there are at best two positions for an advanced assistant or associate professor in her specialty. She looks at her colleagues and sees that in the past five years or even ten, the only assistant or associate professors in her department who have gotten job offers somewhere else are either African Americans or teach in English as a second language—the scenario described above for new Ph.D.'s, only writ large (or small). She looks at her own institution, and concludes that for all the talk about merit, there is little money for raises, release time, or even a trip to a decent library. Compared with her peers at Michigan or Cornell, she is handicapped; to keep up with them, she must work harder than they do. The hinterlands do not, she concludes, offer "access to intellectual circles and institutions that affect the institutionalization process." For the bitter cynic, the periphery is not the center, and there are, effectively, no rewards or incentives for writing. Everything counts, and nothing does. The pace of writing either slows or doesn't; but the bitter cynic becomes unpleasant and mean, particularly toward students.

Third is the preslacker response. I label this response "preslacker" because professors in the posttheory generation hold tenured or tenure-track positions and have access to (limited) institutional support for the research and writing they do. Preslackers are not doing one of the McJobs the academy increasingly offers to new Ph.D.'s., which might then qualify them as potential full-fledged slackers.[31] But preslackers know that being at West Jesus State is and was a step on the institutional slide toward the imposition of permanent McStructorships.

Some cynicism, then, is characteristic of the preslacker response. Preslacker cynicism precludes the embrace of liberal optimism and its faith in the eventual disposition of just rewards, its faith in ambition. Like the bitter cynic, and for the same reasons, the preslacker knows he is never . . . going . . . anywhere . . . else. With tenure, he knows his star will have shined its brightest; he knows he has in fact grabbed the gold ring, the right to write without a concern for the requirements of professional ambition. Preslackers write and can rival liberal optimists in output, but preslackers write for themselves only, or maybe for their friends as well: abandoning "serious" scholarship, or their original fields of expertise, preslackers write what they enjoy: journalism or commentary for National Public Radio; scripts for *Star Trek;* or personal criticism before "they have earned the right to do so." Preslackers can be cranky in their enjoyment, and resist the various cultural impositions of their elders in the profession, such as identity politics or affirmative action; they write "metaprofessional" discourse because they recognize a moral and practical imperative to reorganize academic life, as I hope this chapter demonstrates.

Preslackers know they are lucky. At least once or twice a year, preslackers look at Bettina Huber's statistics drawn from MLA joblists, and then they gasp—a brief but meaningful expression of survivor's guilt. If conditions in the academy change so that it is possible to grab a bigger and flashier ring, preslackers will accept those new conditions—and that bigger, flashier ring—as the accident of nature, of luck, that it is: like winning the lottery, rather than like receiving one's just reward for effort, talent, and ambition. Preslackers know that the periphery is not the center, but that sometimes the profession cannot tell the difference. It is this knowledge that allows them to resist the bitter, envious response of some in the posttheory generation; this knowledge allows preslackers, well, to be happy. In this situation, stars do fall on Alabama.

## Notes

This chapter originally appeared in the *Michigan Quarterly Review* 36, 4 (1997): 607–627.

1. George Levine, "The Real Trouble" in *Profession* 93, (1993): 43.

2. Jeffrey Williams, "The Posttheory Generation" in *symplokē* 3, 1 (1995): 60.

3. David R. Shumway, "The Star System in Literary Studies" in *PMLA* 112, 1 (1997): 88.

4. Michael Bérubé, "Peer Pressure: Literary and Cultural Studies in the Bear Market" in *minnesota review* n.s. 43/44 (1995): 139, emphasis mine.

5. Obviously, other factors, such as demographics and the state of the economy, also affect the job market for Ph.D.'s in English.

6. See also Williams who at least acknowledges that the "contemporary job crisis began about 1970" before going on to cite the statistics about numbers of positions in 1975, without citing any statistics about numbers of Ph.D.'s awarded (58, n.7). Bettina J. Huber, "Recent Trends in the Modern Language Job Market" in *Profession* 94 (1994): 87–105. Eric D. Curren, "No Openings at This Time: Job Market Collapse and Graduate Education" in *Profession* 94 (1994): 57–61.

7. Curren, 57.

8. Curren actually cites data only through 1992–93. I base my figures on Huber's statistics, which include 1993–94. Since there were even fewer positions in 1993–94 than in 1991–92 or 1992–93, to include 1993–94 in my calculations does not bias my argument in my favor. That is, leaving out 1993–94 would only strengthen my argument by raising the average and thus making 1991–92 and 1992–93 seem even more normal.

9. Curren, 57.

10. Curren, 57.

11. Huber, 101.

12. The reader may have noticed that Huber's data for this category is not restricted to tenure-track jobs. This discrepancy between her data and mine does not affect the overall argument for two reasons. First, my look at the 1996 data suggests that virtually all positions in minority literatures are tenure track. Second, since the category of tenure track is more restrictive than the category of all positions, my figure of 14.9 percent must err on the low side.

13. Huber, 103.

14. Huber, 95.

15. I created a broad category in tallying up the positions listed in the October 1996 joblist, one that includes several distinct categories in Huber's analysis. These are rhetoric and composition; technical, business, and professional writing; developmental English; English education; journalism; and linguistics. In determining the totals from Huber, then, I added together all of the above-mentioned categories, so that I would not be mixing my apples with her oranges. To arrive at these figures from Huber, I used data from tables 3 and 7, and from the listing of percentages of tenure-track jobs in composition on page 103. It is unclear even in Huber which "writing" jobs she includes in this listing, since she alludes to both rhetoric and composition and "writing," which in table 7 includes not just rhetoric and composition, technical writing, and developmental English but also fiction writing and poetry. Given that even Huber is unclear about this, I don't feel disempowered to apply her percentages to other specialties of writing such as English education or journalism. I acknowledge therefore some distortion in these figures. I performed the following algebra: from table 7, I determined the number of composition jobs by dividing the total number of jobs by the percentage of composition jobs. I then divided the number of composition jobs by the percentage of tenure-track positions in composition, listed on p. 103, to arrive at the number of tenure-track positions in composition. I then divided the total number of positions by the percentage of jobs that are tenure track, which is found in table 3, to arrive at the number of tenure-track jobs. I then divided the number of tenure-track composition jobs by the number of tenure-track jobs to arrive at the percentage of tenure-track jobs that are in composition.

16. Anecdotal evidence suggests that the necessity of early publication is not necessarily good even for those graduate students who are successful at it. A graduate student at Alabama published an essay on *Hamlet* in *ELH* several years before finishing her dissertation. She has not submitted an essay to a journal since, paralyzed by the fear that she cannot live up to her past success. An assistant professor I know is currently working through the stings brought to her by inevitable rejections of her work, stings she hadn't anticipated after early publishing success

in graduate school. Increasingly over the past few years colleagues have bemoaned the number of bad books being published, as assistant professors rush to turn their dissertations into books: one senior colleague joked that no professor under the age of forty should be allowed to publish a book, and another confessed to me that her disposable income has increased tremendously of late, since she has stopped buying books, not because of the expense but because the quality of the work is so poor. At the end of this cycle of anteing-up are the university presses who find themselves in financial difficulty when their books do not sell.

17. William Galston, "The Education Presidency" in *The New Republic,* November 11, 1996, 35.

18. Claude S. Fischer, et al, *Inequality By Design: Cracking the Bell Curve Myth* (Princeton: Princeton University Press, 1996), 152. I must point out that matriculation figures do not coincide with graduation rates. As Lawrence Mishel and David M. Frankel point out in *The State of Working America: 1990–91* (Armonk, N.Y.: M. E. Sharpe, 1991), currently only approximately 25 percent of the workforce holds a college degree, and this is the case even for those workers aged 25–34. By the year 2000, it is expected that "at least 70 percent of the workforce will not be college graduates" (95, 7).

19. In "Spin Doctorates," published in the *Village Voice Literary Supplement,* November 1995, Williams argues that stars serve a public relations function for universities; stars are "poster professors" who increase the prestige of their employer and attract a paying clientele. This argument seems to me to be reasonable, and in line with my argument here; but where Williams emphasizes what I would call external relations (legislatures, funding agencies, parents of undergraduates), I emphasize what I would call internal relations, relations specific to the profession, such as the promulgation of a reward structure and the ways we entice people to enter our profession. Interestingly, and in contrast to Williams or myself, Shumway deemphasizes, though he does not ignore, institutional interests in the development and maintenance of the star system. Shumway prefers to concentrate on psychology, "the construction of personality crucial to the star system" (91) or the "identification and desire" that fuels fans' relationships with stars (87).

20. Bérubé, 139.

21. Gerald Graff, *Professing Literature: An Institutional History* (Chicago: University of Chicago Press, 1987), 20.

22. Langbauer is cited by Bérubé, 137.

23. One might argue that such calls are unnecessary, that the profession has already been detenured, since it is easy to look around and see among one's colleagues an increasing number of instructors not on the tenure track, and since, as Richard Ohmann points out, "in the mid-1960s over 90 percent of new humanities Ph.D.'s had full-time tenure-track appointments; in recent years the figure has hovered around 40 percent" ("English after the USSR" in *After Political Correctness: The Humanities and Society in the 1990s,* C. Newfield and R. Strickland, eds., (Boulder, Colo.: Westview, 1995), 231. In itself, however, those numbers establish little with respect to the strength of tenure as institutional practice, since they do not take into account the size of the pool of applicants or the number of positions available in the mid-1960s or in recent years. To establish whether de-facto detenurization has occurred, one would need

to know over time the percentage of courses in English departments taught by tenure-track faculty. But the increasing availability of Bérubé's "new kind of job," the tenure-granting instructorship, would argue against de-facto detenurization or at least against a weakening of professional support for tenure. Indeed, the tenure-granting instructorship seems to be a maneuver to reverse whatever tendency toward de-facto detenurization has developed.

24. Shumway, 98.

25. Bérubé, 134.

26. Harriet Hawkins, *Classics and Trash: Traditions and Taboos in High Literature and Popular Modern Genres* (Toronto: University of Toronto Press, 1990), 107–108.

27. Michèle Lamont, "How to Become a Dominant French Philosopher: The Case of Jacques Derrida" in *American Journal of Sociology* 93, 3 (1987): 587.

28. The effects of a prestigious affiliation or of a powerful mentor or of trendy discourse are not entirely undocumented. Psychologists Douglas P. Peters and Stephen J. Ceci wanted to know whether the peer review process reveals "systematic bias in favor of authors from prestigious institutions." As reported in "Peer review: Beauty is in the eye of the beholder," published in *The Behavioral and Brain Sciences* 8, 4 (1985): 747–50, Peters and Ceci submitted twelve previously published essays to the scientific journals in which they had appeared, after first changing the institutional affiliation of the authors from high prestige (e.g., Harvard) to low prestige (e.g., Central State University). What they found was that the vast majority "were rejected upon resubmission—mainly for reasons of design and methodology," for reasons, that is, of intellectual quality. More recently, Alan Sokal's seduction of *Social Text* (14, 1/2 [1996]: 217–52) underscores the same point: a powerful scientist with a prestigious affiliation engaging in postmodern critique of science was a plum *Social Text*'s editors could not resist. Like Peters and Ceci, I wonder whether a similar critique by a scientist from Central State University would have made it onto the pages of *Social Text*. It is also noteworthy that efforts like Peters and Ceci's or Sokal's are roundly demonized by the academic profession. To reveal the nonobjective nature of gaining "access to . . . the institutionalization process" is, perhaps, the ultimate academic transgression.

29. Williams, "Posttheory," 68.

30. My point here is not to equate the University of Alabama with West Jesus State, but to suggest that the structure of our profession is such that the hinterlands begin almost as soon as you leave one of the institutions at the very top of the prestige hierarchy.

31. In *Generation X* (New York: St. Martin's Press, 1991), Douglas Coupland defines a McJob as "a low-pay, low-prestige, low-dignity, low-benefit, no-future job in the service sector. Frequently considered a satisfying career choice by people who have never held one" (5). Dating from around the turn of the century, *slacker* is a colloquial term of abuse applied to those who shirk work or physical exertion; during World War I and again in World War II, the term gained currency in reference to pacifists and others who refused to participate in those conflicts. Since 1991, which saw the publication of Coupland's novel and the release of Richard Linklater's film *Slacker*, the term's earlier meaning has regained currency, specifically with reference to (parts of) the post-babyboom generation. Ironically, however, *slacker* is a term applied (at least originally) by slackers to themselves: being slack is a logical response to the conditions in which they live and work. Consider the "numbers" appended to *Generation X*: percent of U.S.

budget devoted to the elderly (30) juxtaposed with the percent devoted to education (2); the number of people in the workforce for each recipient of Social Security: in 1949: 13; in 1990: 3.4; in 2030: 1.9; the percentage of income necessary for a down payment on a home: in 1967: 22; in 1987: 32; and the percentage of 25 to 29 year-olds who own homes: in 1973: 43.6; in 1987: 35.9 (181–82). Given "numbers" like these, it is not surprising that slackers think ambition is futile. As Linklater observes in an interview with Lane Relyea, "no one in *Slacker* thinks they're going to remake society. They're more satisfied to hang out and snicker ironically with their friends" ("What, Me Work!" in *Artforum* 31 (April 1993): 75).

# THREE

# PHANTOM NARRATIVES:
# TRAVEL, JOBS, AND THE NEXT GENERATION

## *Terry Caesar*

*Flying down to Charlottesville is just an ordinary
piece of business in the life of many academics.*
—Stanley Fish (interview)

A friend of mine writing his dissertation currently is on a one-year contract at a Midwestern liberal arts university. Nelson teaches three sections of Spanish per semester for a salary of $30,000. He has an office, which he shares with another temporary instructor. She arrived first and took the lone desk. Nelson has a table. If anything about his position bothers him more than this table, it is the fact that the chairwoman extended her welcoming greeting to him in the hallway one day between classes.

My friend is paid to be a teacher in the department, not to be a member of it. Nelson is not expected to attend meetings or participate in committees. Nonetheless, some concession has been made to the fact that his present job abides within the larger, more permanent expectation of a career. This concession is represented by travel. The department will pay 50 percent of the expenses of anyone—temporary, tenure track, or tenured—who delivers a paper at a conference.

At one point during his first semester, Nelson had to go to a conference in New Orleans. His paper—based on a chapter from his dissertation—would be his first professional presentation. But what to do about his classes? The departmental policy was clear: all classes must be taught. Fortunately, Nelson was able to schedule a flight plan that would enable him to teach each of his Friday morning classes, leave in time to deliver his late afternoon paper, and return Sunday afternoon in plenty of time to prepare his Monday morning classes.

Alas, there were flight delays. The exact reasons were never clear. It turned out that Nelson did not get back to his town until 3:30 A.M. Monday. He set his alarm clock, but overslept anyway, and missed his first class. Awakening just in time to make the second, he rushed over to campus. But he was not successful in avoiding the department secretary, whose proprietary airs were the scourge of temporaries and teaching assistants alike. As Nelson hurried by, the secretary snarled: "You'll have to make up the last class."

How typical is Nelson? In their chapter on college teaching in *The Jobless Future,* Stanley Aronowitz and William DiFazio estimate that "[i]n many teaching institutions, the proportion of classes taught by part-timers has reached 50 percent, and the ratio is even higher in community colleges" (235). Cary Nelson reaches the same conclusion: "recent studies suggest that nearly 40 percent of all faculty in higher educational institutions are now part-timers, compared with 34 percent in 1980 and 22 percent in 1970" ("Lessons," 126–27).

In contrast, there is no way of accurately estimating how many of these part-time faculty have access to travel funds in their respective departments. My impression is that Nelson is luckier than most; in my own former department, for example, no part-timer who has a conference paper to deliver merits funding (which is down from a maximum of $500 to $400 a year for everybody else). His luck, I would argue, is not only financial but professional: he has a way into (or onto) a tenure track, and thereby toward a permanent position, if only because the department has conceded that he cannot be denied outright a way out for the purpose of professional travel. That this access ultimately attests more to *lack* will, however, be a central assumption of the following discussion.

An even more fundamental one will be the following: the opportunity to travel is central to academic life. Its peculiar securities depend upon the acknowledged necessity for faculty to accept invitations to participate in panels or give talks at special scholarly occasions, to submit applications for awards that enable study or teaching abroad, or to compete for the chance to deliver papers at conferences on the regional or national level. Furthermore, travel constitutes the very definition of academic prestige. The most luminous stars of any discipline are its frequent flyers; David Shumway notes that the growth of the lecture and conference circuit—inseparable from, if not constitutive of, the star system—could not have occured without the advent of jet travel (92).

Conversely, the dimmest lights are those who stay on the ground. It will be another assumption that the plight of part-timers is nowhere more glaringly revealed than by the fact they are more or less permanently grounded; even those, such as my friend, who can be permitted an occasional takeoff may as well have stayed put for all their trouble, and it can be further argued that the proliferation of local or even national conferences during the past decade only confirms the prospect of so many being grounded.[1] If the future of the next generation of academics is accurately reflected in the present of part-time faculty, then nothing about their future experience—not a chair who greets them in the hall, not a table rather than a desk available for the office—better represents its depleted prospects than the absent or marginalized opportunity to travel.

Conversely, nothing for past generations has represented the rewards of a career more handsomely and expansively than travel. It is with good reason, for example, that Harvard's famous Dean, Henry Rosovsky, chortles at one point, while speaking of "abuses" of frequent travel by university professors, that "some of my friends . . . have been referred to as the 'Pan American Airways Professor of Sociology,' the 'Swissair Professor of Physics,' or the 'El Al Professor of Sociology'" (166). In order to assess the cost of this reward being lost, we first need to understand the value of its being possessed, as it has been variously represented in fiction and scholarly literature. In the next section of this chapter, I will consider the traditionally high mystification of travel—at once comprehended as absolutely central to the scholarly enterprise and as its own enterprise. In a final section, I will suggest two things. First, lack of access to professional travel opportunities does not exhaust the ways travel of some sort continues to abide in the profesion. Second, travel of perhaps any kind can be both demystified and revalued by demonstrating how the most elite level of professional activity participates in the most subordinated.

## SABBATICALS PERMANENT AND IMPERMANENT

David Lodge's *Small World* is arguably the most celebrated academic novel of recent decades. Its fame seems directly related to its scale. The narrative takes place far away from campus, and over its expansive horizons there is nothing of the '90s public outcry against higher education or private desperation by young professors—nothing, for example, about state legislatures considering the revocation of tenure at public universities, or professional journals running articles extolling the expedient virtues of secondary school teaching. (For this last, see Smith.) One of Lodge's principal characters, the peripatetic academic insider, Morris Zapp, explains the academy in the following terms: "There are three things which have revolutionized academic life in the past twenty years . . . jet travel, direct-dialing telephones, and the Xerox machine. Scholars don't have to work in the same institution to interact, nowadays: they call each other up, or they meet at international conferences. . . . I work mostly at home or on planes these days. I seldom go into the university except to teach my courses" (43–44).

The vast scale of Zapp's own interaction is the precise measure of the authority by which he can make such statements. We recall Stanley Fish on Charlottesville. Or, we might say it is as if one of Rosovsky's friends is talking, rather than Rosovsky himself—who in fact cites Lodge at one point, in order to reassure us that "the alleged abuses can be more apparent than real" (167). In *Small World,* to the contrary, the "abuses" are so total that some site from which they could be termed abuses in the first place has been used up. Lodge's young hero, Persse McGarrigle, is bemused to hear Zapp's pronouncements, yet in no hurry to see the world. We are given to understand that the only thing he does is to teach his courses, which require that he be on campus all the time. He can only travel by requesting a leave.

The narrative cannot very well deny him the request. Without a leave, McGarrigle could not easily be positioned as a member of the same profession as Zapp, for *Small World* virtually converts academics and travelers into equivalent categories. The very subjects of the profession of English become stops along a profesionalized Grand Tour: "Zurich is Joyce. Amsterdam is Semiotics. Vienna is Narrative," explains Zapp. "Or is it Narrative in Amsterdam and Semiotics in Vienna . . .?" (65). Conversely, what is the profession of English? A discipline that offers fresh subjects for conferences to attend, rather than classes to teach. The traditional, on-site narrative of academic life is something Zapp and McGarrigle leave behind, and increasingly the novel reveals that the older narrative has at most a vocabulary of only one word to describe their activity. Zapp reflects at one point on "the beauty of academic life," whereby, with just one good book, you could get a grant to write a second, and then, after promotion enables you to design your own courses, you would be eligible for more promotion, more grants, and still less teaching. "In theory, it was possible to wind up being full professor while doing nothing except to be permanently absent on some kind of sabbatical grant or fellowship" (152).[2]

How better to characterize the superstar politics of academic life as they have evolved in the decade since the publication of *Small World* than to say that the top, flying high, is like being away on permanent sabbatical? Some institutional connection is of course required; hence, even Zapp has to locate his activity by means of the customary idiom for being granted "leave." But he apparently does not have to make the requisite request because he is presumably expected to do research, not teach. (Or to teach as a function of doing research.) Therefore, the very word *sabbatical* becomes a hapless designation to account for the activity of people already scheduled and salaried to live a professional life apart from circumstances weighed down with inexorable teaching demands, inescapable meetings, and assorted measuring of departmental coffee spoons, now all wondrously escaped, not to say transcended.

The travel in such a life can be conventionally referred to, and is, on a regular basis. Thus, for example, Henry Louis Gates, Jr., thanks two editors for their help on a special issue to *Critical Inquiry,* consisting in part of "establishing a productive timetable that enabled me to undertake research in Africa as planned" (18). (He goes on to thank both his research and administrative assistants, for "enabling me to coordinate the editing of this issue while commuting for a semester between New Haven and Ithaca.") But the travel itself cannot be described as such, lest it appear to exist in its own right.[3] Perhaps one of the reasons fiction better represents the solicitations of travel in academic life is so that the temptations can be indulged, while the responsibilities can be ignored. Morris Zapp is interested in travel, not ideas; or rather, insofar as it concerns ideas, travel to Zapp is the ecstatic, exteriorized exercise of a species of intellectual activity pure and simple, served up according to the menus of individual conferences but ultimately prepared for his own consumption.

Michael Malone's more recent academic novel, *Foolscap,* stages a more consistent comedy of the responsibilities, through the figure of Dean Buddy Tupper, Jr., provost of "Cavendish College," as he tries to keep track of the highest flyer in the English Department, Jane Nash-Ganz. At one point her secretary calls ("she had her own secretary!") to inform the provost that she has flown away to be the keynote speaker at an international women's conference in Warsaw, prompting Tupper to do a double-take: "Warsaw?" (48). At another point, Tupper is given a stack of receipts, among them one from Nash-Ganz for a helicopter from Nice to Monte Carlo. Reason? "Plenary Speaker—Ovidian Joyce: Hermaphroditic Transformations." "What in God's blue heaven," Tupper thinks, "did that have to do with what she'd been hired for? Hadn't her vitae said her training was in American poetry? Well, pardon Dr. Tupper for asking, but as far as he knew, James Joyce wasn't an American, or a hermaphrodite either" (295). Once more, nonetheless, he is compelled to acknowledge that Nash-Ganz is a celebrity who cannot be fired, and therefore a traveler—and therefore someone who crosses boundaries, disciplinary as well as administrative.

How to be responsible to, not to say for, these boundaries? If the Zapps's and Nash-Ganz's flaunt them in their professional conduct—just as they dispute them in their theoretical discourse—it is necessary for someone else to stand in for the dull classes that must be taught, the fateful bills to be paid, or the uninteresting facts to be admitted. Even if the halcyon days of Big Theory are now past, novels such as *Small World* and *Foolscap* could still be written today. But they are no longer, I think, so comically or innocently readable—at least not by the next generation of academics. Such lavish travel might one day be possible for a few of them, as it has been in the past. Yet even these are going to have to depart under an entirely different comprehension of the scholarly enterprise. Daniel O'Hara, for example, compares the profession to professional sports: "A few 'irreplaceable' superstar 'free agents' and a mass of interchangeable 'utility' or 'role' players, most of whom do not have, and cannot get, long-term contracts" (43).

The rest of the next generation is already having to learn new rules, at a time when, according to Aronowitz and DiFazio, the job security of university and college teachers "is more tenuous than at any time since the 1930s" (237). Guidelines follow from an institutional model based on widespread corporate practices of dowsized employment, research cutbacks, mandated productivity and time-based accountability in the workplace; specific rules insofar as hiring is concerned include various redefinitions of what a long-term contract is, such as a series of one-year contracts in perpetuity or a tenure-track position without the possibility of promotion. The rules will not include travel. That is, it simply will no longer be possible to conduct academic life on the order of the venerable ideal of profesional mobility, as articulated lately by James Phelan: "Professors are all finally free agents, able to move wherever someone else would have them, able to renegotiate their contracts whenever they can produce an offer sheet from another school" (195).

Phelan's idiom is strikingly similar to O'Hara's. The difference lies in the analogy: Phelan's professor is an individual entrepreneur, while O'Hara's is a member of a team. This reflects, in turn, an abiding tension in academic life: an individual is affiliated with a department and an institution, yet can achieve a reputation apart from either of these. Magali Sarfatti Larson notes one significant difference between the consulting or academic professions and technobureaucratic ones: "Achievments in the former are highly personalized," which "seems to allow for an ideological blending of personal and organizational prestige" (205). Thus, for example, a professor carries with him some of the aura of Harvard as he moves to a state university. But you have to be in place to move, and in order to be able to move, you have to command the freedom of an individual. Travel is so important in academic life because it ratifies this freedom.

The loss of the opportunity to travel matters because it instead confirms *lack*—of equal opportunity, of freedom, and even of individuality itself. As Jeffrey Willaims remarks: "Many people at less than elite universities—the remaining 90 percent of us—rarely see a grant or do much jetsetting, and time is taken up with teaching four, five, and even six courses a term, grading piles of papers, holding office hours, doing 'service' work, and so on—regardless of discipline" (130). Indeed, the prestige of travel not only vexes the activity of those who manage to travel at less elite institutions but misrepresents the fundamental stasis of their professional lives. Professionals who have basically no chance to travel are comprehended utterly in terms of their departmental circumstances or their institutional status.

In a recent article on metaphors of travel in cultural studies, Janet Wolff examines the ideological gendering of travel as male, which "both impedes female travel and renders problematic the self-definition of (and response to) women who *do* travel" (234). "In a patriarchal culture," she continues, "we are not all, as cultural critics any more than social beings, 'on the road' together. We therefore have to think carefully about employing a vocabulary which, libratory in many ways, also encourages the irresponsibility of flight and misleadingly implies a notion of universal and equal mobility" (235). What conclusions can be drawn if we examine the ideological positioning of travel in academic discourse?

One conclusion is that we understand travel as an elite activity, which *is,* exactly, prestigious because we are not all equally on the road, and cannot be. Another conclusion is more elusive yet perhaps even more important: faculty who enjoy some opportunity (including funding) to travel, if only to a conference or two a year, are embedded in professional conditions that have more in common with part-timers than with elites. It may be more feasible for the next generation to realize this point than for the present one, whose imaginary relationship to the real conditions of their existence has already been formed, as past ones have been, by an ideological acceptance (not to say celebration) of the whole project of people such as Morris Zapp and Jane Nash-Ganz.

A more demystified relation to this project falls upon the members of the next generation, if only because the real conditions of their existence have already changed so drastically from those of the past. The near-exhaustion of Phelan's free-agentry model, after all, will not need to be argued if agentry itself is at stake because fewer jobs are available than ever before. The pressure exerted by yet more reduced chances for professors to stop grading papers and go somewhere else for a weekend or a semester will be more clear on the discourses of even the most sophisticated educational theorists, such as Henry Giroux, who urges, for example, that teachers "are also cultural workers who need to engage other educators in a variety of sites in order to expand the meaning and places where pedagogy is undertaken" (166). If it will still not be possible for an academic fully to *see through* travel, any more than for a feminist in a partriarchal culture to see through it, then there might be some chance for the next generation to make better, more discerning use of its idioms and tropes.

## EQUIVALENCES DISTURBING AND LIBERATING

John Guillory puts the situation of graduate students at the present time very succinctly. Speaking of how the job market has determined the course of professionalization in recent years, he notes "the penetration of graduate education by professional practices formerly confined to later phases of the career," and sums them up as follows: "Students do everything their teachers do—teach, deliver conference papers, publish—without the assurance that any of these activities will secure them a job" (92). How can we understand the consequences of this situation?

In some respects, they might first of all already be more incredible than Guillory makes out. "What the market demands, incredibly," he continues," is a graduate student who is already in some sense a successful professional before that student can be considered for a position as a professor" (92). What the market offers, on the other hand—and will offer the next generation if, as expected, the ratio of part-time, temporary employment to permanent increases more dramatically—is the position of a professor for which the preeminent professional practices of graduate school (that is, conferences and publication) will cease to be relevant at the moment of hiring. It might be necessary now at some institutions to have a book just to get a job. (See Nelson, however, on the paradoxes of this particular point, 121–23.) It will not be necessary at most to write another one—or anything else. A part-time job will not require scholarship. The job may not even exist in another year.

What sort of relation to the profession can we expect a generation shaped by this state of affairs to have? It might be more grim that Guillory allows. He states that "the penetration of this norm of productivity [publications] into graduate education only extends the logic of professionalization already internalized in the professoriat" (98). Yet can we assume that this logic, in turn, will be extended when the admittedly "phantasmic mode of professional desire" (in Guillory's phrase) graduate students are presently having to enact no longer pays off in jobs, or, worse, is revealed as ultimately only expressive of the imaginary of those who already have jobs? The reason to publish a book, in other words, was so you could be like Morris Zapp. What follows once it is clear that publishing a book, as we say, gets you nowhere?

Similarly, the reason to keep traveling back and forth between New Haven and Ithaca is so that one day you could have the security, if not the eminence, of Henry Louis Gates, Jr. But once it is clear that you're only staying in place, with part-time jobs in two institutions, no prospect of anything better at either, and nothing more on the horizon, what then? Of course, no attitude necessarily follows. You remain free to dream that a book will get you tenure, or a commute will get you Harvard. A phantasmic mode is not relinquished just because the material basis for it becomes exhausted; indeed, lack of material basis might drive a phantasmic mode the more. In any case, as Larson explains, elites in a profession control both material rewards and esteem. I think we must inquire into the possible logic that follows when esteem threatens to detach itself from the whole notion of a career.

Larson puts the matter thus at one point: "While esteem is, ultimately, easier and cheaper to dispense than power or income, it holds for the recipient something more than the promise of influence; it is intimately bound up with the sense of self, precisely because professions are *ideologically* constructed as occupations that one enters by *calling,* or at least by choice" (227). The notion of calling is crucial. No calling, and no career, at least in professional terms. What the next generation may well face, it seems to me, is the loss of this notion, which is already in its preprofessional phase being constructed not in venerable ideological terms but instead by the new logic of the technology driven, globally restructured corporate economy. In this economy, as Aronowitz and DiFazio state, "there is absolutely no prospect, except for a fairly small minority of professional and technical people, to obtain good jobs in the future" (9). Under such circumstances, being forced to prepare for employment by acting as if one already has a career before even being certain one has a call threatens to make esteem a purely external thing, arbitrary when it comes, ephemeral if no job follows.[4]

What is a "good" job? For an academic, I would maintain, one that affords security, pays well, and, just as significant, enables some real measure of ambition, defined not only in terms of autonomy in the workplace but the opportunity to travel away from it for perfectly professional reasons. Such travel, in turn, renews the freedom by which an individual chose the profession in the first place. By a grim irony, however, it is precisely the loss of such freedom, most especially by part-time faculty who have jobs rather than careers, as well as classes rather than conferences, which the next generation will have to face in their professional lives. Of course I refer only to those individuals who are fortunate enough to get some sort of job in what they once felt "called" to do.

The irony can be more amply characterized. Although there is of course a difference between being embedded above and below a structure, you can nonetheless be so far above or else so far below that you are effectively uncomprehended in either case—and so not embedded in the structure at all. To this measure, you become free, and can even be understood as making good the chances for freedom which elude the rest of your fellows, all more formally or permanently embedded. What I mean is this: with respect to travel the most elite practioneers in the profession and the most subordinated ones converge in strange and disturbing ways. Perhaps some of these ways can be made productive by the next generation.

We begin at the top. The doyen of international theorists in *Small World* is Arthur Kingfisher, "the only man in academic history to have occupied two chairs simultaneously in different continents (commuting by jet twice a week to spend Mondays to Wednesdays in Switzerland and Thursdays to Sundays in New York)" (93). The frenetic Zapp takes off within an older, settled idiom of sabbaticals and grants. Kingfisher represents an eminent level of activity that cannot be described within some known institutional structure; his travel is beyond the kind to which any academic on any rung of the hierarchy can coherently either achieve or aspire. Furthermore, Zapp has a home. Kingfisher, on the other hand, is so exquisitely decentered (as well as mysteriously endowed) that he only has a destination.

It is not at all clear how intelligible in academic terms would be the great fictional prize of *Small World:* the UNESCO chair of literary criticism. It is to have virtually no duties. Its $100,000 salary is to be tax free. Perhaps most wondrously of all, the chair will be connected with no institution, in no particular country; there is no obligation to use the office or secretarial staff at the Paris headquarters of UNESCO. Since the chair is "purely conceptual," the successful candidate "would have no students to teach, no papers to grade, no committees to chair. He would simply be paid to think—to think, and, if the mood took him, to write" (120–21).

Compare the following part-timer quoted by Emily Abel:

> I did have a good publications record in the past but . . . now I don't have the money to fly to major conferences. Of course full-time tenure track position people get that from their departments to go to one and sometimes even two major conferences. . . . Also, when I teach three courses in three places I don't have time to write. It's a vicious circle—with more publications I would have a better chance to get a job, but teaching this way, there's no chance to turn out publications. (115–16)

Of course there are enormous differences of salary and distinction between the two figures. Kingfisher is defined by not having to teach; the part-timer is saturated by teaching. In addition, Kingfisher's position is nothing if not a theoretical project, whereas the part-timer's position is theoretically vacant. But all is not said about the comparison between them by marking their vast differences, and emphasizing that travel for the one results in freedom and success, while for the other it results in servitude and marginality. Travel also provides a disturbing and provocative equivalence between the two figures.

Neither Kingfisher nor the part-timer has a home in some institutional sense as much as a series of fixed destinations. The fact that the profession is in place to extend great esteem to the one and none to the other should not obscure how decisive is mobility to each. Just so, the two share a common relation to writing: it doesn't matter in terms of their respective positions if either one writes. What matters instead is that each keeps moving—Kingfisher between two continents and the part-timer among three places. Of course Kingfisher is going somewhere; he eventually gets the UNESCO chair (and an erection). Yet even with respect to this prize, an intriguing similarity exists to the position of the part-timer, which is purely "conceptual" insofar as it has no fixed center, lacks a necessary relation to staff, and is conducted wholly in individual terms.

Both Kingfisher and the part-timer are equally the product of highly professional circumstances, which offer unparalleled rewards to a very few and equally unparalleled lack of rewards to a great many. Nevertheless, the same structure that makes both possible cannnot easily explain either one, at least through the customary professional discourse about everybody else up and down the tenure track in terms of theories and jobs, or faculty responsibilities and public perceptions. Neither Kingfisher nor the part-timer has anything to do with tenure! In fact, the figure of each is provocatively distant or evacuated. The ideas of the one are surely so wondrously lofty that it scarcely matters to all but a few who thinks them (or perhaps even whether they are thought), while the classes of the other are undoubtedly so basic that it scarcely matters to more than a few who teaches them.

It may not appear likely that in the next generation someone will write a fictional romance concerning inhabitants of the degraded depths, such as David Lodge has already written of the exalted heights. And yet if such a narrative is conceivable it will, I believe, be grounded just as much in travel as *Small World* is, but travel now acting to recuperate all the disdained professional energies and the disused faraway realms of faculty who never appear to go anywhere. It could well be, for example, a narrative of nomads. "One of the primary objects of discipline is to fix," states Foucault. "It is an antinomadic technique" (216). No matter how exquisitely apprenticed to the conditions of the contemporary market, the most mobile part-time, temporary professors are already present nomadically, both in and out of the profession, moving among jobs almost invisibly. The problem to date is that they are merely type-cast as "gypsy scholars."

Caren Kaplan, for example, admits the nomad "as a sign of pure circulation or deterritorialization." She goes on to imagine how the "metaphor" is susceptable to "intensive theoretical appropriation," because of the fit between the "mythological" elements of migration (independence, alternative organizations, lack of accumulated surplus) and "Euro-American modernist privileging" of solitude (in places far from metropolitan centers) (90). What I am speculating about, on the other hand, is a narrative appropriation of the same elements, through which a migrant class of professors will be rethought. The story will not emphasize their subservience to social control but instead their capacity to elude it, and will not detail how they are fixed by discipline so much as how they are in place to resist it.

Such a narrative might well seem fatuous at present. Another part-time voice from Emily Abel's *Terminal Degrees,* which she characterizes as a "freeway flyer":

> During the fall term I was driving to three places. One is one and a half hours to the north, a little more than sixty miles from here. The second is just twenty miles from here and the third is seventy-five miles from here. Sometimes I could go from one to the other, but, in general, I was driving at least forty and frequently eighty miles a day. . . . I've hardly met any of my colleagues because I drive to a place, park, and run up to teach and then get back in the car and drive some place else and run up to teach. I can't publish because half my time is spent driving from one place to another. (119)

The problem with this travel is how utterly it has been negated by being fixed in place. The rigorously antinomadic discipline of professionalism (which the flyer has internalized under the imperative to write) and the inescapably nomadic circumstances of employment (which the flyer has to accept in order to work) merely cancel each other out. To speak more positively of nomadology here is to try to imagine *another* story released by the distance crossed and recrossed, one that grants the traveler more of his or her customary power: a wilder mode of affiliation than academics normally realize, or a more hybrid identity that other marginal figures in the larger society often enjoy. At present, the freeway flyer is just a figure of pathos, as well as a cliche.

Compare the representational potential available in Derrida's "Back from Moscow, in the USSR." Invited to Moscow for ten days by the Institute of Philosophy of the Academy of Sciences, Derrida produces a text which is and is not a narrative, because it both is and is not travel writing; citing by his title the name of a travel book to the same destination written by Andre Gide over forty years earlier, Derrida locates his text generically (as one with rich utopian possibilities) and then repudiates it for the same reason, for he himself comes too late in the tradition, and appears too personal to the degree that he comes as a travel writer at all. Why too personal? He mentions at one point a "phantom narrative" (211). I would have the "phantom" refer in one aspect to his vacant identity as an academic, including his missing institutional affiliation; it is not clear where Derrida was teaching when he accepted the Soviet invitation, or if it was the same place (the University of California at Irvine) where he subsequently wrote his account.

Undoubtedly this is as it should be for "*the* jet-set academic," as Shumway terms him, who holds or has held recurring or regular visiting appointments at three elite American universities while holding two permanent appointments at two equally prestigious French ones (95). Indeed, Derrida openly wonders "what I am doing with my life today when I travel between Jerusalem, Moscow, and Los Angeles with my lectures and strange writings in my suitcase at this precise moment in History" (202). My concluding point would be this: whatever Derrida is doing, he is a traveler of a peculiarily academic kind inseparable from the freeway flyer. The same structure—of institutions, of esteem, of settlement—finds it difficult to understand why each is spending so much time away from home. Although the system celebrates the one for achieving the distance, and barely recognizes the other for being unable to close it, nothing satisfactorily explains why, through the very fact of their travel, they exhibit a freedom from familiar campus securities and normal constraints that makes them compelling figures.

Of course each is not compelling in the same way; once more, it is important to note that the freeway flyer has no professional honor, and enjoys no institutional or material basis to secure any. Nonetheless, my sense is that a more redemptive narrative is possible. It will not simply see the one figure lost in the other, any more than it will see the notion of a calling lost to market conditions, a career lost to jobs, or jobs lost to people who have done everything in their power to prepare for them. A liberating idea of travel—nomadic or not—may be all that is left to the next generation to deal with loss, including the loss of dignity. (For another theoretical setting of this same point, see Caesar, "Back.") I began by recounting a story about my friend in the

Midwest going to a conference. He's from Venezuela. He's not an exile, though he's got an interesting story, which is only partially the situation of a part-time would-be academic barely holding on.

My guess is, the phantom narratives of people like my friend comprise some of the most powerful ones available to the profession.[5] The trouble is, they have no flesh and blood. The profession continues to proceed largely on the basis of familiar narratives of tenure and its discontents. Broader possibilities of success, deeper resonances of failure, and more wayward sources of connection need to be discovered across the entire spectrum of professional life, especially at a time when its permanent occasions are growing more precious and rare. These might involve repudiation of these very occasions, or they might entail renewed dedication to them. In either case, a generation that isn't going to get more jobs is going to need more stories, including one or two about the relation between someone who is flying all over the world and someone who cannot leave for a weekend without making up his last class, as well as about the common activity that seems to make it all worthwhile.

*Notes*

1. This is of course an intricate question. Just as the circumstances of your contract determine whether or not you can go in the first place, the circumstances of your institutional affiliation determine—if, for example, you teach at Clarion University—whether you normally take off to Charlottesville (as Fish suggests in my epigraph) or instead usually drive to Cortland, New York, where the state university hosts an annual conference in Modern English and American Literature. Not everyone who gives a paper at this conference is from the immediate area. But most are.

Moreover, this regional conference is typical in one crucial respect to those special ones on a national scale, such as the 1990 Conference on Cultural Studies, hosted by the University of Oklahoma, about which Cary Nelson writes: "Essentially everyone who volunteered to give a talk was placed on the program. The result was about 350 papers given in 100 sessions over three days" ("Always Already," 29). The essence of all these many and varied conferences, more numerous than ever in the '90s, is simple: unlike elite ones (such as, preeminently, the MLA) participation in each of them is secured not through competition or invitation but simply on the basis of submission.

Anyone can give a paper at these conferences (especially, more recently, graduate students). Thus change in the profession thereby appears to be expanded at the base, where "business" now seems to have a bit more room, while being consolidated at the top, where institutional hierarchy remains unchanged, especially regarding crucial routes to publication. Few in fact get to go to Charlottesville, although now more get to have their own personal Charlottesvilles, many now located close to home.

2. Compare the bland way Rosovsky puts the same thing: "Faculty members love sabbaticals. Projects can be completed, sites visited, colleagues in distant places consulted. Professors tend to be enthusiastic travelers and their way of life encourages their natural proclivity" (166).

What Zapp suggests, very much to the contrary, is that he is so enthusiastic about travel because his way of life does *not* encourage it.

Indeed, the narrative of virtually any academic novel enacts the moment whereby the hero has to get away from campus, in order to open fresh avenues of experience and new sources of identity. It is the moment, for example, in Bernard Malamud's *Pictures of Fedelman* when Arthur Fedelman (who arrives in Italy to be addressed as "professor," although the narrative does not specify an academic affiliation) is forced to bear the judgment that he needs to lose the study of Giotto he has brought with him; as the man who steals the manuscript, and burns it, tells him: "The words were there but the spirit was missing" (41).

3. Compare Gayatri Spivak, asked—in Australia (one of many locales in *The Postmodern Critic*)—what effect travel has had on her work: "Well, you know, I think for a time I will stop traveling. I became caught up in this traveling circus, and I think I've kept doing it for so long because it undermined some of the seriousness with which I was beginning to take myself" (37). A consideration of the imbrication of travel in Spivak would virtually require a separate study. Of particular interest is her recent discursive performance, "Acting Bits/Identity Talk," described by the editors of the volume as "a dazzling series of geographical excursions (from Algeria to Bengal to Bangladesh to Italy to Canada—where our point of entry will be through someone who is Lebanese)" (628).

4. The effects of literary stardom remain to be seen in the lived experience of the next generation. How much esteem does one need to receive in order to be a star? How much does one need to aspire to in order not to be a fan? How many publications? How few? At the conclusion of his discussion of the star system, Shumway makes the following statement: "The star system depends on fans, an impoverished community focused on individuals who are not part of that community. It would be better for literary scholars, teachers, and students to stop being fans and to recognize that they can authorize knowledge without the name of a father or mother" (98). Perhaps so, but Larson's point is that esteem is a crucial motive in the construction of professional identity. In dismissing how profoundly the text of esteem has been rewritten—for better or worse—by celebrity culture, Shumway threatens to banish the presence of esteem itself.

5. At present they are represented in the displaced form of postcolonial reading practices, whose recent prominence, in turn, reflects not only the effects of the new global economy but the American academy's employment opportunities, which have reduced many young professionals to the felt status of migrant workers, if not diasporic ones. On this point, see, for example, Caesar, "Theory," 226 and 235. More generally, I think we can say that the terminal lack of a professional "center" has already driven young scholars to seek in literature a source, if not a mirror, either for their own subalternity or more simply their own ungroundedness.

*Works Cited*

Abel, Emily. *Terminal Degrees: The Job Crisis in Higher Education.* New York: Praeger, 1984.

Appiah, Kwame Appiah, and Henry Louis Gates, Jr. "Editor's Introduction: Multiplying Identities." *Critical Inquiry* 18, 4 (Summer 1992): 625–29.

Aronowitz, Stanley, and William DiFazio. *The Jobless Future: Sci-Tech and the Dogma of Work.* Minneapolis: University of Minnesota Press, 1994.

Caesar, Terry. "Theory in the Boondocks." *Yale Journal of Criticism* 6, 2 (Fall 1993): 221–35.

———. "Back to the Future: Mourning and the Career of Specialization." *M/MLA. The Journal of the Midwest Modern Language Association* 32, 2/3 (Winter/Spring 1999): 70–87.

Derrida, Jacques. "Back from Moscow, in the USSR." In Mark Poster, ed. *Politics, Theory, and Contemporary Culture.* New York: Columbia University Press, 1993.

Fish, Stanley. Interview. *Thinking in the Twentieth Century.* Prod. Joel Foreman. Maryland Public Television. 1985.

Foucault, Michel. *Discipline and Punish: The Birth of the Prison.* New York: Vintage, 1979.

Gates, Henry Louis, Jr. "Editor's Introduction: Writing 'Race' and the Difference It Makes." *Critical Inquiry* 12, 1 (Autumn 1985): 1–20.

Giroux, Henry. *Disturbing Pleasures: Learning Pop Culture.* New York: Routledge, 1994.

Guillory, John. "Preprofessionalism: What Graduate Students Want." *Profession 96.* Modern Language Association, 1996: 91–99.

Kaplan, Caren. *Questions of Travel.* Durham: Duke University Press, 1996.

Larson, Magali Sarfatti. *The Rise of Professionalism.* Berkeley: University of California Press, 1977.

Lodge, David. *Small World.* New York: Macmillan, 1984.

Malamud, Bernard. *Pictures of Fidelman.* New York: Dell, 1970.

Malone, Michael. *Foolscap.* New York: Washington Square Press, 1993.

Nelson, Cary. "Always Already Cultural Studies: Two Conferences and a Manifesto." *M/MLA. Journal of the Midwest Language Association* 24, 1 (Spring 1991): 24–38.

———. "Lessons from the Job Wars." *Social Text* 44, 13 (Fall/Winter 1995): 121–34.

O'Hara, Daniel. "Lentricchia's Frankness." *Boundary* 2 21, 2 (1994): 40–62.

Phelan, James. *Beyond the Tenure Track: Fifteen Months in the Life of an English Professor.* Columbus: Ohio State University Press, 1991.

Rosovsky, Henry. *The University: An Owner's Manual.* New York: W. W. Norton, 1990.

Shumway, David. "The Star System in Literary Studies." *PMLA* 112, 1 (January 1997): 85–100.

Smith, Alison. "Secondary Education: Still an Ignored Market." *Profession* 96 (1996): 69–72.

Spivak, Gayatri Chakravorty. *The Post-Colonial Critic: Interviews, Strategies, Dialogues.* New York: Routledge, 1990.

———. "Acting Bits/Identity Talk." *Critical Inquiry* 18, 4 (Summer 1992): 770–803.

Williams, Jeffrey. "The Life of the Mind and the Academic Situation." *College Literature* 23, 3 (October 1996): 128–46.

Wolff, Janet. "On the Road Again: Metaphors of Travel in Cultural Criticism." *Cultural Studies* 7, 2 (1993): 224–39.

# FOUR

# TO BOLDLY GO WHERE NO MLA HAS GONE BEFORE

*Crystal Bartolovich*

*For Michael Sprinker, who always fought the good fight.*

—In this life, we want nothing but Facts. . .[1]

I playfully invoke the "Star Trek" series in my title not only because this collection's subtitle (*The Next Generation*) does so, but also because the crews of the "Enterprise" in both its old and new dispensations (as well as those of "Voyager" and "Deep Space Nine"), for all their highly visible "multicultural" inclusiveness, project into the future the very problem that concerns me here: a "community" which presents itself as a utopia of freedom and independence for its members, and yet seems capable of functioning only as a rigid hierarchy. Academic "communities," like those of the Star Trek star ships, often pride themselves on their ostensible enlightened distance from the rest of the universe: sexism, racism, homophobia are all—at least in theory—banished from their domains; women and minorities are not only encouraged to apply, but may end up stars. *Freedom* (as in "academic freedom") is one of the most bandied-about words in academic space. However, in actual practice this "freedom" is predicated, in a Hobbesian paradox, on deference to senior members of the profession and administration. Indeed, academic communities, like those of the military-modeled TV star ships, are intensely devoted to rank, with the gulf separating the untenured from the tenured, the "part-time" from the "full-time," and the graduate students from the faculty, looming especially large, though they may all teach in classrooms right next to each other, and follow similar itineraries through the library. In spite of their supposed "enlightenment," the capacity for—and accomplishment of—brutalities, from the petty to the severe, of such "communities" are an open secret of academia.[2] Yet the system persists, and, indeed, manages to mystify its practices as benign and just, or at least necessary. It is perhaps not surprising that participation in this myth is rather less eager at the lower end of the hierarchy.

What *is* surprising, however, is how very rarely open struggle breaks out in such putative "communities" even when the conflicts of interest are clear. Indeed, one reason why the Yale strikes of 1995–96 commanded such dramatic and sustained attention, it seems to me, is that they concretized contradictions which many of us feel in our own academic lives, but which are rarely addressed openly. On the one hand, many of us aspired to academic life precisely because it seems to offer a measure of freedom and control over time, thought, and labor largely unavailable elsewhere under conditions of capitalism. On the other, what we actually encounter en route to a Ph.D. and tenure rarely conforms to the fantasy we nurtured while applying to graduate school. We soon learn about the vagaries and impossible odds of the job market (and, later, for tenure), which gives rise to "disciplined" subjects whose anxieties leave little room for pleasure in the modicum of "control" we have over our labor. We discover, too, the hierarchy of institutions, and what this hierarchy will mean, materially, for our lives after graduate school should we manage to get a job at all. In addition, it does not take long to find out that "research" (of the "right" kind—depending upon fashion and the workings of the star system at the moment) is the dominant demand placed upon us for advancement to the upper echelon of the profession.

Above all, however, we learn that departments (much less universities) are rarely "democratic"—even formally. Where "democracy" does exist, there are, nevertheless, powerful pressures on junior (and other "marginal") members to "fit in" and "not rock the boat," though these demands are, of course, not clearly articulated in the faculty (or graduate student) handbook. By recording here what, in any case, every one already knows, I am not suggesting, of course, that differences of "knowledge" and "experience" do not exist or matter; however, I *am* contesting the implication of the hierarchy that, at all times and in all situations, these differences can be assumed to correspond to the existing academic pecking order, such that full professors (especially those at elite institutions) always know best. In the response of the senior MLA staff and officers to the passage of Resolution 6, which censured the administration of Yale University for strike-breaking activities in response to graduate student attempts to organize, we saw, I would argue, just such an assumption at work. And while this response is not especially surprising, it is nonetheless troubling. I want to take a closer look, then, at the official response of the senior MLA officers to the Yale situation, as well as the MLA membership's response to it more generally, and consider what these different responses might reveal about a "generational" (or, more broadly, a "situational") rift in both universities and the MLA today.

I will begin with a symptom: while reading the fall 1996 *MLA Newsletter,* largely devoted to fallout from the Yale resolution, I noticed that there were more references in it to the need for "facts" to understand the Yale situation properly than even Dickens's Mr. Gradgrind could shake a stick at. This obsession with the "facts" on the part of the (then) MLA president Sandra Gilbert and the Executive Council members who commented on the resolution process in the *Newsletter,* piqued my curiosity from both a theoretical and a political perspective. For one thing, such a firm, uncritical faith in "the facts" seems at odds with the usual positions taken by humanists on these matters. Whether because they ally themselves with the Dickensian view that "the facts" can't get at everything (which is why we *need* poetry, ethics, and humanistic thought in the first place), or because they have kept up with the most cutting-edge work in critical theory, which suggests that the processes of meaning-production call into question any simple division of labor between "fact finding" and "interpretation," few literary critics these days would accept that "fact" bears any simple relationship to "truth," or that either of these categories can be separated from problems of interpretation. Remarkably, however, nowhere in the *Newsletter* does anyone raise the possibility that we might be dealing primarily with a problem of *interpretation* in the various controversies and disruptions which have ensued in the wake of the Yale strikes, and Resolution 6 in particular. Pursuing the reasons for this curious neglect might tell us something, it seems to me, about how the Yale strikes—to which most of this concern over "the facts" has been directed—could shed some light on problems of vision, and why the next generation might not see the world in quite the same way as their senior colleagues.

As a starting place, I can cite one of the MLA's own publications, *Redrawing the Boundaries.*[3] An article on "Cultural Criticism" in that volume suggests that

> theory . . . has become a name for the reflective or second-order discourse that breaks out when a community's previously unspoken assumptions are no longer taken for granted. These assumptions then become objects of explicit formulation and debate—very likely because the confines of the community are breached. Literary theory emerges when critics and teachers of literature no longer share agreements on the meaning of terms like literature, meaning, text, author, criticism, reading, aesthetic value, history, teaching, discipline and department—and, of course, culture. (428)

When there is agreement about the keywords used in a specific discourse community, the definitions of these terms appear to be common sense or "the facts." Disagreement, on the other hand, exposes a certain ambiguity about determining the facts, and reminds us that what we see is irreducibly dependent on our frames of reference.

Resolution 6—I do not think anyone would dispute—has brought to the fore numerous disagreements: about the mission of the MLA, the organization of the university, the relationship of graduate students to universities, and the legitimacy of unions in an academic context. It has also, discomfitingly, exposed a rift between senior members of the profession and the most junior. After reading the fall *MLA Newsletter,* however, one might think that the only issues it raises concern the mechanics of the resolution process—the difficulty of ascertaining "facts," and the ethics of censure. I do not wish to belittle these concerns; what does trouble me though is that they seem to have entirely overshadowed the substantive issues of Resolution 6. What we should be seeing in the Resolution 6 dilemma, it seems to me, is not *primarily* a problem with the resolution process, but rather a breakdown in fundamental assumptions, a disagreement about values and basic definitions. "Union," "University," "MLA," and "academic community" have become "community-breaching" concepts, in Graff and Robbins's terms. Raymond Williams has not only suggested that such keywords signal sites of social struggle, but also that they often do so in generational terms, as groups who forge their identities under vastly differing conditions simply don't "speak the same language."[4] However, examination of disputes around these keywords, and the role of the un- or under-employed in calling them into question, has been rather peremptorily laid aside as the MLA officers direct us to the presumably more important work of "getting the facts"—or, more accurately, talking about the importance of getting the facts (which takes us even further away from the important issues raised by Resolution 6).

Here are a few examples of comments from the Executive Council on the resolution process as they appear in the fall 1996 *MLA Newsletter* (emphasis mine):

> I have serious doubts about the appropriateness of resolutions censuring individuals or institutions, since these imply quasi-judicial *fact-finding* procedures that the MLA is not equipped to conduct. (15)

> I'd propose that all resolutions citing by name a specific person or educational institution be sent directly to a standing committee on *fact-finding*. (15)

> *Fact-finding* takes time, and as scholars and in the interest of fairness, we owe it to ourselves to take that time before risking that divisiveness. (14)

> Emergency resolutions seldom afford adequate opportunity for *checking facts* or soliciting other opinions and should therefore be abandoned in their present form. (16)

> When a resolution includes complicated and controversial issues, it is difficult to *amass enough information* to foster judicious decisions." (14)

The headnote introducing these comments helpfully points out that they were generated in response to "questions about emergency resolutions and resolutions that censure institutions or individuals [which] came up after the 1995 convention." The 1995 convention was, of course, the very one at which Resolution 6, an "emergency resolution" censuring the administration (individuals) of a particular institution (Yale), came onto the floor. Although Resolution 6 is not explicitly mentioned in the comments by Executive Council members from which the above-cited quotations are drawn, the repeated references to "emergency resolution" and "censure" keep pulling it in as a subtext—but not in order to consider any of its substantive issues; the council appears to see such resolutions only as dangers to be avoided. Indeed, aside from a repression of "Yale" while talking of it constantly, what all of the writers for the Executive Council seem to share is a fear that (1) because of resolutions like 6, the MLA is vulnerable to lawsuits if its resolution process is not changed, and (2) a proper defense against such legal challenge is to institute a committee (between the Delegate Assembly and the membership) to facilitate the collection and "checking" of facts in proposed resolutions. This is not so simple a proposition as it sounds in the abstract, as I will argue below, nor are its difficulties primarily ones of amassing and checking as the executive council implies—but first, back to the facts at hand.

A obsession with the facts—similar to that found in the Executive Council members' comments cited above—also manifests itself in the three letters from Yale senior faculty which accompanied the printed texts of the 1995 resolutions, circulated to the membership after the MLA that year. In the first of these letters, Annabel Patterson establishes this theme in her opening sentence, which claims that she will reveal "the facts that lie behind the graduate students' inflammatory rhetoric" in Resolution 6. Likewise, Margaret Homans contends that Resolution 6 is "factually erroneous, slanderous and personally motivated," while Linda Peterson and Ruth Yeazell critique the Delegate Assembly for passing the resolution before "ascertaining the facts." Homans additionally calls for the emendation of the MLA constitution to prevent the passage of such "groundless" resolutions in the future. I draw attention to this particular theme in these letters because we find it repeated so emphatically not only in the comments of the Executive Council which I quote above, but also, even more forcefully and explicitly, in Sandra Gilbert's analysis of the Yale situation.[5]

In her "President's Column" in the fall 1996 *Newsletter*, Gilbert presents numerous objections from the membership to the passage of Resolution 6 on evidential, political, and other grounds, including the claims that the accused were given insufficient opportunity to defend themselves, that the membership who voted in favor of the resolution improperly leapt to the conclusion that the complainant was right, and—the unkindest cut of all—that the presentation of facts in the case of Resolution 6 on the part of its proposers was so shoddy that it "betrays the ordinary standards of scholarship." The bulk of Gilbert's column is given over to the reported speech and writing of those MLA members who think that the resolution process in general, and resolution 6 in particular, is silly at best, and perhaps even evil and destructive of our professional practice. Lurking behind all of these comments (reinforced by the constant repetition of this theme in the Executive Council members' remarks), is the assertion that, the facts were never properly established in the case of Resolution 6, a view which Gilbert herself admits to holding: "I too am deeply disturbed by the same questions about standards of evidence that have troubled others who had procedural objections to the Yale resolution." This announcement is followed by a paragraph in which she details in the most incriminating way possible, the ostensible bad behavior of proponents of Resolution 6 at the delegate assembly meeting. The story—for her column—ends there.

However, in the "real world," as opposed to the "made for *MLA Newsletter*" version, the story does not end there. Gilbert fails to mention the eight pages of dissenting letters from Yale faculty and administrators (cited above) which went out with the first mailing on the 1995 resolutions, a forum which gave these members of the Yale community ample opportunity—an opportunity denied to the "complainants" it should be added—to present, at length, both a defense, and the facts as they saw them, to the membership as a whole. Additionally, no mention is made by Gilbert that, in spite of the attempt by these Yale faculty to discredit the resolution—which, one would presume, was through the best possible case that they could devise—the membership who voted was not convinced by their "facts."

One possible explanation for why these two niggling little matters are left out of Gilbert's account, is that if this longer story is told, it becomes rather more difficult to describe the Resolution 6 dilemma in terms of a crisis over "facts" and "standards of evidence." Although they claim to be bringing the flaming sword of the facts to cut through to the truth obscured by the "rhetoric" of Resolution 6, the letters from the Yale senior faculty actually offer little evidence of disagreement about any significant facts whatsoever. If one does not assume from the get-go that unions are inappropriate at Yale, or in general, the letters actually *corroborate* Resolution 6, by indicating that the striking graduate instructors were motivated by an attempt to have their elected union recognized by the administration, that they had made many other attempts through less drastic means to gain this recognition, and, most importantly, that threats of firing and other repercussions were directed at these instructors.[6] These are the crucial facts, the very ones that the National Labor Relations Board found easily determinable, and upon which they based their decision that the Yale administration behaved improperly.[7] What the National Labor Relations Board calls "the facts" and what the Yale administration does are separated by significant differences over the proper relationship of graduate students to universities, the status of academic labor, and the value of unions for academic organizing. However, instead of focusing on the politics of facts—the power relations which might influence what are called "facts" in the first place and who has the right to identify them—the presentation of the resolution dilemma in the fall *Newsletter* seems to claim that the 3,828 members of the MLA who voted for Resolution 6 must be poor scholars, swayed by "passion," who did not have the best interests of the profession, the MLA or "scholarship" in mind.

To see if there is any merit to such a view, let us examine the actual sites of disagreement as the letters of the Yale anti-union faculty indicate them: (1) the letter writers contend that the graduate instructors' union is illegitimate and therefore cannot serve as an appropriate motivation to action; Resolution 6 contends that the union is legitimate, and is being treated unfairly by the Yale administration. (2) the letter writers aver that conditions at Yale are not so bad that they warrant a union in any case; Resolution 6 asserts the right of the grad instructors to make their own decisions on this score. (3) the letter writers argue that threats of firing and academic blacklisting do not constitute inappropriate responses to what they see as unwarranted and inappropriate actions on the part of the grad instructors; Resolution 6 sees these threats as union-busting "academic reprisals" in the sense that they disrupt the possibility of "academic community" in any but the terms of the Yale administration (about which more below). These disagreements, I think it is rather easy to see, arise not at the level of "the facts" (in spite of the claims of the letter writers), but rather at the level of *interpretation*.

Let us assume for a moment, then, that an MLA "fact-finding" committee *had* been in place, and that Resolution 6 had been referred to it. On what exactly would they have ruled? On the simple facts (graduate instructors did not hand in their grades; they were threatened with disciplinary action and loss of jobs) there was *no* disagreement between the claims of Resolution 6 and those of the Yale senior faculty who wrote their letters attempting to undermine it. Indeed, a letter (from senior Yale administrators) threatening the striking student-instructors with the loss of their jobs is actually included (as an attachment) with the materials sent out by the Yale senior faculty. Given this mass of "evidence," what would a fact-finding committee decide? Whether or not unions were appropriate organizing agents for graduate instructors? Whether or not grade strikes were appropriate activities? Whether or not the Yale strikers' grievances were "real"? The persons (senior faculty from elite institutions) most likely to be asked to serve on a fact-finding committee to answer such questions given current MLA structures and habits are precisely those least well positioned to understand (much less empathize with) the plight of graduate students at the current conjuncture. Thus, I for one would be extremely unhappy with the insertion of an MLA committee between the membership and the Delegate Assembly on these matters of interpretation—a profoundly undemocratic move. Before we shift to any such system, then, we should be clear about its potential implications, especially given the tendency the MLA leadership has shown to displace issues of "interpretation" into issues of "fact" in the case of Resolution 6.

That so many of the anti-union commentators on the strike have failed to notice this odd equivocation of interpretive problems as "factual" ones, seems to stem from a fantasy that if only the facts were known, then the Yale administrators obviously would have been exonerated, and the grad instructors exposed to be ungrateful, spoiled children acting up. Instead of admitting the possibility that conflicting visions of the relations of students to universities are at stake here—and, in fact, that the world might look like a quite different place from the empyrean height of the Karl Young Chair and the more earthy plane of graduate life, even graduate life at Yale[8]—many MLA officers seem to assume that those who voted in favor of Resolution 6 must have misunderstood, been deluded by, or blinded themselves to, the "factual" situation. This astonishes and dismays me, not only because of the implication that a vote for Resolution 6 necessarily indicates shoddy scholarship and "prejudice," but also—more importantly—because I think that in the displacement of a question of "interpretation" into a question of "the facts," one of the most important issues of the Yale strikes for the MLA is being occluded; namely, that the visions of "scholarly community" which underlie the various positions taken are radically different. On the one hand, the Yale senior faculty seem to assume that "academic community" is something that we already have, a given, and that a union is, thus, a threat to the very "ideals and standards" upon which that community is based. On the other hand, the striking grad instructors seem to be suggesting we need to rethink "academic community" altogether.

As I reread the letters from the senior Yale faculty, I was struck by their reliance on a certain vision of academic community as opposed to corporate community or a wage relation. The senior administrators at Yale, for example, described their rationale for refusal to recognize the union as "educational," emphasizing the difference between the university and other payers of wages. In other words, the university community is special and fragile, and unions contaminate it. Margaret Homans puts it this way: "it is not possible for Yale students—in training, after all, to occupy professional positions—to constitute the proletarianized body they claim to be." What both the administrators and Homans take pains to assert is that universities in general—and Yale in particular—are qualitatively different spaces than corporations, and that the universities internal relations *cannot*, then, be ones of exploitation but must, rather, be ones in which its members will, in time, be able to work things out in "an atmosphere of mutual respect." It does not seem to be thinkable—or at least not admittable—to many of the senior administrators and faculty at Yale that the possibility for "mutual respect" is actually *structurally* impeded by the very hierarchical privilege that they cling to in their relations with graduate students. Because of this remarkable (or remarkably cynical) metanymic thinking, these senior faculty are capable of casting themselves in the role of unjustly wronged champions of the *university's* (and therefore the graduate students') best interests while defending their own.

For example, Annabel Patterson, after pointing out—emphatically—early in her letter that unions are not conducive to "an appropriate relationship between students and faculty in a nonprofit organization" concludes her letter with the observation that the faculty "regret that graduate student anxieties, especially about their future in a constrained job market, have led to such alienation" and offers the assurance that the Yale faculty "continues to work hard to improve morale and communication, and to persuade students that the teaching profession has ideals and standards which can never be identical with those in an industry or corporation." The great divide between the material conditions of existence of graduate students and the faculty suggest that something more substantial than "communication" and "persuasion" is needful to improve these conditions. Nevertheless, it is easy to sympathize with Patterson's assertions; the myth of "academic community" is one of the most powerful ideologies in the academy—and it *is* attractive: a fantasy of the space outside of capitalism where scholars think deep thoughts and organize their relations with receptive and supportive colleagues in an "atmosphere of mutual respect" with no exploitation or pettiness anywhere in sight.[9] The problem, of course, is that it bears no resemblance to actual relations and the institutional structure which underwrites them. For this reason, "Academic Community" is a myth in which the next generation cannot afford to indulge uncritically. If we attempt to examine this myth out of the sentimental haze produced by hooding ceremonies and their appeal to the "ancient and universal community of scholars," we can begin to ask questions of power which paint a different landscape than the idyllic scene of the grove of academe (now disrupted, alas, by those unruly and indecorous graduate students) the senior faculty from the putative Garden of Yale attempt to conjure up.

To consider these questions of power, it might be helpful to recall that people can (and necessarily do) occupy multiple subject positions at the same time. It is possible to be "a student" and "an employee" simultaneously—and for the interests of each of these roles to conflict with the other, depending upon the structuring relations. For example, if we change the above formulation to "a woman" and "an employee" it probably would be relatively easier for most readers to see what I am getting at. Although as an "employee" a woman may be "well paid" and have "good benefits" as these are understood under conditions of capitalism, she might at the same time be treated in patronizing or unprofessional ways by male colleagues who rationalize their behavior by appeals to certain male and female roles in the social order. Or, alternatively, an employer might claim he is treating a female employee "well" even while paying her less than men who perform comparable tasks, on all sorts of grounds that now seem questionable to most people, but not so very long ago seemed perfectly natural.[10]

With this in mind, going back to my example of students who are also employees, I want to open up the possibility of imagining that what might *appear* to be treating "students" well, according to a certain set of traditional hierarchical (even quasi-feudal) assumptions (e.g., graduate students are bound to the senior faculty by ties of duty and should rely on them to manage their relations with the administration rather than acting as agents on their own behalf), might well leave them exploited as "employees"—especially under current conditions in which so-called apprenticeship leads so infrequently to tenure-track employment. At Yale in 1994–95 school year, for example, the combined placement record of ten humanities departments was only 27 percent, which must have left many students—not to mention the 73 percent of candidates who remained unplaced—doubtful, if not rueful, that they were "in training . . . to occupy professional positions"—as Margaret Homans asserts—since painfully few of these positions seemed to exist (Young 184). In any case, surely the senior faculty at Yale can't really believe that they are simply doing graduate assistants an educational favor by hiring them to grade papers for the large lecture classes? And that the department and the university benefit not at all from this arrangement? Only according to the logic of a Tom Sawyer tricking his friends into whitewashing the fence for him can we be expected to go along with such a ruse.

Of course it is important to be able to point out the ways in which the university is not exploitative in the same way that a factory is, but it is also helpful to be able to see in what ways it *is* like a factory if one is interested in creating real alternatives to capital, to whose needs the university, as well as factories, are subsumed. Willy-nilly, universities *are* increasingly taking on the practices and discourses of corporate capital. Jeff Williams recently catalogued many instances of this trend, noting in particular an administrative fascination with "productivity" in publications from the *New York Times* to the *Chronicle of Higher Education.* One of my own former employers, Carnegie Mellon, has even been praised by *Business Week* magazine as exemplary in its move toward corporate-style management: "Managing a university as if it were a business seems to pay off. . . . Research money pours into [Carnegie Mellon's] computer science department. Industry pays for fully half of the engineering department, with each professor bringing in an average of $215,000 a year in outside research money" (Baker 116). In 1994 alone, Carnegie Mellon received over a million and a half dollars in royalties for its technological and other inventions. This performance was not singular; thirty universities earned even more that year in this way—*including Yale.*[11]

Indeed, in spite of the confident assertions of the senior faculty in English that

Yale president Richard Levin is one of them, and that he does not see the university as a corporation, the president's actual practice suggests otherwise. A recent *Business Week* article reports that "Levin has for several years mulled what many of his peers have considered for their colleges—running the place like a business. 'We have to manage this institution efficiently,' he says, 'we cannot do everything under the sun'" (Jackson 102). Only faculty and alumni resistance, the article goes on to claim—not a devotion to the singularity of academic community attributed to him by Annabel Patterson, et al.—have limited his efforts to downsize Yale as rapidly as he would like. Meanwhile, numerous other institutions *are* downsizing at more or less rapid pace, increasing their use of part-time and graduate student instructional labor with alacrity, as well as increasing teaching loads and course enrollment numbers.[12] Hence, Evan Watkins has observed recently that though "the analogy [between a factory and a university] doesn't yield a point-by-point comparison, . . . there seems to me good reason to suspect that the dominance of a capitalist mode of production has involved structurally comparable transformations of 'intellectual' work as well, such that it would be no more possible to imagine a university English department as Samuel Johnson's study writ large than to imagine a factory as a giant artisan's workshop" (14). Watkins's point is that while it might not be accurate strictly speaking to analyze English teachers as proletarians (a view he vehemently rejects), it might be important to wonder how the structure of the university as a workplace changes as capital restructures, and what impact these changes have on English—and other—teachers.

One of the changes that occurs in such a situation is that "academic community" comes to signify differently as the vast majority of its members find themselves in an unanticipated position relative to both the institutions in which they work, and to each other. Stanley Aronowitz has chronicled the declining power of faculty organizations relative to administrative staffs backed by boards of trustees over the past two decades as universities modeled themselves more on corporate and less on communal models. He observes: "Nearly all institutions of higher education maintain the formal apparatus of faculty sovereignty. . . . But in both public and private university sectors, power to make decisions has slowly shifted to administrators who now retain final determination of nearly all university issues" (91). Aronowitz, rightly I think, sees this as an assault on academic freedom—not in the sense of an *individual's* freedom to think, research and write as he or she sees fit, but rather in terms of "the rights of the faculty as a collectivity to retain sovereignty over the educational process" (91). This important reminder that "academic freedom" is an issue for a *community* and not just of individuals is salutary. At a time when—especially for humanists—the university is changing radically, we find ourselves in a position to rethink not just what the university should be, but to whom it belongs: questions which crises such as recent labor unrest at Yale bring to the fore dramatically.

These questions of "belonging" confront the next (potential) generation of scholars most immediately and painfully. When only 46 percent of all job candidates in English—according to the MLA's own data—are likely to land a tenure-track job, it is not surprising that graduate students are not willing to suffer their graduate years in silence.[13] For many of them, unions have come to represent a chance at belonging, after all, to an "academic community" of which they too have dreamed but which seems increasingly elusive. To anyone who thinks that unionization is, of itself, the death of that community, and that unions, like the resolution process, *incite* divisiveness, this must seem misguided at best. But I would like to put forth another reading: that neither unions nor the MLA's resolution process *cause* divisiveness; they are, rather, symptoms of divides that are already here. To fail to recognize this is to continue to see an imperiled (but pure) community where there is actually already (to borrow from the Graff and Robbins article I cite at the beginning of this chapter) a breach. For this reason, I found it disturbing that Sandra Gilbert refers (in the Fall *MLA Newsletter*) to the "sides" of the dispute in the Yale strikes as "the union" and "Yale," with the unfortunate implication that the striking graduate instructors—most of whom had been at Yale longer than at least one of the letter writers among the full-time faculty—are not part of Yale. For the grad instructors, however, the union is not a declaration of independence from an actually existing academic community called "Yale." It is rather an assertion of rights to some meaningful powers of self-determination in a community-to-be called Yale toward which they contribute their labor, pedagogic, scholarly—and political.

Hegemony theory offers us a way to analyze this situation in a more helpful manner than accusing dissenters of inciting divisiveness (see note 3, this chapter). It directs us to examine the dynamic among competing group interests and consider why the "consent" of subordinated groups (such as, in this case, graduate students) to the rule of the dominant academic ideology of "community" has broken down (another way of saying "the confines of the community are breached"). Seen from this perspective, the function of the call for "fact" collecting on the part of the senior faculty at Yale emerges as an attempt to "define the situation" in such a way that it can be resolved on terms most favorable to them, at a moment when dominant ideology is in crisis. Ideology works by naturalizing a partial view as universal and necessary: as "fact." Hence, the senior faculty at Yale want to try to make it seem to be a fact that unions are inappropriate organizing vehicles for university teachers, that grad instructors are simply students and not in any sense employees, and that the university is somehow outside of capitalism. Other definitions of the situation are, of course, possible. Graduate student unions disrupt the balance of power in the universities—including the power of the senior faculty to "define the situation." Rather than relying on their advisors to see that they are looked after when departmental largess is handed out, or assuming that the very senior faculty who benefit from the pleasures of graduate teaching—and a decrease in their own work load provided by graduate assistants and instructors—can be relied upon to advocate student interests at all times, graduate students are increasingly taking matters into their own hands. In doing so, they define the situation of graduate study and employment rather differently than their senior colleagues. If the MLA senior staff and officers could manage for a moment to think of the ensuing disagreements as a struggle among competing definitions of the situation rather than a stark black and white of facts (a position so un-nuanced that they would be unlikely to bring it to their study of literature), they might be able to see how they have simply taken on, in their discourse of facts, the definition of the situation of one side in the Yale dispute. A more balanced perspective would prompt them to bring the interpretive skills and appreciation of complexity gleaned from their professional practice to bear as forcefully upon this social text as literary ones.

Of course if it is so, as I am suggesting, that the senior faculty at Yale who wrote the letters, as well as the senior MLA staff are interested rather than neutral fact amassers, then what of the striking students: are their positions "interested" too? Surely, yes. It is here that the question of justice—and some recognition of the ways that different relations to concrete, material conditions of existence can lead to quite different definitions of the situation—must come into play. One of the striking students has described a moment of recognition and politicization in his graduate career when, as a young and doubtful-of-unions newcomer to Yale, he had listened to the narrative of an older graduate student who, because he had a wife and child who needed to be included in his health plan, ended up being forced to give "roughly half of his income back to Yale for health care" coverage. Coming up against the hard realities of graduate life for himself and his peers caused him to conclude that "there really are issues of justice here. GESO [union] has the moral high ground; it's not *just* Yale [corporation] trying to do what's in their interest and we're trying to do what's in our interest" (emphasis mine, quoted in Robin and Stephens, 60). This sorting out of "interest" in a materialist analysis proceeds by way of examining the relative structural positions of the speakers. In this instance, we might well ask whether it might not be possible that graduate students are in a better position than the senior faculty at Yale to see the "facts" that matter and the interpretations that matter *for justice* in the case of resolution 6.[14]

So what is to be done? I propose first of all that the next generation think about what "academic community," as we wish to have it, means in explicit terms, without assuming that academic community is some timeless, obvious and perfect thing that we already have, that has somehow suddenly become threatened by unruly graduate students and pesky unions as some of our senior colleagues have done in relation to the Yale strike. Community is, rather, what its potential members must imagine and work *for,* with clear-eyed analysis of the complex material conditions in which we all (currently, unequally) work. Moving the debate in this direction will push the emphasis from the local divisiveness unions supposedly generate to the long-term possibilities for an academic community that is democratic and broad based in ways we might not yet be able to comprehend fully. This is not to say that there is—pluralistically—room for everyone; the members of the profession who confuse the capitulation of graduate students to administrative interests with "mutual respect," are, it must be said, not very promising candidates. In the meantime, the next generation cannot permit the MLA to give in to a fear of taking stands because powerful groups (such as the Yale administration) might be unhappy about it and threaten lawsuits. Such threats would be possible no matter how many facts are collected so long as fundamental disagreements about how to interpret them are in force. Dismissing the perspective of an opponent as due to passion rather than reason, rhetoric rather than fact, and prejudice as opposed to objectivity—as the senior Yale faculty and MLA officers have attempted to do—stops the debate to be sure. But at what cost? Graduate students and un- and under-employed faculty are a significant percentage of the profession and of the MLA membership, but not, of course, of its leadership. Surely, then, it is not impertinent at this juncture to consider the power relations which have structured the MLA's representation of what counts as "fact" and what does not, what counts as "reasonable" and what does not, what counts as "neutral" and what does not, in the case of Resolution 6.

This said, let me be perfectly clear about what I am *not* saying. I am not suggesting that "evidence" is unimportant and that resolutions should be free-for-alls in which anyone can say anything whatsoever and that the membership should simply go along. Resolutions should be carefully scrutinized by the membership, and as much information should be circulated concerning them as is possible. The recently instituted revision to the resolution process—which provides a forum for members to comment on the resolutions prior to voting—is very helpful. Given that safeguards such as this are already in place, however, what I *am* suggesting is that a situation in which a resolution composed of out-and-out lies would be proposed strikes me as extremely unlikely; establishing the facts simply is not so much of an issue as the Executive Council and president of the MLA are claiming.

The vague and obsessive focus upon "the facts" seems to function as a distraction, a red herring, more than anything else, especially since Resolution 6, the motivating case for "reform" of the resolution process (in ways that render it less democratic), does not really fit the "lack of facts" thesis when examined carefully. MLA members are sophisticated readers of text, and those who actually vote on resolutions have numerous means to become well informed on the issues under discussion (which in these days of the computerized databases and email is easier than ever before). I myself read the (anti-union) comments on Yale's official webpage and many articles in major U.S. papers written on Yale and strikes since 1984 to get a sense of its administration's past behavior in labor disputes (not very nice). I also saw a great deal of diverse and thoughtful material written on the strikes, including a widely circulated letter penned by Yale senior faculty who *supported* the striking instructors (a view not explicitly represented in MLA publications at all). Given a highly literate, engaged, and research-skilled membership, I think a case of outright fraud in a resolutions extremely unlikely—and its passage even less likely.

What is likely, however, is that numerous issues will arise which will be contentious, and in which each side's position might well look outrageous, unfair, and impossible to the other. The NLRB's list of faculty and administrators at Yale who threatened students during the strike is unlikely to convince the offending parties that they acted improperly if they do not accept the students' right to organize and strike, however incriminating the list might look to those readers who see the strike differently. On the other hand, the declaration of Yale's PR department on its webpage that "Yale is a good employer!" with its list of aspects of life at Yale that support this contention to its own satisfaction, is unlikely to convince unsatisfied workers (or their supporters), whether they are in the library, the classroom, or the kitchen. The point here is not that there are no "facts," but rather that no amassing of facts—without attention to the underlying issues through which we see them—is going to get us very far in the debate over how to conduct the resolution process.

So I think it is lamentable that the important issues raised by Resolution 6 (about the status of graduate students, their labor, and academic community) have been displaced onto an argument about how the resolution process should be conducted—an argument which seems to keep us from looking at (and dealing with) the problems which gave rise to the resolution as we go around and around about the process of generating them.[15] At this rate, those (few) of us from the next generation who do make it onto the ship will have to keep dealing with the same old stars while we talk about the miserable injustice of our world, when the point (as always) has been to change it.

*Notes*

A shorter version of this chapter was part of the panel "What Does Literary Criticism Have To Do with the Yale Strikes?" at the 1996 MLA Convention. It was organized by the Division on Literary Criticism in order to consider the impact and meaning of the Yale Strikes of 1995–96, which included a graduate student "grade strike" (refusal to hand in grades at end of term) for union recognition and a strike of service workers (including kitchen and grounds crew staff) and how their lessons might be useful to thinking through problems facing higher education today (for an excellent general overview of the issues posed by the strike, see the essays collected by Cary Nelson in *Will Teach for Food: Academic Labor in Crisis*). The title of the MLA panel in which I participated refers to Yale strikes, not just the graduate instructor's strike, even though, because of the particular emphasis of Resolution 6 (a MLA delegate assembly resolution censoring Yale's administration for its treatment of striking graduate students), the grad instructors have received most of the attention among MLA members. Nevertheless, it is important to recall that students were not the only group engaged in strike action recently at Yale; clerical workers, librarians, and dining-hall workers were striking as well. In joining a union, the grad instructors have allied themselves with these workers (and vice versa), as well as with a long history of labor struggle both at Yale and in the United States. They have opened the possibility of forging an "academic community" which includes all university workers, professor and kitchen staff, librarian and secretary, as our colleagues in Britain have done in the General Strike of the Universities in November of 1996 (see Meikle's "One Out, All Out"). They have forged lateral alliances with other universities where students are unionized (or hope to be) rather than thinking of their own predicament or the predicament of others as isolated and isolatable. The problems that confront us are collective problems, requiring collective solutions. As capital and the university restructure themselves over time, we will find ourselves in the position of having to reassess assumptions, concepts, and relations previously taken for granted. Unions might not be the only, or even the best, solution to the problems we confront along the way, but at the current conjuncture they have provided a collective structuration for thinking and organizing that for too long has gone on in an atomized fashion. To these collectivist ends, in this chapter I was particularly concerned with the fall 1996 *MLA Newsletter*'s representations of Resolution 6 (censuring the Yale administration's behavior during a "grade strike" waged by graduate student instructors), and how these representations seemed to foreclose the complex analysis of the situation necessary to gleaning any lasting lessons from that resolution. I attempt to open up the possibility for an ongoing conversation on some of its fundamental issues in these remarks. I am grateful to Andrew Ross for asking me to participate in the MLA panel for which this chapter was originally written, and to those colleagues, especially Tim Brennan, Lisa Frank, Keya Ganguly, Paula Geyh, Jeff Williams, and Yu Mi Yang, who commented on it before and/or afterward. Thanks also to Ivo Kamps who solicited this essay for *Journal x* when he got wind that it had (unsurprisingly) been turned down by *Profession.* Thanks as well to Peter Herman who later solicited it for *Day Late, Dollar Short.* In the rejection letter from *Profession,* Phyllis Franklin suggested that "more space than was needed" was given in this article to the critique of the MLA. I hope that other readers might see this as a matter of interpretation. I have here slightly revised the text that originally appeared in *Journal x.*

1. The epigraph is borrowed from Mr. Gradgrind in Dickens's *Hard Times,* a book which reminds us that there are more than "facts" in this world.

2. Of course not all senior members of university faculties participate willingly in the perpetuation of the mythology of the school; Indeed, as Althusser's "Ideology" essay recognizes, in terms appropriate to my own argument as well, a few resist: "I beg pardon of those teachers who, in dreadful conditions, attempt to turn the few weapons they can find in the history and learning they 'teach' against the ideology, the system and the practices in which they are trapped. They are a kind of hero. But they are rare . . . " (157).

3. I chose to cite this text primarily because it is collected in an MLA publication, and, thus, I assumed that its position would carry at least some weight and legitimacy with members of that organization, whether they agree with it or not. My own position on theoretical work, which I will develop through the argument of this chapter, is actually closer to Stuart Hall's neo-Gramscian "ideology critique," which relies upon a complex theorization of hegemony. See, for example, "The Problem of Ideology: Marxism without Guarantees."

4. Williams opens his *Keywords* with an anecdote about just such a process. As a young man, just back from the war, he realized that he did not "speak the same language" as the pre-war world. This theme can be tracked through his work in various guises. For example, in his discussion of "structure of feeling" in *Marxism and Literature* he observes that "no generation speaks quite the same language as its predecessors" and links these differences to altered "practical consciousness" formed under conditions unlike those experienced by the previous generation in significant ways (131). Of course, Williams does not assume that it is impossible for generations to identity with and understand each other; he is simply observing *tendencies,* which (as in the case of the Yale strike) often correspond to (and thus are reinforced by) differences in *interest,* as well.

5. I am not implying that this similarity necessarily points to "collusion" on the part of the MLA officers and the Yale faculty who wrote the letters complaining about Resolution 6—ideology does not work that way for the most part. What interests me is that so many MLA

officers—probably with the best of intentions—consciously or unconsciously bought into, and reproduced, the claims of the senior Yale faculty as "true" when these same claims appear to be patently "rhetorical" to other readers. Leaving open the possibility for the moment that the attempt to place all the facts on one side and all the rhetoric on the other in this dispute simply will not bear up to scrutiny, we must consider, then, the implications of the MLA officers' discursive alliance with the Yale senior faculty, as I attempt to do in this chapter.

6. Linda Peterson and Ruth Yeazell note in their letter, for example, that "for a number of years now, some graduate students at Yale have been agitating in various way in support of a union—meeting, pamphleteering, picketing, even engaging in temporary 'job actions'." Annabel Patterson points out that a letter from senior administrators at Yale "explained to the part-time acting instructors that those who failed to turn in their grades [that is, participated in the grade strike] . . . would not be allowed to teach in the spring."

7. The *New York Times* reported in November of 1996 that "lawyers for the National Labor Relations Board . . . plan to charge Yale University with acting illegally by punishing teaching assistants who staged a grade strike last December in a drive to unionize" (Greenhouse 6). The Board's determination to pursue this course was based on the collecting of evidence of numerous threats by various members of the senior faculty and administration of Yale toward striking graduate assistants. Representatives of the administration never have denied the making of these threats; their position was rather that, as the *New York Times* article notes, "in the past, the board's lawyers treated graduate assistants as students rather than employees" and thus their treatment of the striking teachers was justified.

8. The thorny question of how to deal with the relatively elite status of Yale graduate students in relation to other graduate students (which they would hardly deny) raises itself here. One thing that is clear, however, is that no matter how privileged they may be in relation to graduate students in other sites, they are not privileged in relation to the senior faculty in their departments. Furthermore, I think that an important analogy can be drawn through an examination of labor history. It has often (though, of course, not exclusively) been the case that relatively well-off groups were organized before other groups (Northern factories before Southern ones; "Big Steel" before the small plants)—and that the organizations established by the somewhat more secure workers provided a structure for the more vulnerable groups to join, offering them an otherwise unavailable margin of protection. Without claiming that graduate students are exactly like steel workers (obviously not so), I think that one can claim that elite graduate students are in a position relative to more exploited graduate students which is analogous to Big Steel's relationship to smaller plants earlier in the century. If it succeeds in unionizing the teaching staff at a major private university, GESO will have set an important precedent which will be helpful not only to graduate student organizing, but also the organizing of part-time faculty and even full-time faculty at private schools far less privileged than Yale. Hence, Margaret Homans misses the point in her observation that "it would be appropriate for students to unionize at those schools where teaching loads are much higher than at Yale and where reliance on graduate teaching is greater. Part-time and adjunct faculty with Ph.D.'s present an even more legitimate motive to unionize, although they are not part of the union movement at Yale. But it is not possible for Yale students—in training, after all, to occupy professional positions—to

constitute the proletarianized body they claim to be." The unionization of Yale students might well *enable* the unionization of the other groups Homans names. In any case, "students . . . at those schools where teaching loads are much higher than at Yale" are also in "training . . . to occupy professional positions"—so it is not entirely clear why it is proper for them to unionize but not Yale students on that ground alone. But more importantly, while Yale students are undoubtedly better off financially, in work conditions and even in future prospects than many of their graduate student colleagues at other schools, this by no means suggests that within the local power dynamic they have no legitimate grievances. In addition, the part-time workers with Ph.D.'s, who Homans admits are an exploited group at Yale, can certainly benefit from a graduate instructor's union, which, should it ever be recognized, would provide a site in which they could organize in relative safety from reprisals (such as being fired) fear of which no doubt contributes to their current nonparticipation in GESO.

9. Jameson's dialectic of ideology and utopia is pertinent here. At the conclusion of *The Political Unconscious,* he argues that even retrograde ideological positions can contain the germs of utopian hope, and thus that they should be read in such a way that "a functional method for describing cultural texts is articulated with an anticipatory one" (296). In other words, one might (and should) explore the work performed by particular texts toward reproducing the status quo, or a specific nexus of interests, while also recognizing the desire for a nonexploitative, democratic "collective-associational" future which might be expressed simultaneously with it (in concepts, to take the case in hand, such as "academic community"). Problems arise in assuming that the latter already exists in the guise of the former.

10. One of the main issues of the staff strikes at Yale in the mid-eighties was, as a matter of fact, such gendered discrepancies in pay. Though hotly disputed at the time, the case for equal pay now seems practically incontrovertible, and the case against preposterous (which does not, alas, mean that inequalities do not persist). On such a model, one wonders what the case against graduate student unions will look like in ten years time!

11. Data culled from the Association of University Technology Managers' survey of "Gross Royalties Received . . . for Fiscal year 1994"—part of its *Licensing Survey* for that year.

12. See Cary Nelson's much cited article for *Social Text,* and the essays collected in *Higher Education under Fire,* edited by Michael Bérubé and Cary Nelson.

13. If these figures are "disquieting" (as she puts it) to Sandra Gilbert, imagine what they must be like for those people more immediately affected. The passage in which she makes this admission bears quotation in all its grim detail: For the 1993–94 graduating Ph.D.'s who got postsecondary academic jobs (75 percent) "only 45.6 percent of the jobs in English . . . were full-time tenure-track positions. The smaller percentage of tenure-track jobs is especially disquieting. . . . I remind myself that the placement survey is several years old and the number of advertised positions has dropped since then!" (4).

14. "Standpoint" theory provides a rationale for this position. See, for example, Hartsock.

15. This is not to say that these issues are not being discussed by MLA officers, or in forums the MLA provides; I am simply suggesting that it is unfortunate that Resolution 6 has been excluded as a site for these discussions, especially since it offers a specific, concrete site to evaluate and work on.

*Works Cited*

Aronowitz, Stanley. "Higher Education: The Turn of the Screw." *Found Object* 6 (1995): 89–99.

Baker, Stephen. "Carnegie Mellon's Secret? Sticking to What it Does Best." *Business Week* May 24, 1993: 116.

Bérubé, Michael, and Cary Nelson, eds. *Higher Education under Fire.* New York: Routledge, 1995.

"Council Members Comment on Resolution Process." *MLA Newsletter* 28,3 (1996): 14–16.

Gilbert, Sandra. "President's Column: (Re)solving Our Differences." *MLA Newsletter* 28, 3 (1996): 3–4.

———"Business Week." *MLA Newsletter* 28, 2 (1996): 3–5.

Graff, Gerald, and Bruce Robbins. "Cultural Criticism." *Redrawing the Boundaries.* Ed. Stephen Greenblatt and Giles Gunn. New York: MLA, 1992, 419–36.

Greenhouse, Steven. "Labor Board Plans a Suit against Yale." *New York Times* November 19, 1996: B6.

Hall, Stuart. "The Problem of Ideology: Marxism without Guarantees." *Stuart Hall: Critical Dialogues in Cultural Studies.* Ed. David Morley and Kuan-Hsing Chen. London and New York: Routledge, 1996. 25–46.

Hartsock, Nancy. *Money, Sex, and Power: Toward a Feminist Historical Materialism.* Boston: Northeastern University Press, 1985.

Jackson, Susan. "Meanwhile, the Ivy League Is Rolling in Clover." *Business Week* December 22, 1997: 102.

Jameson, Fredric. *The Political Unconscious.* Ithaca: Cornell University Press, 1981.

Meikle, James. "One Out, All Out." *Guardian,* Higher Education, Tuesday November 19, 1996: 2.

Nelson, Cary. "Lessons from the Job Wars: Late Capitalism Arrives on Campus." *Social Text* 13, 3 (1995): 119–34.

———ed. *Will Teach for Food.* Minneapolis and London: University of Minnesota Press, 1997.

Robin, Corey, and Michelle Stephens. "Against the Grain: Organizing TAs at Yale" in *Will Teach for Food,* 44–79.

Watkins, Evan. *Work Time: English Departments and the Circulation of Cultural Value.* Stanford: Stanford University Press, 1989.

Williams, Jeffrey. "Renegotiating the Pedagogical Contract." *Class Issues: Pedagogy and the Public Sphere.* Ed. Amitava Kumar. New York: New York University Press, 1997.

Williams, Raymond. *Keywords* (revised ed.). New York: Oxford University Press, 1983.

———*Marxism and Literature.* Oxford: Oxford University Press, 1977.

Young, Cynthia. "On Strike at Yale." *minnesota review* 45/46 (1996): 179–95.

# FIVE

# "IT'S A BEASTLY ROUGH CROWD I RUN WITH": THEORY AND THE "NEW UNIVERSITY"

## Kalí Tal

*It's a beastly rough crowd I run with. No doubt about it, junior faculty are getting out of shape and out of hand. . . . Even to the enemy of our enemies, it seems, we look something like a cross between Johnny Rotten and Cotton Mather: just take the Sex Pistols' political tact and respect for authority, toss in the Puritans' good cheer and sense of rhythm, and presto, you've got Rotten Mather, assistant professor of English, thirty years old and not to be trusted.*[1]

On April 2, 1997, I came home to find an unopened certified letter on my kitchen table. My roommate was staring at it like it was a dead rat. He'd signed for it, which made me unhappy. "Never sign for someone else's certified mail," I told him. I never sign for certified mail myself, unless I know what's in the envelope. But I knew what was in this envelope. I'd been anticipating its arrival for about three days. It was a notice of nonrenewal for my position as "founding faculty member and Professor" at Arizona International Campus (AIC), a new experimental nontenure college of the University of Arizona (UA).

In less than ninety days I'd be unemployed, a grim prospect under any circumstances, but after moving from New Haven, Connecticut, to Tucson, Arizona, to accept this job with the understanding that the original one-year contract would be renewed on a multiyear continuing basis, it was a shock to find myself stranded thousands of miles from my support networks without a penny of savings. There had, in fact, been no warning. Neither the provost of AIC nor the director of the academic house within which I worked had ever given me either oral or written notice that there was a problem with the performance of my duties. I was the only faculty member whom the provost declined to provide with a written evaluation letter. When queried, the provost claimed that the terms and conditions under which I was hired stated he was not required to provide a reason for my nonrenewal. This was news to me. I'd never seen the terms and conditions under which I was hired.

There had been rumors flying among the faculty for a couple of weeks, but there were a lot of rumors at AIC. I'd thought that nonrenewal was a distant possibility for a little over a month, but the first confirmation that I was in serious trouble came on 27 March, when the provost canceled my scheduled evaluation meeting. He canceled it for no reason I could understand. He was there. I was there. We met at the appointed hour but he told me that he was not going to talk to me about my evaluation. I asked if there was a problem. He answered that if I didn't know what the problem was, he wasn't going to tell me. He asked me if there was anything else I wanted to talk about. I told him I didn't have anything to talk about except my evaluation, and I couldn't understand why he was withholding it. He again refused to discuss it. That was, without a doubt, the most surreal conversation I've ever had. Colleagues and attorneys have listened to it and they agree it's surreal. I've got it on tape. In Arizona, you're allowed to tape a conversation even if the other parties don't know you're doing it. If they ask you, you're supposed to tell them. The provost didn't ask. I'd been told to tape the meeting by a colleague on the UA main campus faculty, who was suing over a tenure decision. She'd been sure of the worst. She was wiser than I, and she was right.

Though the rhetoric of "shared governance" had permeated the promotional materials on AIC, the provost ruled the campus with an iron hand. With only seven faculty members, all on one-year contracts, he didn't have much opposition. We were isolated from the faculty on the main campus both because of our distant location (about fifteen miles from the mothership) and because many UA faculty were suspicious of the nontenure campus, so we weren't welcomed into the UA community as colleagues and didn't have access to main campus support networks. Furthermore, there had been a concerted effort to keep us in the dark about our status—we'd been promised an opportunity to take part in drafting the terms and conditions of faculty employment at AIC, but somehow neither the opportunity nor the terms ever actually materialized.

From the beginning, mine had been the voice raised most insistantly in faculty meetings to ask questions about the structure of the institution, our workload, the resources which would be made available to us. In some cases, I was backed up by others, but I've never seen a more cautious and fearful group of faculty—for good reason. I spoke up out of principle, but I don't fool myself into thinking that there was any sort of nobility involved: I've got an outgoing nature, I'm extremely stubborn, and (most important) I realized that of all of that small group, I was the one least likely to be devastated by the loss of my job, even if there was retaliation and I was fired—I am trained in graphic and web design, so if necessary I can find employment outside the academy.

When we were hired, we were told we'd be protected by "due process" and have "academic freedom" under terms and conditions which were still under development. But when I was fired, it was as "professor (nontenure eligible)," a position which guaranteed no right to expectation of continuance from year to year. Renewal occurred at the sole discretion of the chief administrative officer, and faculty had the right to appeal only to the same administrator who had denied them renewal in the first place. Once dismissed, I had ninety days to find another job before facing the grim reality of unemployment in Tucson. When the power to renew a contract is so arbitrary and it is in the hands of one man, from whom no one representing faculty can demand accountability, it is surely unreasonable to expect that it will be exercised fairly and dispassionately.[2]

The larger issue was not whether my own contract was renewed, but whether this "experimental" new campus was going to set a precedent for other nontenure campuses by stripping faculty of all rights. I had come to AIC a believer in the notion that tenure could be replaced by a more equitable contract system, and that the tenure system could be improved upon by an alternative structure which culled out "deadwood" teachers and rewarded good teaching and good scholarship at the same time it guaranteed due process and academic freedom. But now I have my doubts that such a structure is possible or, more precisely, that those who advocate the abolition of tenure ever *intended* to create such an alternative structure. By the time my contract was not renewed, I had been transformed into an activist by my simple refusal to stay silent in the face of administrative dishonesty. This was not a comfortable role, particularly when other faculty did not vocally support me (though almost every other faculty member did share, privately, his or her concerns over the lack of due process and academic freedom). The Damoclean sword of nonrenewal hung over us, and kept most of us mute in our own corridors.

I'm sure that the provost expected me to quietly disappear—he'd survived a long time on the UA campus as an unpopular administrator and was locally famous for involvement in scandals and for high-handed decision making. Terminating my employment may have seemed to him business as usual, consolidation of power, a chilling warning to those under his direct control. But it didn't work out that way. Instead I waged a successful campaign for reinstatement, using the Internet as an organizing tool to mobilize support within the profession. I possessed a wealth of documents to back up my position, and though the outgoing president of UA, Manuel Pacheco, turned down my first appeal, the combination of pressure generated by publicity, support from the chair of the Faculty Senate, and the timely (and welcome) appointment of a new president, Peter Likins, worked in my favor and a reinstatement agreement was reached at the end of October, 1977. The provost stepped down in July of 1998, returning—ironically enough—to the tenure-track position he'd never given up in the Sociology Department of UA. He currently earns about $140,000 a year—I understand that he got a $10,000 raise this year. I'm sure Sociology is thrilled to have him back.

One of the unintended results of my Internet campaign was that I briefly became a national poster child for the tenure system. Though tenure, at least in regard to my problems at AIC, was never the immediate issue (the position was nontenure track from the outset), it was and is certainly an issue on the mind of just about everyone in the profession. Friends and colleagues forwarded me various posts from electronic discussion lists where my situation was the topic of conversation. Though most folks deplored the conditions of my nonrenewal, there were a number of academics who said (in crude paraphrase): "That's what you get when you take a nontenure-track job." As if I deserved it. As if I had a choice. As if, today, any of us do.

I was offered the position at AIC after three years on the market, and I'd applied for over eighty positions each year. I received my Ph.D. in American studies from Yale University in 1991. If I'd gone on the market then, I'd likely be tenured today; most of my friends are. At that point, the cachet of a Yale degree still gave an applicant an edge in the market. But my then-husband had finished his computer science Ph.D. in 1989, and had accepted a position in Washington, D.C. at a cool $50,000 a year. No starting salary in the humanities could possibly match that and I was still working on my dissertation, so we moved to D.C. together. I taught part time at George Mason University and at University of Maryland at College Park and I took a job at the U.S. Holocaust Memorial Museum, working first in their oral history department and then in their multimedia center. I kept the job at the museum even after finishing my dissertation—it was in D.C. and the pay was far better than a university job would have been. But in 1992 I went on the academic market seriously because teaching and research were what I'd always wanted to do.

When I went on the market, I was "armed" initially with a book contract (and, as the years passed, a published book) out of Cambridge University Press.[3] I had strong recommendations from well-respected Yale professors and, later, from other well-known scholars. I had peer review article publications, anthology chapters, and had started my own interdisciplinary journal, *Viet Nam Generation,* which had become known as the journal of record in the field of Viet Nam War and sixties studies. I'd begun as a teaching assistant in 1984, and I'd been teaching my own classes since 1986, always with excellent evaluations. In 1993 I received a Networked Associate Fellowship from the Institute for Advanced Technology in the Humanities, where I built the Sixties Project website (http://jefferson.village.virginia.edu/sixties) and ran a popular listserv called SIXTIES-L. In short, I should have been—from what all of my mentors told me—a prime candidate for a job.

My job-seeking history is enough like others that I will not go on at length about it. I will say, though, that I endured the same sort of mistreatment at MLA that many have described—interviews that were clearly not serious, or where everyone except the unsuccessful candidates knew that the job already belonged to someone else. By 1996, when I received the job offer from AIC, I was separated from my husband (and his salary), living in poverty in New Haven where the glut of unemployed and under-employed Ph.D.'s made finding even part-time work almost impossible, trying to make a go of running a small press, earning a little money building websites on the side, and looking for a full-time teaching job continuously. That year's applications seemed, once again, to have borne no fruit. When I received a late March phone call from AIC requesting an on-campus interview, I had just declared bankruptcy. I didn't have the luxury of turning down a nontenure-track position if I wanted to stay in the profession.

According to the American Association of University Professors, in 1995 52 percent of full-time professors have tenure. An additional 20 percent are on the tenure track. That means that 28 percent of the full-time positions (almost 1 in 3) are non-tenure track. And it's worse now than it was in 1995. Part-timers now make up about

42 percent of instructors nationwide,[4] so that means that over 55 percent of the jobs on the market (and the percentages will likely continue to grow) are never going to lead to tenure and most of the available nontenure jobs aren't even going to lead to full-time employment. So when AIC called, I said, "Sure! I'd love to come out and visit your campus!" And when they offered me a job, I took it. I had reservations about the one-year contract, but the provost assured me that it was only a formality and that the regents would approve multiple-year contracts for us in 1997. (I didn't know at the time that the state of Arizona had decided in 1995 that oral contracts for employment were no longer binding.)

This volume focuses on the way "shifts in the material conditions affecting the academy have influenced the theory and praxis of the next generation."[5] The story above outlines some of the material conditions of my environment. The next section underlines how these conditions, and conditions which preceded them, have affected my theoretical stance and the manner in which I practice my trade.

Peter Herman is quite right in placing me in the next generation, since I did receive quite a bit of my theory second- and third-hand, albeit in two of the hallowed sites in which that theory evolved. Paul de Man died the year that I arrived at Yale Graduate School. I did try taking a course from Harold Bloom, but fled after several sessions convinced me that a student of African American literature would have a hard time finding his classroom a hospitable environment. Because I'd come from the UC Santa Cruz American Studies Department (a hotbed of theory in the late 1970s and early 1980s), I was already familiar with feminist and literary theory, some of which *did* come from the source. My dissertation director at Yale, Robert Stepto, is, of course, a theorist, and through the African American studies courses I took, I was introduced to the work of Houston Baker and Skip Gates and Cornel West. I actually picked up most of the rest of my theory outside of the classroom, in conversation with other grad students, who pointed me to books I'd never heard professors mention. That was how I came across Derrida, Barthes, and Bakhtin, and learned Eco and Calvino were more than good novelists.

When I was at Yale I bought anthologies on semiotics and deconstruction, on literary theory in general, and devoured them with avid excitement. I found psychoanalytic criticism and then tried to lose it, though it's dogged me lo these many years. In the American studies program at Yale, theory seemed to be something that one absorbed through one's own reading, and then brought back into the classroom for various purposes—among them, of course, intimidating other grad students who *didn't* know theory. (I was sure, the first year I was at Yale, that I must be stupid because I didn't know what "heuristics" meant or what a "hermeneutic circle" might be. By the next year, I'd wager that I similarly terrified other students because such terms had been absorbed into my vocabulary so completely that the definitions went without saying.)

In short, my education in theory at Yale was random but voracious, carried out in the company of my peers, and almost entirely outside of (or parallel to) the institutional structure except in my African American studies courses. The truth was that most of my professors at Yale weren't interested in "theory." It would have been a different story, I'm sure, if I'd been a Comparative Literature student, but in American Studies I found that interest and competence in theory were certainly not required of faculty members. Those of our generation who were "taught theory" are, in my experience, rare, even at elite schools. I think instead that most of us had few or no committed theory teachers, learned theory largely on our own from books, and brought those books back to the classroom where at least some of us engaged in "visceral, if not vicious, rejection"[6] of our own teachers' work. And because what moved us were books, we tended to use those books when we later put our own classes together, accounting, perhaps, for Peter Herman's claim that we seem to use the same books our teachers did, rather than rejecting those teachers.

I have outlined my approach to theory and praxis in the introduction to my book, *Worlds of Hurt: Reading the Literatures of Trauma*—an introduction in which my references might be listed as a pedigree, in order of their appearance: Alice Miller, Gregory Bateson, Terrence Des Pres, Elie Wiesel, Philip Halle, Valerie Smith, Joan Cocks, Gerald Graf, Michel Foucault, Daniel Goleman, James Young, Timothy Luke, Jean-Paul Sartre, James William Gibson, Harry Haines, Chaim Shatan, Émile Beneviste, Paul Fussell, Roland Barthes, Joan Scott, Jorge Luis Borges, Judith Herman, Andrea Dworkin, Claudia Tate:

> I believe that the responsibility of the cultural critic is to present a continuous challenge to the assumptions upon which any communal consensus is based—to insist that nothing go without saying. When cultural critics seek to expose and then question the rationales for specific community practices, we situate ourselves in opposition to dominant discourse. We question our own beliefs, and the beliefs of others. We appeal to people's "good sense," and we measure our success by the amount of argument we generate. We actively work towards the breakdown of consensus, at which point, "assumptions that could previously be taken for granted become one set of theories among others, ideas that you have to *argue for* rather than presuppose as given." . . . Cultural critics seek to establish a mode of discourse in which each person can first uncover and acknowledge his or her beliefs, and then test them, compare them to the beliefs of others, understand their implications, and modify them to reflect a changing understanding of the world. Our end goal is a community based on the full and informed participation of all its members—a community where difference is not only accepted but cherished because it provides us with new frames of reference and new ways of understanding ourselves.[7]

And the cultural critic is always in dialogue with her colleagues, her mentors, and her readers—which accounts for the insistant way I weave quotes into my articles, twining my words around the words of other scholars, using them as starting points for discussion, as evidence, as grist for the mill.

Completing my dissertation in the midst of the "culture wars" of the late 1980s and early 1990s, I was well aware that my position as an unapologetic feminist, a Marxist, a semiotician, and an African Americanist automatically guaranteed I'd be under suspicion as an ideologue in the classroom, an enforcer of that rightist bogey-woman, "political correctness." It's that laundry list of appellations that makes me a "theorist" on the contemporary scene. To expand on the Gerald Graff quote embedded in the above excerpt:

> Theory is what breaks out when the rationale for the community's practices is no longer taken for granted, so that what could formerly "go without saying" becomes an object of dispute, a dispute, moreover, that may lead to no final resolution. Once consensus breaks down, assumptions that could previously be taken for granted become one set of theories among others, ideas that you have to *argue for* rather than presuppose as given.[8]

I suppose that's why I always find myself in trouble. The supporters of what once was consensus don't seem to much like having to *argue for* their position. While feminists, Marxists, semioticians, and African Americanist scholars (among others) are all used to justifying their stance, providing supporting evidence, and defending themselves against all challengers, contemporary conservatives tend to view criticism as persecution and to see themselves as disempowered by the mere existence of contrary views.[9] For example, when I arrived at AIC it was immediately apparent that all the senior administrators were male, while all administrative assistants were female. All the senior faculty were male, while all the junior faculty were female. (The highest paid female faculty member—me—made $8,000 a year less than the lowest-paid male faculty member.) At the orientation-day activities, all presentations but one were made by men, and the metaphor used to describe the way the institution should run was a sports team metaphor—in fact, the provost opened the proceedings by telling us he didn't learn about "teamwork" in the academy, but on the basketball court. Toward the end of a day of canned presentations, where there had been no opportunity for discussion, the provost opened up the floor—finally—for comments from the new faculty. When I pointed out—as tactfully as possible—the way the men had dominated the presentations and the gender imbalance at the institution, the provost hit the roof. Flushing red, and in angry raised tones, he told me that AIC didn't need people who were going to come in and criticize it. He attacked me so savagely that I was stunned and so, apparently, was every other woman faculty member and a fair number of the female staff members. When he called an adjournment, we found ourselves clustered in the women's bathroom, huddled up and talking in whispers, illustrating the oppressive sexism of the institution far better than any argument I could have made. A lesson, though not my first, in the disrespectful manner those who do not wish to *argue for* their views will treat those who dare to question them. Theory bumps up against practice and leaves bruises.

Graff's definition of "theory" (though I think it is absolutely correct) is so broad as to make it necessary for an academic to be specific about what *kind* of theorist she is—a problem which Cary Nelson underlines in his recent comment about the job market:

> Departments occasionally advertise for specialists in theory and talk of teaching courses in theory, a conversation in which phenomenology, deconstruction, narratology, postmodernism, and other bodies of theory all seem more or less interchangeable, but in the 1990s the universal category has widely been abandoned for more specific searches and courses.[10]

In other words, while the conservatives will refuse to make a distinction between theorists (they're all bad), hiring committees are specifically concerned with filling positions based on quite narrow areas of specialty. Of course, there are usually conservatives on hiring committees and they will, often, take "antitheory" positions, which means that they will oppose the creation of job slots specifically for feminists, Marxists, and the like, and they will oppose the filling of "neutral" slots with persons who take those theoretical approaches. And since the granting of a tenure line is such a rare thing in institutions today, and the field of applicants is so wide, it's likely that few theorists will be hired into "neutral" slots because there will almost always be conservative faculty who oppose their appointments vocally enough to tip the scales against them. As I've come to learn, hiring is the result of a great deal of intradepartmental compromise—a system in which the least controversial candidate often gains the job over the most excellent candidate. In my own case (rumor has it) the provost opposed my hiring, but had used up political capital opposing the hiring of so many other faculty members that the committee was able to override his veto. In that particular case, the pro-theory forces won, though they didn't (as we later saw) hold the balance of power.

Contemporary graduate students—particularly in literature—are being trained in "theory." But they're often learning it in a class taught by a part-time or nontenure-track faculty member, unless they are at one of the elite institutions which house the leading lights of theory—the profession's "stars." The work of the previous generation of activists (many of them also theorists) has served as a wedge to open the humanities—and, particularly, the literary profession—to previously underserved groups, benefiting those who work in feminist studies, ethnic studies, and postcolonial studies a great deal, while shaking the previously solid foundations of the traditional world of mostly white, mostly male humanities scholars. Annette Kolodny, however, points in her recent book, *Failing the Future,* to the fact that though more women and people of color are receiving more Ph.D.'s than ever, there hasn't been much change in the makeup of the full-time faculty as "the percentage of full-time faculty members remain overwhelmingly white and male."[11] White men comprise 58.9 percent of the faculty, white women 27.9 percent. Minority professors make up about 10 percent of the faculty combined and "were more likely to be squeezed into the lowest echelons of academe."[12] Though recipients of the Ph.D. are growing more diverse, nonwhite and female scholars aren't getting hired into full-time or tenure-track jobs in proportion to their presence in the population. Instead, they're filling the ranks of the unemployed and underemployed, and the balance of power is maintained.

Young humanities faculty members feel the generation and "theory gap" quite painfully in many institutions, and often work in an environment in which their scholarship is not only incomprehensible to their older peers, but regarded with suspicion and hostility. Even older peers who have some background in theory often think the next generation has *gone too far.* John Carlos Rowe, interviewed in *The Chronicle for Higher Education,* responds to a recent movement to return to "aesthetics" in the study of literature with the following:

> Older scholars trained in high theory broke down the idea of universally shared literary standards, allowing younger scholars to import popular culture into the classroom. "Now overwhelmed by art forms they just don't get, senior professors take refuge in aesthetics, says Mr. Rowe. "There's an emotional appeal to it," he explains. "You hear again and again, 'I entered this profession because I loved to read. Don't you love to read?'" His answer: "Sure I love to read. But there are limits to enjoyment."[13]

The situation is made even worse by the tendency of graduate students to ally with these young theory-trained professors, emphasizing generational differences. At my parent institution, UA, which is a decent research university, I hear again and again from graduate students in the humanities that they are frustrated because the university allows them only one nontenure-track faculty member on their dissertation committee, and they can't find two tenure-track professors who will support their work (particularly if that work is very theoretical and/or rooted in popular culture). The few theory-oriented tenure-track and tenured faculty are swamped with grad students, but they are reluctant to turn these students away because they know that those grad students have few other options.

The bond between graduate students and young faculty in nontenure-track positions deepens because graduate students—who are very smart people—can see the writing on the wall. They understand that in today's market they are more likely to wind up as itinerant intellectual labor than they are to land that elusive tenure track position which provides them a reasonable course load and time for research. The exploitation of graduate student labor by universities is well documented in recent books by Cary Nelson, Michael Bérubé, and Annette Kolodny, as well as in *Workplace,* the journal of the MLA's Graduate Student Caucus.[14] The theory gap merely underlines the sense that the older generation has collaborated in pulling the temple down around its own ears. It seems no accident to many young scholars that just at the moment at which women and nonwhite scholars are making gains in real numbers, percentage of the labor pool, and in elite intellectual circles their power and the power of the profession is being undermined by radical reorganization of the structure of universities and colleges. Kolodny states:

Between 1995 and 2010 . . . over 300,000 faculty are expected to retire, leaving vacancies in all fields across higher education. At the same time, in almost every discipline, women have been making "dramatic gains at the Ph.D. level," almost doubling "their share of the doctorates granted in English and increas[ing] their representation among foreign language degree recipients by just over half." As a result, especially in the humanities disciplines, the 1990s are certain to be the last decade in which tenured white males over fifty control what gets published and who gets tenured.[15]

Unfortunately, it may also be the last generation in which it is *possible* to be tenured. As Bill Readings argues in *The University in Ruins,* the corporatist contemporary university is a "bureaucratic system rather than . . . the ideological apparatus that the left has traditionally considered it. As an autonomous system rather than an ideological instrument, the University should no longer be thought of as a tool that the left will be able to use for other purposes than those of the capitalist state."[16] Bérubé and Nelson, too, focus on the corporatization of the university, its embrasure of what Readings calls "the techno-bureaucratic notion of excellence."[17]

Nelson presents the case that the discipline which most ardently embraced theory is the discipline that also embraced corporatism:

English, I would argue, is the discipline most responsible for laying the groundwork for the corporate university. I refer to our employment practices. For English departments above all have demonstrated that neither full-time faculty nor Ph.Ds are essential to lower-level undergraduate education. What's more, we've shown that people teaching lower-division courses need not be paid a living wage. We can no longer claim that such courses have to be taught by people with years of specialized training.[18]

Everywhere graduate students and recent Ph.D.'s look there is evidence that their elders have sold them down the river. One can find it even in the relatively staid *Chronicle of Higher Education:*

"English departments have been built on the systematic exploitation of teaching assistants and, more recently, part-timers," says James Sledd, a professor emeritus of English at the University of Texas at Austin. "But nobody does a damn thing about it because to challenge it is to challenge the whole economic system of higher education, which smells."[19]

Institutions' increasing reliance on non-tenure-track instructors is driven by cost. Universities facing budget difficulties can hire instructors for a small fraction of what they would pay tenured professors. Many instructors, particularly part-timers, get by without an office, a telephone, or even a campus mailbox. Most are not allowed to serve on faculty committees or apply for research grants. And if they are encouraged to participate in activities other than teaching, they typically are not paid extra to do so. . . . Many full-time instructors have health insurance, but most part-timers do not. Worst of all, the longer they work in such positions, the slimmer their chances are of ever landing tenure-track jobs.[20]

And so on. Articles stating the problem aren't hard to find. What *is* hard to find, however, are tenured faculty members who are willing to do anything about it. Aside from the usual suspects (Bérubé, Kolodny, Nelson, and a few others) the tenured members of the profession are largely silent on the issue. Most are not about to sacrifice their own salary or benefits to supplement the woefully underfunded folks off the tenure track. Part-timers and graduate students' attempts to organize are often unsupported by the majority of tenured and tenure-track faculty members on campus, or—as in the well-documented Yale graduate student grade strike of 1995[21]—vehemently opposed.

As one might expect, I had a particular interest in the Yale strike, since it was my alma mater, and since the graduate student organization, GESO, was born in the Yale clerical and technical worker's strike of 1984–85, in which I was active as a graduate student working to support the union. At that time, pro-union organizer though I was, I couldn't see the connection between our work as teaching assistants and the "real" work done by the members of Locals 33 and 34. I remember trying to make a clear distinction between my position and theirs, trying hard not to "pretend" to be a worker, because back in 1984 it was still possible to think of graduate teaching as an apprenticeship, as a gateway into a profession that would keep me *out of* the working class. That was 1984. Ten years (and a long job search) later it was hard for me to imagine that anyone could still believe that a Ph.D.—even a *Yale* Ph.D.—was a sure ticket to a tenure-track job. But it wasn't hard for me to believe that the Yale faculty could turn on its own students with such viciousness. After all, I knew these people. As a student I'd been totally turned off by the contradictions between Nancy Cott's and Margaret Homans's claims to feminism and their pumps-and-pearls self-presentation, and I must admit that I got a small thrill of vindication from hearing about their censure of striking GTAs. The few faculty that stood against that wave—Michael Denning, Hazel Carby, David Montgomery—are admirable for the consistency between their scholarly work and their activism, a consistency I strive to emulate.

Species that eat their young have a hard time surviving unless, of course, they produce so *many* young that a few get away every time. This seems to be the strategy of contemporary graduate programs in the humanities, and especially in English. Literature in general, and theory in particular, has turned into, in Bérubé's words, a "family drama of good rebel children and bad rebel grandchildren,"[22] where the children-turned-parents seem to be content with the fact that their children will never achieve a standard of living equal to their own. (Similar, in some ways, to the diminished expectations of Generation X.) In conversation in the electronic world of LambdaMOO, a graduate student (let's call her Piglet, though that's not her "real" MOO name) said to me, "I keep noticing, for instance, that certain members of the faculty who have not yet retired are very suspicious of this thing called 'theory,' apparently because they don't think they use it themselves." Polarization is not just along lines of employment status—it's generational as well, with the last generation (theorists and nontheorists) often aligned against the next generation. But the two-tiered system that has developed (privileged tenured faculty on the top level, underprivileged nontenure-track faculty and graduate students on the bottom level) is reaching critical mass, as demonstrated in the recent MLA election in which populist Cary Nelson was voted onto the seven-member executive committee of the organization. Nelson has articulated a lot of ideas for reforming the MLA, and now we'll get the chance to see if he (and we) can put them into practice. But in addition to fighting the entrenched oldsters in the MLA, he'll be battling the beast that is the corporatist university.

At Arizona International, the environment in which I'm working may well be the profession's future:

> Professors at AIC are true liberal arts educators: dynamic professionals dedicated to teaching. They're open-minded, current, and responsive. They offer global perspectives, know how to facilitate learning, and show connections between varied coursework. What's more, every professor takes the time to know you personally. They realize that you are not a number, but an individual with your own unique combination of talents and experiences. They help you adjust to college and provide the guidance and support that works best for you. And, AIC faculty are easily accessible to students and to the community.[23]

AIC students might not be "numbers," but AIC profs are another matter. One of the reasons I became persona non grata at AIC was that I began to work with spreadsheets, calculating the number of tasks we were delegated, and the number of hours each would require, in an attempt to figure out how many hours our work week would total. There were obvious problems from jump street. First, we were expected to spend twelve hours a week in the classroom, teaching. If one estimates a minimal two hours of preparation and grading time for every hour in the classroom (a conservative estimate), that already totals thirty-six hours. We were required to spend an additional six hours a week advising and mentoring, which brought us to forty-two hours. And we were also responsible for "academic planning, program and curricular development and searches." So that'd come to maybe another two to three hours a week. Since college professors tend to work long hours, coming in under fifty hours a week wouldn't have been too bad. But given the student-to-faculty ratio, if we were going to meet our commitment to giving individual attention to students, working out "Learning Contracts" with them, sitting on various review boards, doing community service projects, and so on (all while putting together completely new courses which no one had ever taught before), we were either going to have to hire double the current projected number of faculty or we were going to be working over eighty hours per week. At faculty meetings and general meetings, I wound up asking a lot of questions no one could answer.

What became clear over time was that the administration (in the person of the provost, had promised then-president of UA, Manuel Pacheco, and the Arizona Board of Regents that he could accomplish a certain set of tasks with a limited amount of resources. He'd promised that individualized instruction would be cost effective, "cognizant of, and . . . sensitive to, the needs of a free-market economy."[24] The new college was funded on the promise that it could be done on the cheap. But as Annette Kolodny points out again and again in *Failing the Future,* education is *not* cheap, and good education is downright expensive, though it's an excellent long-term investment for the nation. In a system where all decision making is concentrated in the hands of administrators, though, and the faculty is stripped of power, job security, and, hence, academic freedom, it's possible to continually increase demands on faculty workers and thus meet nearly impossible goals with heavily exploited labor—especially when there's an enormous pool of unemployed academic workers hungry for jobs. Any jobs. This was the system the provost was determined to create. I didn't start off at AIC wedded to the notion that tenure was an essential part of the university system. Like many other young Ph.D.'s and grad students, I'd resented the tenure system for sheltering certain professors who didn't seem to be accomplishing much useful work, or who were bad teachers. But what I learned in the course of my fight for reinstatement is that those in administration who support the eradication of tenure are neither friends of faculty, nor advocates of education. They are corporatists whose interest is the bottom line, who resent faculty powers in university governance, and want to eliminate them from the decision-making process. The elimination of faculty power is essential to the smooth operation of for-profit institutions like University of Phoenix, and traditional universities have begun to see the financial and organizational advantage of hiring voiceless graduate students, part-time and contract employees over tenured faculty with rights to shared governance.

Among the ideas which have gained general currency in this environment are: (1) Hiring part-timers instead of full-time professors; (2) Emphasizing teaching instead of research; (3) relying on technology to allow fewer professors to teach more students. All three of these strategies will have long-term damaging effects on the university system and will undermine the ability of the university to serve the purpose for which it was created—educating students. The drawbacks of part-timers have been detailed in numerous places, many of them mentioned already in this article. The emphasis on teaching (also widely discussed) is a way of wringing more classroom hours out of professors at the expense of work which advances the field and thus enriches the profession. And the reliance on technology is misplaced, as anyone who seriously explores the body of available educational software will be forced to confess. Not only is there a dearth of decent educational software, but purchasing, maintaining, and upgrading software and hardware is often far more expensive than faculty salaries. And, as Kolodny points out, "An exclusively cost-driven dependence on computers and telecourses may instruct students in a subject: but only the professor with passion and disciplinary expertise can help students understand why a subject is important to think about and *how* to think about it."[25]

If the above three ideas are placed fully into effect, their chief combined result will be to shut down intellectual production so that the current generation of scholars has neither the resources nor the time to augment the body of intellectual work upon which future generations of scholars and students would ordinarily expect to draw. Much as a factory can show short-term profits by neglecting its infrastructure or refusing to invest in new machinery, the university can show short-term profit by creating an environment in which professors are teaching under conditions which do not allow them to research or write. Neither is a sustainable strategy. The machines will break down or need to be replaced, just as, eventually, we will notice that the materials we are using in our classrooms are outdated and obsolete. In both cases, the strategy puts those who choose it behind the eight ball, and recovery is doubtful. Under deepest suspicion today are scholars engaged in humanities research and writing, since the current emphasis in the corporatist university is on "practical" applications of knowledge. Theory, of course, is at the top of the list of "useless" activities in which humanities scholars engage. Unsurprisingly, theorists are the academicians most likely, as a group, to question the "natural" evolution of the corporate university.

To assert that one "does theory" in this time and this place is to stake a claim not only to a particular intellectual position, but to a set of political and even generational affiliations. Theory, though ostensibly popularized by the last generation, is actually not the tool of that generation, but of our own. Far, however, from dismantling the master's house with the tools we've been handed, we find ourselves barred from the grounds and forced to watch while the big house and its outbuildings fall apart before our eyes. To carry the metaphor further, it seems to me that while we're sitting out here in the cold, the folks who live in that house are pulling out the supporting walls and burning them in the fire in an attempt to keep warm. I am not hopeful about any of this.

As for me, I return to a reorganized Arizona International College after a two-year appointment on the UA main campus. AIC has been relocated to the central campus, though plans are afoot to build it a new "co-campus" north of Tucson in cooperation with Pima Community College. Our survival depends upon whether we can increase our enrollment quickly enough to please the regents and the legislature and to convince them that we are "cost effective." A widely-respected dean has replaced our unpopular provost, and this has greatly improved our working environment and boosted our morale. I'm on a three-year contract which (if we survive) I can reasonably expect to be extended for another five years. Terms and conditions of employment now protect me and my colleagues by specifying a process of formative and summative evaluations, and a twelve-month notice of nonrenewal at the termination of a continuing contract. This is the good news. The bad news is that the workload, from my current calculations, continues to be unrealistic given the liberal arts curriculum and the personalized plans of study we advertise. The gender imbalance is still evident in the current composition of administration and faculty. As the sole nontenure college on a campus where the faculty is strongly committed to supporting tenure, we continue to be an isolated island and a target for hostility rather than the recipients of collegial support. Most AIC faculty would like to see the college converted to a tenure-based system, but we are not hopeful about the outcome of any tenure-seeking effort. Since this is Arizona (well known for its hostility to labor), a real faculty union seems unlikely to evolve, thought the graduate students at UA, like elsewhere, are fighting for their rights. I can't offer comforting words or neat solutions. As a college, we mirror in microcosm the divide between an older university structure and some as-yet-undetermined new structure which, from all the signs will not be an improvement.

*Notes*

1. Michael Bérubé, *Public Access: Literary Theory and American Cultural Politics* (New York: Verso, 1994, 43).

2. The text of the letter I sent to the faculty prior to my non-renewal follows:

Administrative hostility to faculty criticism is nothing new in academia. What is new is that this criticism is taking place in an environment in which faculty have none of the protections of the tenure system, and in which—despite promises to the contrary—no system of due process or academic freedom has yet been installed. For example, all faculty are currently on one-year contracts as "professor" (nontenure eligible)," a position which guarantees no right to expectation of continuance from year to year. Renewal occurs at the sole discretion of the chief administrative officer—and faculty have the right to appeal only to the same administrative officer who denied them renewal in the first place. Until notice of renewal is given in writing, no faculty member can rest easy. At any time until we receive a written notice of renewal we can be dismissed, with only ninety days notice. And though multiyear contracts were advertised last year and this year, it appears that in actuality, none will be forthcoming.

Arizona law changed last year, and it seems now that no oral contracts are binding, and so it does not matter that the provost led each faculty member hired in spring of 1996 to believe that we would be employed beyond the first year, or that he assured us that the sole reason for starting us with one-year contracts was that he could not get us multiyear contracts at our current salaries through [Arizona Board of Regents]. Under current conditions I may do an excellent job in every area of responsibility (teaching, service work, mentoring, recruitment), and still not have an expectation of re-employment. When the power to renew a contract is so arbitrary and it is in the hands of one man, from whom no one representing faculty can demand accountability, it is surely unreasonable to expect that it will be exercised fairly and dispassionately. What is the mechanism at AIC which protects dissent or secures academic freedom? . . .

The larger issue here is not whether my own contract will be renewed. What concerns me more—and will continue to concern me whether I am employed by AIC or not—is the fact that AIC promises one thing, and apparently is content to deliver another. I came to AIC a believer in the notion that tenure could be replaced, and the tenure system improved upon, by an alternative structure which guaranteed due process and academic freedom. But now I have my doubts that such a structure is possible or, more precisely, that those who advocate the abolition of tenure ever *intended* to create such an alternative structure.

My fellow faculty members may or may not vocally join in my complaint about AIC's policies. Everyone has their own reasons for speaking out or for keeping silence. But I do know that there is not a single full-time faculty member, except for the two who started in January, who has not shared his or her concerns over the lack of due process and academic freedom with me and with other faculty members and/or students behind closed doors. It is our dedication to AIC's mission that enforces silence on these matters outside of the walls of the institution, but it is the Damoclean sword which hangs over us all that keeps us mute in our own corridors. The provost may decry the traditional division between faculty and administration, but he does his best to foster that split by refusing to grant faculty real power or any measure of autonomy, instilling in his professors a fear of retaliation for criticism, apparently reneging on his promise of shared governance, and failing to communicate directly with us when he perceives there to be a problem.

3. Kalí Tal, *Worlds of Hurt: Reading the Literatures of Trauma* (New York: Cambridge University Press, 1996).

4. "Contracts Replace the Tenure Track for a Growing Number of Professors," *Chronicle of Higher Education* (12 June 1998), http://chronicle.com/che-data/articles.dir/art-44.dir/issue-40.dir/40a00101.htm

5. Peter C. Herman, "Introduction," this volume, 1.

6. Ibid, 2.

7. Kalí Tal, *Worlds of Hurt*, 5.

8. "Why Theory," Gerald Graff, *Left Politics and the Literary Profession*, Lennard J. Davis and M. Bella Mirabella, eds. (New York: Columbia University Press) 1990, 23.

9. See, for example, the journal *Academic Questions*, produced by the National Association of Scholars, in which articles claim, over and over, that the universities have been taken over by the left and that conservative scholars are being driven out of the profession, attacked and silenced. Michael Bérubé argues: "For this is a new American conservatism that regards any opposition as de facto 'oppression,' just as it regards all criticism as de facto censorship, and it is accordingly outraged not to have rooted out its widespread and principled liberal-left opposition in universities, even though so much of its opposition has crumbled elsewhere. Conservative attacks on academic life, then, should be understood as the consequence of conservatism's failure to achieve among the academic American intelligentsia the kind of hegemony it has enjoyed in American economic and social policy, not to mention the federal judiciary. But there is one novel element about the antiacademic attacks of the 1980s and 1990s: American conservatives have now been alerted to the strange posthumous career of Paul de Man, with the result that deconstruction—and therefore, 'theory' in general—can now be vilified by the right as an academic form of Nazism" (*Public Access: Literary Theory and American Cultural Politics* (New York: Verso) 1994, 67).

10. Cary Nelson, *Manifesto of a Tenured Radical* (New York: New York University Press, 1997, 16).

11. Annette Kolodny, *Failing the Future: A Dean Looks at Higher Education in the Twenty-First Century* (Durham: Duke University Press, 1998, 71–72).

12. Ibid.

13. "Wearying of Cultural Studies, Some Scholars Rediscover Beauty," Scott Heller, *Chronicle of Higher Education* 4 December 1998: A15.

14. Cary Nelson, *Manifesto of a Tenured Radical* (New York: New York University Press, 1997); Michael Bérubé, *The Employment of English: Theory, Jobs and the Future* (New York: New York University Press, 1998); Annette Kolodny, *Failing the Future: A Dean Looks at Higher Education in the Twenty-First Century* (Durham: Duke University Press, 1998); *Workplace:* http://www.workplace-gsc.com/workplace1/workplace.html.

15. Annette Kolodny, *Failing the Future: A Dean Looks at Higher Education in the Twenty-First Century* (Durham: Duke University Press, 1998, 100).

16. Bill Readings, *The University in Ruins* (Boston: Harvard University Press, 1996, 41).

17. Ibid. 54.

18. "What Hath English Wrought: The Corporate University's Fast Food Discipline," Cary Nelson, *Workplace* 1, 1 (Feb. 1998): http://www.workplace-gsc.com/features1/nelson.html

19. "Bad Blood in the English Department: the Rift Between Composition and Literature," Alison Schneider, 13 Feb 1998, *Chronicle of Higher Education*, A14.

20. "Scholars off the Tenure Track Wonder If They'll Ever Get On," Robin Wilson, *The Chronicle of Higher Education*, 14 June, 1996. Special Report: A12.

21. For full coverage of the strike see Michael Bérubé, *The Employment of English*, 37–64, and Cary Nelson, *Manifesto of a Tenured Radical*, 194–216.

22. Michael Bérubé, *Public Access: Literary Theory and American Cultural Politics* (New York: Verso, 1994, 221).

23. *Arizona International Campus: The New Choice for College Education*, promotional pamphlet.

24. *New University in Pima Country: A Report of the Community Advisory Committee to Manuel T. Pacheco, President, The University of Arizona and for Consideration by the Arizona Board of Regents*, The University of Arizona, July 1994.

25. Kolodny, *Failing the Future*, 35–36.

# SIX

# BREAKING THE MONOPOLY: THE NEXT GENERATION AND THE CORPORATE ACADEMY

*Jesse G. Swan*

Numerous challenges face the next generation, not least of which is the increasingly popular conception of the university as a corporation.[1] The challenge is not simply academic: the more people think of universities as corporations, the more they are able and desirous of "downsizing" them, which means reducing the number of tenured and tenure-track faculty members and increasing the number of part-time instructors, among other things.[2] The next generation in these circumstances will likely become a new lost generation. And the possible transformation of the public university into a business threatens more than the next generation's scholarly and professional plans: It portends the babyboomers' failure to ensure the extension of American democracy to as many citizens as possible.[3] A corporation does not make citizens; it makes, whenever it can, wholly dependent consumers. The next generation needs to alert itself to the signs of this transformation of the university and appreciate the effects on it in order to consciously, conscientiously, and effectively offer the public alternative figurations of the university.[4]

There are multiple ways some people are beginning to think of the university as a corporation. One way replaces the objective of higher education: no longer are professors to teach, they are to turn a profit. Because the university, like the church, is not a wealth-producing entity, though, we have had to have a concerted public spectacle to create the illogical though now palpable sense that universities, like everything else, should generate profits. To accommodate the public spectacle acted out by moderately attractive, mostly white men winning public office in the 1980s and 1990s, from the school board to the white house, some college administrators have provided the illusion of profitability by metaphorically suggesting that a large number of students is the same as an excess of material wealth. As profit, in the business sense, is popularly conceived of as currency, students have been transformed into units of currency for a public university. Professors now, to be profitable, and even to keep a course from being canceled, must have remarkably high numbers of students, regardless of the course.

Although at first such requirements may sound economically sensible, the next generation should be attentive to likely detrimental effects that such requirements, based on such thinking, can eventuate. Even though we can "compete" in such circumstances—we can offer sensational courses, for instance—we need to realize that doing so makes us accomplices in the demise of our profession. By gratifying dominant discourses of profitability with popular courses or even with silence, we reify the discourses, dehumanize students, and make ourselves inessential. As Linda Ray Pratt exhorts, rather than accommodating such discourses, "we must devise public strategies that challenge consensus, not reinforce it."[5]

The possible refiguration of the university by the metaphor of profit effects not only the conceptualization of students as currency but also knowledge and courses as property or objects suitable for trafficking. The Western Governors' University serves as an extreme example of such a model of "brokering courses." A primary goal of this experimental institution is to incrementalize university study into salable units: a student no longer passes a course, she instead purchases various competencies. So many competencies buys credit for a course, regardless of how or in what manner or order the competencies were proven. Once a competency has been met, it has been securely bought and the student holds on to it until she can redeem it, with other competencies, for a larger unit of academic property called a credit. Eventually, students will have purchased enough "competency-based credentials" from distant "education providers" that they will be able to exchange them for "competency-based degrees and certificates." As "chief academic officer" Bob Albrecht describes the distinction of his new education delivery system, "While there are a number of distance education programs around the country, the Western Governors University is unique with its focus on competency-based credentials and its involvement of multiple states and institutions."[6] In this corporate academy arrangement, education is reduced to trafficking, credit is made into property, and educators are made into vendors. There's no sense of the social—never mind spiritual—dimensions of education.[7]

Concurrent with the transformation of students and courses into objects of currency and traffic, the corporate model and its monolithic drive for profit also turns the university into a large discount store. In the retail model of public education, students are sale hounds, faculty are customer-service representatives, and administrators are managers and manager-trainees whose primary job is to keep an exploited and disgruntled workforce smiling and accommodating. This model informs speeches and evaluations by some administrators and senior faculty when worrying over head counts. It is manifest in the examples already given, but it seems most integral to recent projects for addressing the age-old problem of students flunking or dropping out of college.[8] Because the business-minded conceive of students as currency and academics as goods to be hawked in volume, and because students praise and blame faculty members for their own success, failure, and decisions to postpone continued, higher education, which certainly is not the same as failure as our many returning or nontraditional students beautifully illustrate, the corporate-minded administrator proposes pressuring faculty into conforming to the customer-service model of interpersonal relations. If only faculty were more customer oriented, rather than knowledge-, skills-, and/or socially oriented, the figurative reasoning goes, students who presently choose to drop out would much rather stay and consume. Because everyone has direct experience with delightful as well as unpleasant sales clerks, thinking of the more alien professor-student relationship in terms of the retail circumstance can comfort even if it insidiously harms.

A particularly stressful instance of the malefic effects on academic autonomy and consequently on academic efficacy that such corporate academies can occasion comes from the new anti-intellectual university, Arizona International Campus, currently "under the wing of the University of Arizona," but intended, eventually, "to become a separate institution."[9] Initially setting up its liberal arts institution free from tenure in something resembling an open-air outlet mall, dignified by the appellation, science and technology park, Arizona International was managed by a senior finance officer, David C. Gnage, and a chief executive officer, Celestino Fernandez. Excited about the prospect of servicing large numbers of students without the burden of intellectually free faculty, the executives enticed academicians out to Arizona with implied promises. While the "campus" would be free from tenure, faculty would somehow "have academic freedom to do their teaching, and due process," according to the CEO. For an energetic, broad-minded, trusting '90s Yale Ph.D., the nontenure, due-process promise worked to make her, after only a year, the institution's "sacrificial goat." Though eventually winning her job back, the eminently qualified, if critical, next generation professor was fired for not getting along with others, notably the executives whose policies were the object of much of her analysis and questioning. Under cover of a concern for the customer-student—professor-merchandisers must get along with people because that's what customers like in sales clerks—executives fire at will employees *they* do not like. As the CEO of Arizona's corporate academy concluded firmly, "We're not faculty centered. We're student centered."[10]

The peculiar danger of such figurations lies in the fact that many, though certainly not all, of the next generation, like the "sacrificial goat" of Arizona International Campus before she was fired, think it so absurd that no one could actually think and evaluate with it.[11] Since many cannot or do not want to believe that such corporate conceptualizations are increasingly monopolizing discourses about higher education, many fail to engage the public discourse in terms that challenge, subtly or overtly, the figurative monopoly.

That most of us need to challenge the developing figurative monopoly and that most of us need to do so even hyperbolically at times becomes still more evident once we read and listen to the views of extremist businessmen and women. Such businesspeople do not mince words or worry over civility when they attempt to sell the public on their ways of thinking. For instance, in praising the customer-oriented efficiency of "cyberprograms"—that is, electronic correspondence courses—Lisa Gubernick and Ashlea Ebeling rave that "[m]odern technology brings education to the students rather than forcing students to subsidize fancy campuses and featherbedding faculties." Besides the glories of television and home computers for student-consumers, the corporate academy promises to pluck "conventional educators" as well as their beds. Contrasting the faculty salaries and benefits of a real university with those of a for-profit syndicate, our "reporters" find the source of profitability: Unabashedly, Gubernick and

Ebeling explain that "Arizona State professors get an average of $67,000 a year. The typical University of Phoenix on-line faculty member is part time and earns only $2,000 a course, teaching from a standardized curriculum." And, finally, characterizing the reactions of American professors who have been instrumental in extending postsecondary educations to over 20 percent of our population,[12] Gubernick and Ebeling cry that "the academic establishment has adopted a Luddite approach." Clearly, there are forces at work attempting to transform our democracy-making academy into "For-Profit U."[13] When we do not counter these venal projects, we allow the academy to become another dehumanized site for playing out further fantasies of the free market. In the process, students fail to change, fail to become the sort of people a democracy requires, since no one changes, no one becomes a better person by purchasing an object—a competency or a piece of costume jewelry—even from the most congenial sales merchandiser managed by the most cunning executives.

In addition to the influence on the academy and the country, the potential transformation of the university into a corporation yields immediate as well as remote degenerative effects on the next generation. In our teaching, the increasing conceptual monopoly enjoyed by corporate tropes makes it difficult—and in some instances impossible—to teach and cultivate alternative, expansive ways of knowing. Confronted by a classroom full of bottom-line, service-oriented thinkers, the next generation professor faces pedagogical challenges that could be ignored by the previous generation. One way to address the problem is to change the subject from the old and alien to the new and popular, from the linguistic to the visual, from the intellectual to the sexy. Such a strategy, though, plays into the increasingly dominant tropes and economy of value in a manner that makes us luxurious and even frivolous, two things no one wants to support with public funds.[14]

As with our teaching, our scholarship and criticism are perniciously impacted. Because administrative evaluators sometimes take a corporate approach to evaluation, the next generation can feel forced into sometimes faux contention for the sake of publishing, which is the material product required by the corporate mind to suggest intellectual activity. We are also pressured into the sexy over the arduous since we all can deconstruct, expose the dynamics of colonial power exploits, champion the subaltern, and reveal latent sexual desires in any text—from coupons to *Paradise Lost*—in far less time than it takes to understand the vicissitudes of the textual histories of authors and their work. When activity must supply material products, and when quantity of material products suggest efficiency of productivity, the next generation is compelled to ingenious criticism over learned scholarship.[15] Ruinously, such circumstances and behaviour offer very limited immediate rewards while establishing the foundation for an eventual elimination of all such activity on the grounds that it is too costly and too political for a frugal, practical, corporate society.[16]

Descrying the sexy and fast criticism of some, I need to make clear, is not to object to the substantive work of cultural criticisms of the previous and next generations. The work of bell hooks and Leo Bersani, for instance, is neither sexy nor fast, though criticism that imitates it often is, with the consequent debasement of the original's achievement and distinction. The crucial differences between the work of a hooks or a Bersani and derivative criticism are etiological and teleological. When the impetus for writing criticism comes from bureaucratic pressures for productivity in a short period of time rather than independent pressures for expression and exposition developed over longer periods of time, the criticism is usually simply derivative, certainly untested, and creates the cultural sense of ease, availability, and consequent discounted value. For all our theoretical sophistication, we seem not to understand such economies of value. When the goal of criticism is personal, immediate, material gain—the scrutiny of annual reviews intensifies this purpose—the criticism, especially when it purports to champion some despised and oppressed people, becomes itself insidiously exploitative. Faculty need to win more control of the culture of academe if we wish truly to advance our cultural-political as well as "academic" causes and pursuits.

In not successfully creating and maintaining an academic culture that nurtures rather than exploits, we are allowing the effects of corporate thinking to produce denigrating conditions not only for students and scholarship, but also for ourselves personally. Most significantly for the individual, the new corporate tropological environment fosters significant psychological, emotional, and spiritual strain. Viscerally committed to ideals of freedom, ethical behavior, and the life of the mind, yet still relatively powerless because untenured or newly tenured, the next generation has to cope with an unprecedented level of dissonance between its values and those of corporate type senior colleagues and administrators. Some, of course, are blessed with noble administrators, but all have encountered the CEO wanna-be who is hyper about FTEs (full-time equivalents) and technology, especially technology involving "distance" learning. The dissonance is dangerous for the next generation in that it invites depression, bilious melancholy, hopeless demoralization. Often, there appears little to be done to alleviate these feelings and experiences, so the next generation lives with the strain of cognitive dissonance, or it gives up its integrity to work the system, or, in extreme cases, it takes more lethal action.

But there are other options available to us. Generally, the next generation must recognize that it must do scholarly as well as public work if it is to influence positively the shape of the academy in the next century. In its scholarly work, three commitments need to be made and maintained. First, the next generation needs to interrogate the methods and values implicit in its work. We cannot, as Peter Herman notes in the introduction, continue to "uncritically and unproblematically" accept the theoretical paradigms of the last generation, not so much because they are wrong, they certainly are not, but mostly because they have very different effects today from the '60s. We know that cultural facts such as race, gender, sexuality, or even the self are in constant flux and only meaningful in context, unlike material facts such as gravity, the basic components of atoms, or the process of mitosis. It should not surprise or offend, then, that the methods and procedures essential for the previous generation need modification to accommodate changes in society occasioned in part by those methods and procedures. The previous generation has made a difference, and mostly it has been a positive difference. We now need intelligently to work from, not in, those differences, which means being as cognizant as possible of the effects of what we do when we do it.[17]

The second commitment we need to make is to keep our sometimes acrimonious fights to ourselves. This means that we need to disagree and we always will, but we can and should do so among ourselves in our expert discourses. For some reason, the only time we seem to make ourselves intelligible to the public is when we fight with each other. We should reverse the pattern: make much of our work in the study of cultural facts more accessible and keep our acrimony, which is often as personal as it is academic, to ourselves by expressing it in our professional idioms.

Related to the second commitment is the third, which is to make alliances with clearly ethically minded senior colleagues and with colleagues from very different disciplines. If we are in the liberal arts, we need to make alliances with the sciences and even with business, and vice versa. We all have certain very important common interests, not least of which is tenure, and we need to outline the areas of common interest and then focus on them. If we can find scholarly projects to collaborate upon, we will foster an impenetrable collegiality.[18]

In our public work, we need always to understand what needs to be said in public and we need to resist the fear to say it. Perhaps following Dominick LaCapra's suggestion for yet another category for evaluating faculty, a "critical intellectual citizenship" category, we need to promote visions of faculty and the academy that foster increased possibilities of intellectual and cultural critique.[19] About visions of faculty, about what a faculty is, what material conditions a faculty requires to critique and promote criticism, we need to cultivate figuratively appealing and captivating arguments and performances that communicate the need for tenure. Just as the authors of the U.S. Bill of Rights understood that protection from recrimination is essential in creating a critical public culture—a public culture unified by its thoughtful suspicion of power—the authors of the U.S. tenure conventions understood that protection from recrimination is essential in creating a critical academic culture—a culture that teaches suspicion of power.[20] Likewise, opponents of tenure understand that the best way for power to control the suspicious and critical is to make them vulnerable and dependent. David Breneman understands this as his recent attempt to lure the next generation with flattery, money, and assurances of freedom in exchange for tenure makes clear.[21]

Besides requiring tenure, we must also clarify, the academy needs a preponderance of tenured and tenure-track faculty members, certainly at the level of tertiary education, but even, I believe, at the secondary and primary levels. Whatever the value of tenure at the primary and secondary levels,[22] at the college level, tenure is crucial for the advancement of a culture that critically engages dominating interests, which at present involves those of putatively apolitical global capitalism, a.k.a. the corporate world.[23] In advocating a preponderance of tenured and tenure-track professors, we must be prepared publicly to address, among other issues, the deleterious effects on the academy triggered by the downsizing of tenured faculties in favor of increased reliance on part-time instructors. Saying things like, "reliance on part-time, adjunct faculty is detrimental to programs, universities, and America," however, may frighten some next generation intellectuals not only because careerist administrators find it expedient to exploit such workers and punish those who criticize such exploitation, but also because many of our dear and esteemed friends are presently laboring in such positions.[24] Criticism of the overreliance on adjunct instructors is often viciously turned into criticism of the instructors, a spin that we know we cannot always control.[25] Similarly, we must also be prepared to explain why and how real private and public universities free from the contamination of exploitation and subservience are better for our society than for-profit, monopoly-desiring enterprises are, even though tenure antagonists will likely try to spin such explanations into evidence of an unmeritorious elite coterie jealously protecting its sinecures.[26] Many of our detractors are out for money, so they will do and say just about anything against anyone, which makes our task of promoting conditions necessary for a free and critical society daunting, indeed.[27]

Dispiriting though they might sometimes be, public expressions of alternative images of the academy are required. In this regard, two interesting and contending models for explaining the value of a free academy might help suggest some currently useful patterns of figuration for the next generation. Like any expression, though, these are mostly useful presently to create circumstances conducive to a critical society. Just as the discourse of liberal democracy has been perverted by material and generational changes and made to serve dominant interests rather than critiquing them,[28] any pattern of discourse can devolve into complicity, accommodation, or simple innocuousness. Though we generally appear to live, as Carolyn Heilbrun has said of women, with the dream and "the delusion of a passive life,"[29] we should instead be vigilant about attending to the effects of any discourse we engage as we engage it.

In an energetic, intelligent book on the academy and its future, the late Bill Readings appraises the condition he calls *The University in Ruins* and proposes a performative commitment for faculty.[30] Supporting the interpretation that "The replacement of culture by the discourse of excellence is the University's response to 1968" (150), Readings provides a scathing critique of the administrative standard of excellence—disembodied, unessentialized, always contingent and highly arbitrary—over the cultural or ideological standards of the past. To counter excellence as a unit of measurement and subsequent basis for decisions, Readings argues that we must insist upon "value," and the best way to uphold "value" rather than "excellence"—wholesome human interaction rather than bureaucratized measurement—is to cultivate an "institutional pragmatism . . . that dwells among the ruins of an institution" (129–30). Because the administrative discourse of excellence is "dereferential," Readings proposes a pragmatic practice he playfully calls "Thought." This "Thought" that does not refer outside of itself for validation is the product of Readings' pedagogy that "is a *relation, a network of obligation*" (158) and promises to put the curriculum back in the hands of faculty (177) since it is a faculty role to Think and to model Thought. "Dissensus" becomes the mode of being of such an institution in ruins, and "[i]n the horizon of dissensus, no consensual answer can take away the question mark that the social bond (the fact of other people, of language) raises" (187). Thought is integrally social and critical, not really measurable because not dependent outside of itself, but always pragmatically interactive with other forces in society. Such pragmatism appeals to those, like Readings, who acquiesce to the corporatization of the academy and think the best strategy is to insist on as much ethical dependency as possible: "My argument," Readings makes clear, "is that the University is developing the status of a transnational corporation" (164).[31]

Sharing Readings' belief that the university cannot refer outside of itself for its value and be what a free, critical society needs, George Allan discerns three competing models of the academy, all of which are flawed by having distinct, extracollegial purposes. Allan's alternative vision in *Rethinking College Education* is like Readings' in that it counters administrative demands for "excellence" with playfulness and thought, but it differs from Readings' proposal by resisting the accommodation of the politics of global capital in favor of propagating the politics of manners, especially of conversation.[32] Wanting both to critique and to model, Allan presents each of the three contending images of the college separately in the voice of each image's champion: The college as a faithful community comes first, followed by the image of the college as a guild of inquirers, which is succeeded by the image of the college as a resource center. Each image has its own traditions, manifest even in documentation style, but each has the major flaw of being validated by some external purpose: saving souls, adhering to a (scientific) method, servicing consumers. Allan's vision of a college is one of a circumstance that encourages students to practice ways of being playfully, that is to say, safely, moral. Offering an answer for "How can a college make it possible for a student to develop character" (138), Allan explains that moral practice—character—is adverbial rather than nominative or verbal, and so "[t]he essence of a college lies not in what it teaches [the nouns] but in fostering an environment in which making the choices [the verbs] is thought less important than learning the moral conditions [the adverbs] for doing so" (145). Allan calls us, then, to insist upon missionless and purposeless colleges so that all missions and purposes might be playfully, morally explored. "A College," Allan explains, "if it has no essential purpose, is able to develop a character of its own" (124). His last chapter, "The Standards of a College [A Quadrivial Conversation]," performs the sort of character Allan, and in many ways Readings, promotes: it expresses four contending views equitably while proving that the moral-ethical commitment to questioning and listening—Readings' "Thought" and Allan's "moral character"—needs to be the defining trait of the academy of a critical, free society.

Though I prefer Allan's vision of the academy to Readings', mostly because I resist succumbing at all to the corporatization of cultures, Readings' vision does offer many ingenious and potentially persuasive critiques of current cultural figurations. Further, by insisting on the intrinsic value of the academy in the playfulness of Thought, Readings may contribute to the successful rejection of inimical, external standards of worth and performance. Similarly, Allan's vision promises to integrate all desires by playfully exploring how all desires effect moral practices of individuals. The value of both of these visions contending with corporate and administrative tropes is that they offer, I believe, what people want: a respectful assertion of the beauty of ultimately inexplicable social commitment. In Readings' words, this "social bond is the fact of an obligation to others that we cannot finally understand. We are obligated to them without being able to say exactly why. For if we could say why, if the social bond could be made an object of cognition, then we would not really be dealing with an obligation at all but with a ratio of exchange" (188). The academy makes such commitments more widely knowable and possible. When the next generation as a generation takes up such positions and vocally promotes them, as Readings and Allan have, I believe, the academy will better its chances of vanquishing the corporate threats of exploitation and subservience it currently faces.

In coming vocally and publicly to promote such counter images of the academy, the next generation needs also to think about the exigencies of public discourse. Though accommodation of dominant ways of publicly speaking certainly is necessary to gain attention, it is imperative that the accommodation extend only as far as is necessary. In a recent *PMLA* letter, Peter Herman rightly exhorts us "to explore making the case that our work is not hopelessly alien to the values and aims of the corporations and marketing consultants hired by many universities."[33] However, in learning "how to talk about literary studies in the language of those who see little use for us except as teachers of technical writing,"[34] we need to do so only in order to gain attention and understanding so that we can then introduce and encourage alternate, competing figurations of the academy. As incredible as it appears to be to many of the next generation, "the public" is comprised of remarkably numerous intelligent and ethical people who are only in need of appealing alternatives to corporate metaphors. No one thinks of the church in corporate terms, or when one does, he wants to tax it. And many people actually have hostile feelings toward business, as was made clear to me by one of my first-year students in the fall of 1997. Writing about the impact of career pressures on family life, one student concluded that "the main thing is family life has gone down due to the importance of jobs."[35] People can understand different purposes and benefits, but they must be offered them by fellow citizens. We must learn the tropics of corporation in order to subvert them for the benefit of everyone, including true corporations.

Lastly, complementing our revised individual commitments and activities, we might reconsider the benefits—and pitfalls—of collective organizations and activities, notably those readily available through faculty senates. Part of the reconsideration of collective activities needs to be soliciting alliances with politicians and business people. Our isolation from the public sphere may not in fact be the product of superciliousness, as many feel, but it certainly is detrimental to us in that it is allowing a figurative monopoly to form concerning the public conception of the academy. No feeling person *wants* to live in anything, even a corporation, like what vocal corporate dreamers, such as Richard J. Mahoney, propose. There are alternatives to turning the university into a mean, skeletal corporation and administrators into "junkyard dogs" as critics like Mahoney advocate.[36] It must be the next generation's commitment to public work as well as scholarly work, as Henry A. Giroux explains, that will offer the knowledgeable, ethical, and even beautiful alternatives many, and hopefully most, people in fact crave.[37] But we must act, and act differently from the way we have been acting. In acting differently, in breaking the corporate monopoly, we can know that, as with Milton's Eve, "though all by mee is lost, / Such favor I unworthy am voutsaf't, / By mee the Promis'd Seed shall all restore."[38]

*Notes*

This chapter was conceived while I was at Eastern New Mexico University, a recipient of the Pew Leadership Award for the Renewal of Undergraduate Education. Information on the Pew distinction may be obtained online by searching for Eastern New Mexico University at ⟨http://www.pewtrusts.com/Frame.cfm?Framesource=Grants/grantee_links.cfm⟩. I would like here to acknowledge the extraordinary kindness and assistance of the editor, Peter C. Herman. Further, for discussions of intellectual ethics and responsibility, I am forever indebted to O M Brack, Jr., Nancy A. Gutierrez, S. K. Heninger, Jr., and Ollie O. Oviedo. For daily support for several years, I am heartily grateful to AnaLouise Keating.

1. While this chapter suggests some cultural symptoms reflective of a nascent corporatization of the academy, it is certainly not the first to point out such phenomena, as the essay and notes reveal. For a good example of unabashed, albeit apparently very well intentioned corporate thinking in "allocating faculty positions" in "these days of academic downsizing" (54) and "overproduction of Ph.D.s" (60), see Carol Christ's "Retaining Faculty Lines." *Profession* 1997 (1997): 54–60. For a critical but still participatory essay about "the academic labor market" (238) and, especially, "the pain inflicted by the kind of academic downsizing that has led campus administrators to substitute low-paying, part-time and temporary 'adjunct' jobs for properly compensated, full-time, tenure-track positions" (236), see Sandra M. Gilbert, "Bob's Jobs: Campus Crises and 'Adjunct' Education." *Profession* 1998 (1998): 235–41. For essays on several issues related to the attack on the academy by business influences, see the special issue of *Sociological Perspectives,* "The Academy under Siege," 41, 4 (1998).

2. See David F. Noble, "Digital Diploma Mills: The Automation of Higher Education." *Science and Culture* 7, 3 (1998): 355–68. Also see Noble, "Digital Diploma Mills, Part II: The Coming Battle over Online Instruction," *Sociological Perspectives* 41, 4 (1998): 815–26.

3. Christopher Newfield describes this movement from expanding democracy to expanding bureaucracy in much of his work. See, for instance, his "What Was Political Correctness? Race, the Right, and Managerial Democracy in the Humanities," *Critical Inquiry* 19 (Winter 1993): 308–36, where he explains that "in the humanities we have managerial ideals instead of politics" (336). Don Ihde discusses these issues as well in "Humanities in the Twenty-First Century," *Postphenomenology: Essays in the Postmodern Context.* Evanston, Ill.: Northwestern University Press, 1993. 137–55.

4. As the notes have already suggested, and as the ones to come will continue to suggest, many intellectuals are alert to the problems of corporatization, but certainly many others are not, as is suggested by Mark R. Kelley, William Pannapacker, and Ed Wiltse's call to action, "Scholarly Associations Must Face the True Causes of the Academic Job Crisis," *The Chronicle of Higher Education* 18 December 1998, B4–B5. Kelley, Pannapacker, and Wiltse insist, rightly,

that academic associations, such as the Modern Language Association of America, must "stop telling us that we should look for non-academic jobs," and start "prodding colleges and universities to end their heavy reliance on part-timers and adjuncts," a reliance reflective of "a corporate mindset in academic administration." As these authors astutely point out, "if all college and university teaching were performed by full-time faculty members who held doctoral degrees, we would be facing the undersupply of Ph.D.'s predicted in 1989." A sanguine response to the techno-business transformations facing the academy may be found in Richard J. Finneran's Presidential Address to the South Atlantic Modern Language Association, published as "Who's Afraid of the World Wide Web? or, The Digital Academy of the Future." *South Atlantic Review* 63, 2 (1998): 1–6.

5. Pratt, "Going Public: Political Discourse and the Faculty Voice." *Higher Education under Fire: Politics, Economics, and the Crisis of the Humanities,* ed. Michael Bérubé and Cary Nelson. New York: Routledge, 1995, 50.

6. All references in this paragraph are to the Western Governors' University press release of 8 July 1997. The developers are quite proud of their business savvy and ability to transform the academy into a profitable enterprise as their webpages at ⟨http://www.westgov.org/smart/vu⟩ and ⟨http://www.wgu.edu/wgu/index.html⟩ indicate. Also see Goldie Blumenstyk, "Western Governors U. Takes Shape as a New Model for Higher Education," *The Chronicle of Higher Education,* 6 February 1998, A21–A24, and Chris Hables Gray, "The Western Governors Virtual University: Politics, Pedagogy, and Progress?" (updated 10 February 1998) ⟨http://www.ugf .edu/CompSci/CGray/VIRU.HTM⟩.

7. Whatever the benefits are for the governors, administrators, and big businesses behind Western Governors' University's development, Roberto Sanchez notes, few students are applying. Sanchez reports "about 100" applications submitted between 3 September and 11 October 1998, which has made officials at Western Governors' decline from "releasing enrollment counts to the public, arguing that those numbers are a bad measure of its success." Instead, these officials cite the high number of "hits" enjoyed by their website since the institution opened: the website has "been getting about 100,000 hits a day," according to Jeff Xouris, Western Governors' spokesperson. See ⟨http://www.peabody.jhu.edu/~fschock/sabb/struggles.htm⟩ (18 March 1999). Also see Jerry Farber, "The Third Circle: On Education and Distance Learning," *Sociological Perspectives* 41, 4 (1998): 797–814.

8. For a reliable history of U.S. enrollment trends for the last half of the century, see Elizabeth A. Duffy and Idava Goldberg, *Crafting a Class: College Admissions and Financial Aid, 1955–1994.* Princeton: Princeton University Press, 1998.

9. Quotes are from the Arizona International Campus website (10 March 1999): ⟨http://www.azintl.edu/FIPSE/home.html⟩. Attaching to legitimate universities is, reportedly, the preferred method around accreditation agencies. Lisa Gubernick and Ashlea Ebeling ("I got my degree through E-mail," *Forbes* 16 June 1997, pp. 84–92.) explain that borrowing the academic credentials of a reputable university is how new ventures do "an end-run around the problem" of accreditation (87). The Western Governors' University also continues to have trouble with accreditation. See ⟨http://www.msnbc.com/news/193021.asp⟩ (posted and copyrighted 9 February 1999).

10. All references in this paragraph are to Courtney Leatherman's report, "Campus

without Tenure Is Dubbed 'Fire-at-Will U." *Chronicle of Higher Education* August 15, 1997, p. A12.

11. Disbelief is but one of many responses of intellectuals, as Sandra Gilbert points out many, including "the passivity, perhaps the complacency or perhaps the anxious denial, with which all too many tenure-track professionals have reacted to a series of crises undermining contemporary study in the humanities." "Bob's Jobs," 238.

12. In 1960, 7.7 percent of Americans completed four years of college or more, whereas in 1997, the percentage had risen to 23.9 percent. See "Educational Attainment, by Race and Hispanic Origin: 1960 to 1997," at ⟨http://www.infoplease.com/ipa/a0774057.html ⟩ (23 March 1999).

13. All references in this paragraph, unless otherwise noted, are to Gubernick and Ebeling's polemical "report," "I got my degree through E-mail," *Forbes* June 16, 1997, pp. 84–92. Also see William Trombley, "Coping with the Tidal Wave II: Florida Gulf Coast University Amid alligators and hurricanes, a new campus is taking shape," ⟨http://www.policy center.org/ct_1096/ctn3_1096.html⟩ who describes the "Sweatshop U" dreams of Floridian academic entrepreneurs.

14. My comments on confronting bottom-line thinkers are most appropriate to state universities with relatively open admissions policies. The most elite and exclusive universities likely have different freshman classes, though Mark Edmundson of the University of Virginia describes the sort of languid consumers and capricious evaluators I am referring to in "On the Uses of a Liberal Education: I. As Lite Entertainment for Bored College Students," *Harper's,* September 1997, 39–49. For some student responses to such characterizations, see Christopher Shea, "A Pithy Critic of Terror on film, Freud, and Passionless Students," *The Chronicle of Higher Education,* 19 December 1997, A13-A14.

15. Rather than point to a less professionally secure next generation intellectual, and since he is an academic "star" whose reputation and livelihood will remain substantively unaffected by any criticism I make, I point to Stanley Fish, in his contentiousness, as an instance of rewarded ingenious productivity. This is not to say all of Fish's work is ingenious contentiousness: much of it is most marked by its substantive contribution to literary criticism and theory in English. For his sensational expressions, though, see, for instance, "No Bias, No Merit: The Case against Blind Submission," *PMLA* 103, 5 (1988): 739–48. Obviously, Fish does not need this publication the way his next generation juniors need publications, but the benefit of publication still accrues to him, not wholly unlike the way the benefit of a savings account at a university credit union would accrue to a millionaire-administrator, to use a corporate analogy. A decade later, this sensational, contentious publication that showed that "there is no such thing as intrinsic merit, and indeed, if I may paraphrase James I, 'no bias, no merit'" (739) is still receiving attention that contributes to sustaining a "national reputation." See, for instance, Domna C. Stanton, "What's in a Name? Revisiting Author-Anonymous Reviewing," *PMLA* 112, 2 (1997): 191–97.

16. On the disagreement over the impact of the politics of our current behaviour inside and outside the academy, especially with regard to what I have just called "sexy" versus "arduous" intellectual work, see Pamela L. Caughie and Reed Way Dasenbrock, "An Exchange on Truth and Methods," *College English* 58, 5 (1996): 541–54.

17. Trying to be progressive, Hans Ulrich Gumbrecht tells us not to worry about the effects of what we do as we follow the lead of other social phenomena in his "The Future of Literary Studies?" (*New Literary History* 26 (1995): 499–518). Gumbrecht's argument rests on many assumptions. The most significant assumptions for the next generation are that the academy does not lead cultural and social realities, and that it cannot. Following his line of argument contributes to the deep sense of the derivativeness rather than generativeness of the academy, something I want to persuade us not to do. Another way of appreciating the need to understand the effect/s of what we do when we do it is to consider responses to the work of Bill Readings, work that I outline below as perhaps one model for an alternative figuration of the academy. In reviewing Readings' essay on the court of Henry VIII (*Rethinking the Henrician Era: Essays on Early Tudor Texts and Contexts,* ed. Peter C. Herman. Urbana: University of Illinois Press, 1994.), for instance, Karen Newman (*Shakespeare Quarterly* 48 (1997): 109–10.) remarks that "Readings's claims are confusing in that he seems to want to relocate the often-remarked 'rise of a culture of spectacle' in early modern England to the court of Henry VIII (285), but he uses *Henry VIII,* a play written in 1612–13, with its notorious series of visual tableaux and the coincidental, spectacular burning of the Globe at its first performance, to support that claim. It is never clear to this reader how a Jacobean play and the historical event, the burning of the Globe in the early seventeenth century, can be adduced as evidence of a culture of spectacle in the 1530s" (110). Newman's reaction signals what happens when purposes and historiographies are different. Readings' poststructuralist commitments allow him to think without the conventions of history that Newman's commitments to diachrony require, and Newman's attempt to clarify Readings' poststructuralist modes and conventions disables her realizing and appreciating that he is being very different from her. Exactly what public effect such divergent historiographies and modes of being have in various sets of social contingencies is what I call all of us to attempt to determine as we go public. For a similar response to Readings' work, see Gerald Graff, "Response to Bill Readings," *New Literary History* 26 (1995): 493–97. Also on understanding the contextual differences between speaking in the academy and speaking in public, see Jacques Derrida, "Canons and Metonymies: An Interview with Jacques Derrida,"*Logomachia: The Conflict of the Faculties.* Ed. Richard Rand. Lincoln: University of Nebraska Press, 1992, 194–218.) who insists that "the political opposition between right and left must, when it concerns a strategic lever, be handled with the greatest care, even with vigilance, with the greatest sensitivity precisely to paradoxes" (206).

18. One example of such collaborative, collegial work among various disciplines is Barbara E. Walvoord and Lucille P. McCarthy, *Thinking and Writing in College: A Naturalistic Study of Students in Four Disciplines.* Urbana, Ill.: National Council of Teachers of English, 1990.

19. Letter to the Forum, *PMLA* 112, 5 (1997): 1134. Also see Ellen Cushman, "The Public Intellectual, Service Learning, and Activist Research," *College English* 61, 3 (1999): 328–36. Cushman critiques views of the public intellectual like LaCapra's in order to advocate the creation of "knowledge with those whom the knowledge serves" (330) in a way that "can have readily apparent accountability, and . . . can have highly visible impact" (335).

20. For a compact history of the establishment of U.S. tenure conventions, see the AAUP "redbook," *Policy Documents & Reports,* Washington, D.C. (1995).

21. *Alternatives to Tenure for the Next Generation of Academics,* AAHE Working Paper 14

(Washington, D.C.: American Association for Higher Education, 1997). For a reply to Breneman, see Matthew W. Finkin, "Tenure and the Entrepreneurial Academy: A Reply," *Academe*
(January/February 1998): 14–22.

22. I do not mean to slight or otherwise denigrate the importance and value of primary
and secondary teaching, or the role such levels of education play in "the academy," by focusing
on the college or tertiary level in this chapter. Alison T. Smith's recent reminder of prejudices
against primary and secondary teaching is a healthy one. See Alison T. Smith, "Secondary Education: Still an Ignored Market," *Profession* 1996 (1996): 69–72.

23. The complexion and value of what is designated "global capitalism" differs according
to one's perspective and purposes. Paul McCarthy, for instance ("Postmodern Pleasure & Per-
versity: Scientism & Sadism," *Essays in Postmodern Culture*. Ed. Eyal Amiran and John
Unsworth. New York: Oxford University Press, 1993, 101–32.), criticizes postmodernism's
methods and assertions for their intimate complicity with global capitalist desires, while Adam
Podgorecki (*Higher Faculties: A Cross-National Study of University Culture*. Westport, Conn.:
Praeger, 1997) diagnoses the problem of the "spreading professionalization in the sciences"
(141) as resulting from the fact that "we live in a world established by the rules of the free market" (138). More charitably toward the condition of global capital, George Soros assumes a
global capitalist condition as well as its general potential for improving living conditions for increasing numbers of people as he attempts a neoliberal, new-deal-like redemption of it. See, for
instance, Soros's promotion of an "open society" in "The Capitalist Threat" (*The Atlantic
Monthly* [February 1997]: 45–58), "Toward a Global Open Society" (*The Atlantic Monthly* [Jan-
uary 1998]: 20–24, 32), and *The Crisis of Global Capitalism: [Open Society Endangered]* New
York: BBS/Public Affairs, 1998.

24. For statistics and discussion of the increased and excessive reliance on adjunct faculty
in languages and literature, see Sandra M. Gilbert, et al. *Final Report, MLA Committee on Professional Employment*. New York: MLA, 1997.

25. Corporate-minded administrators are not the only ones who put such spins on such
public statements as Brian E. Szumsky's "Defense of Adjunct Faculty Members" (*MLA
Newsletter* [Spring 1998]: 34) against my call for vigorous public demands for more tenure-
track jobs for such workers (*MLA Newsletter* [Summer 1997]: 16) indicates. Still, it is important to remember that there are usually opportunities to respond, and it is imperative that we
do so. See my response to Szumsky, *MLA Newsletter,* (Summer 1998): 15–16.

26. Besides Szumsky's attack on tenured professors—they are "pampered" and do far less
"hard work" than adjunct instructors—numerous others are attacking tenure. In addition to
sources already cited, see Annette Kolodny, "'60 Minutes' at the University of Arizona: The
Polemic against Tenure," *New Literary History* 27 (1996): 679–704, and "60 Minutes" producer
Rome J. Hartman's reply following Kolodny's essay, which is then followed by a clarification
by Kolodny.

27. David F. Noble is working on a new book, tentatively entitled, *Digital Diploma Mills,*
and has posted some of his findings on the Internet. Concerning the venal motives of administrators, besides seeing how technology promises figurative profit in the form of reducing labor
costs and selling the same automated "education" to large numbers of consumers, Noble points
out the personal profit administrative technozealots achieve: A former vice chancellor of UCLA,

for instance, left, after committing the university to digital investments, to head up the newly formed Home Education Network, an online, for-profit purveyor of virtual education. As Noble concludes, "Quality education will not disappear entirely, but it will soon become the exclusive preserve of the privileged, available only to children of the rich and the powerful . . . unless we decide now not to let it happen." Online, search ⟨http://www.richmond .edu/~creamer/archive.html⟩ for David F. Noble, Digital Diploma Mills.

28. See bell hooks, *Killing Rage,* New York: Henry Holt, 1995, who explains how liberalism turns oppressive, or, conversely, Satya P. Mohanty, *Literary Theory and the Claims of History,* Ithaca: Cornell University Press, 1997, who describes an "irony" in postmodernist suspicion of Enlightenment values since, he explains, in the eighteenth century, Enlightenment claims were revolutionary (1).

29. *Writing a Woman's Life,* New York: Ballantine Books, 1988, 130.

30. Bill Readings, *The University in Ruins.* Cambridge: Harvard University Press, 1996.

31. And elsewhere, he reiterates that he thinks this corporatization of the academy is "implacable" (178).

32. George Allan, *Rethinking College Education.* Lawrence: University Press of Kansas, 1997.

33. *PMLA* 112, 3 (1997): 442.

34. 442.

35. The student declined to be identified.

36. See Mahoney's "'Reinventing the University: Object Lessons from Big Business," *The Chronicle of Higher Education* 17 October 1997: B4–B5.

37. See Henry A. Giroux, "Beyond the Ivory Tower: Public Intellectuals and the Crisis of Higher Education," Michael Bérubé and Cary Nelson, eds. *Higher Education under Fire: Politics, Economics, and the Crisis of the Humanities.* New York: Routledge, 1995, 238–58.

38. *Paradise Lost,* bk 12, lines 621–23.

# Seven

# New Technology and the Dilemmas of the Posttheory Generation: On the Use and Abuse of Computer and Information Technology in Higher Education Today

*Jeffrey R. Di Leo*

Regardless of how one views the political, pedagogical, and economic impact of computer and information technology on higher education, one cannot deny that the use of this technology within the academy is on the rise as are general pressures on faculty by administrators at many institutions to incorporate computer and information technology into their teaching.[1] Furthermore, it is difficult not to notice that the reactions of those within higher education to this situation can and do differ widely. This chapter deals with a specific set of responses to the intervention of new technology in the academy—responses by a group of academics that for now can be called the "next generation," but will later for our purposes be more precisely labeled the "posttheory generation."[2] After proposing a specific position on just who these people are, we will examine why their response to the changing technological condition of the academy is particularly interesting. I will argue that if we assume the notion of a posttheory generation as presented, then certain problems and prospects will arise for this generation regarding the interventions of new technology within higher education.

The new technological condition of the academy will affect the next generation in ways that will make difficult for them to either globally affirm or unconditionally denounce it. As we will see, some aspects of the technological revolution will clearly work to the benefit of the next generation, while others will clearly challenge their aims and ideals. As I see it, the necessarily conflicted reaction that the next generation must have to this technology will make it very difficult for them not only to voice support for its increased intervention without contradicting a certain set of values that they hold, but that it will also be difficult for them to organize resistance to the rise of new technology within the academy without opposing another set of beliefs. Let's begin though by first providing a rough overview of computer and information technology use and policy within the university today by focusing on the issues and situations most relevant to the next generation. Then, after briefly characterizing the next generation as a "posttheory" generation, we'll go on to look at why the alleged practices of this new type of scholar strongly suggest a mixed response to new technology policy and practice on campus.

## BEYOND BIBLIOPHILES AND TECHNOPHILES

It seems as though more often than not, discussions of the problems and prospects of computer and information technology in higher education lead to arguments about the future of the book, with the defenders of "print culture" squaring off against the proponents of "digital culture." Their disputes generally assume the position most famously stated by Frollo in Victor Hugo's *Notre-Dame de Paris:* "Ceci tuera cela"—"This will destroy that" (197). Hugo's claim that the book will kill the cathedral, and that the alphabet will kill images, implied not only that printing and the resultant rise in literacy rates would seriously challenge the authority of the church, but also that the book would change our mode of expression. An analogous situation may be seen as well to hold in our case.

Many fear that the intervention of computer and information technology in higher education will radically change, if not destroy, higher education as we know it, though we disagree on whether this is a good thing: a disagreement that will even be shared, as we shall see, among members of the next generation. Furthermore, while it is often assumed that the introduction of digital technology into the academy will reconfigure the foundations of authority as well as pose a challenge to traditional modes and means of expression, there is not much consensus on the nature or consequences of either of these events—a lack of consensus which holds as well for the next generation.[3]

In *Notre-Dame,* Hugo tells us that the "book of stone, so solid and durable" would give way to the "book of paper, yet more solid and durable" (178). The question for us today is whether the "university of paper, so solid and durable" will give way to a "university of computer bits, yet even more solid and durable." Should we, as members of the next generation, ascribe to the view that the transition from a print or book culture to a digital culture is a change for the better? If so, in what sense? Politically? Professionally? Economically? Pedagogically? The next generation must try to avoid making quick responses to these questions despite all temptations to the contrary, and even though this is for one reason or another very difficult for many; we must make every effort to steer a path between fascination coupled with attraction to the new(er) technologies of mediating communication, and fear and loathing of any challenge to higher education as we have known it. But this task seems to be more easily said than done, particularly given the extremes to which many take these and related concerns.

On the one side, there are those like J. Hillis Miller who after admitting to a "reasonably benign fetishism of the book" shared by "so many readers of [his] generation, and many generations before," go on to claim that "Not only is the text of the novel caught in the materiality of the book, it is also tied by way of the book's paper, cardboard, ink, and glue to the historical and economic conditions of its production and distribution" (34). The writer E. Annie Proulx, continues this line of thinking by bluntly stating that "books are forever." The information superhighway might be good for "bulletin boards on esoteric subjects, reference works, lists and news—timely, utilitarian information, efficiently pulled through the wires" writes Proulx, but "[n]obody is going to sit down and read a novel on a twitchy little screen. Ever."[4] This view is sometimes characterized as "bibliophilia" (Nunberg 9). In addition to citing the relative discomfort caused by reading material on a computer screen versus the pleasure of reading a printed book, "bibliophiles" also cite the relative portability and inexpensiveness of printed books over "bitted" books as well as the charge that you cannot read your computer screen in bed as major reasons for favoring books over computers. Their arguments—arguments that they share with hard-core proponents of "book culture"—extend as well into the realm of the classroom. For the "bibliophile," few things can take the place of the three basic material elements of the book-culture classroom: the student, the professor, and the book.

But, as George Landow points out in his 1996 contribution to an inspiring collection of essays on the future of the book, "Twenty Minutes into the Future; or How Are We Moving Beyond the Book?" most of the books that we actually "experience," or better yet, that our students experience, are not the kind of books that are the subjects of our bedtime reading dreams. Many of them have "narrow margins, typographical errors, and tiny type," writes Landow, not to mention the fact that "many of them begin to collapse, break apart, and drop pages during the week in which they are assigned" (210). "In ascertaining the present and future position of the book in our culture, one must recognize the way most students today actually encounter the printed book as object," continues Landow. It is not the "well-designed, well-printed, well-bound morocco volume of our ideal," rather it is most of the time an "ill-designed, fragile, short-lived object" (Landow 1996, 211). Such responses by Landow and others to the complaints of bibliophiles, if nothing else, point out deep weaknesses in common lines of argument against computer interventions in the classroom. And, perhaps even more significantly, not only do these responses draw attention to important questions concerning the effect of the material nature of texts on reading that are oftentimes neglected in debates over the use of computer mediated texts in the classroom, they also ask us to compare just what our students actually use as their texts to what they could be using via digital technology.

Furthermore, the bibliophile's line of argumentation is just not in line with what most students actually want regarding computer and informational technology. According to Kenneth C. Green, director of the Campus Computing Project and a visiting scholar at the Center for Educational Studies of the Claremont Graduate University, new technology is an integral part of the campus experience. "Students of all ages and across all fields," says Green, "come to campus expecting to *learn about* and also to *learn with* technology."[5] And universities are increasingly encouraging this student interest. For example, there is a growing demand by universities that students fulfill some type of computer technology competency. According to the Campus

Computing Survey conducted over the summer of 1998—a widely regarded and reliable source of information concerning campus computer and informational technology use based on data provided by officials at 577 two- and four-year colleges and universities across the United States, and now in its ninth year—two-fifths of the survey participants reported having some type of computer competency requirement for undergraduates. This figure is up from one-third just three years earlier.[6] Moreover, some even take this line of thought one step further, arguing that learning about and with technology should even be an integral part of the English department's mandate—that it should be an even more central part of the English curriculum than say reading novels and stories.

In a recent article for *The Chronicle of Higher Education* written by Lisa Guernsey,[7] Richard Grusin, the chair of Georgia Tech's technologically progressive English department, says that "academic leaders should consider their English department as more than places of 'moral inoculation' where students are expected to 'get literature.'" "The departments should also be places where students learn how new technology is shaping and reshaping our understanding of texts." Grusin emphasizes as well that this is particularly the case at technological institutions, though does not elaborate on why the case would be different for them as opposed to say liberal arts universities. The shift in curricular emphasis at Georgia Tech also resulted in a change of name for the English department: the "School of Literature, Communication and Culture" became its new appellation.

The department formerly known as English at Georgia Tech is one of an emerging generation of English and humanities departments[8] where professors will not only require students to spend more time using computers as pedagogical tools through the use of email, hypermail archives, websites, moos, and so on, but will also emphasize understanding how this form of communication functions. As such, time spent learning the moral and rhetoric of the story will be displaced by the study of the epistemological implications of the our new communicative medium: the computer.

The situation alluded to by Green and Grusin is, of course, understandable if not expected when placed in the context of data concerning the growing role of computers as both a source of information and a means of conveying knowledge on the college campus today. According to the 1998 Campus Computing Survey, more college students and courses are using more technology than ever even while at the same time college and university administrators struggle with computer and information technology planning.

The CCS 1999 survey indicated that, for example, the single most important challenge confronting the surveyed campuses regarding computer and information is "assisting faculty integrate technology into instruction." Thirty-three percent cited this as opposed to just over a quarter noting user support and a meager 4 percent citing Y2K problems. Furthermore, the CCS survey documented that the percentage of classes using email has risen from 8 percent in 1994 and 25 percent in 1996 to almost thirty-three percent in 1997 and a whopping 45 percent in 1998. The survey also indicated that one-third of all courses utilize the Internet as part of the syllabus compared with just 15 percent in 1996, and that almost one-fourth of all college courses are using the WWW for class materials and other resources. Use of the WWW for this purpose is up from just over 8 percent in 1996, and a meager 4 percent in 1994.

Findings like these make many university administrators salivate at potential opportunities for economic gain through projects like distance learning based on computer-mediated instruction. The infamous case of UCLA's Instructional Enhancement Initiative, and partnership with The Home Education Network is clear evidence of the promises and pitfalls of such projects—a case which has had and will have deep ramifications for the next generation's response to the intervention of new technology in "higher learning, inc."

In 1997, UCLA passed the Instructional Enhancement Initiative—a move that proved to be most unpopular among the faculty at UCLA. The initiative had mandated websites for all 3,800 of UCLA's arts and sciences courses, and marked "the first time that a major university has made mandatory the use of computer telecommunications in the delivery of higher education."[9] A year after the initiative, only thirty percent of the faculty had put anything online, and several dozen members of the faculty had even actively resisted the initiative. UCLA Extension met with similar resistance when instructors adamantly opposed signing over rights to their course materials to either the Regents of UCLA or The Home Education Network—the initial name of UCLA Extension's corporate sponsor. By this point in time, UCLA had started its own for-profit company based on the sale of online education with private corporations such as the Times Mirror Company.[10]

Similar stories concerning what David Noble aptly terms "the commoditization of instruction" and the "commercialization of higher education"[11] by computer and information technology might be cited, such as the two-month strike by faculty at York University (Canada)—the longest university strike in English Canadian history—over protection against the very type of administrative action taken by UCLA in their initiative. Another, more recent example, is the resistance which faculty and students in the California State University system raised to the California Educational Technology Initiative, a deal between CSU and Microsoft, GTE, Hughes, and Fujitsu which would have given this consortium of firms a monopoly over CSU's telecommunications infrastructure and the marketing and delivery of their courses online. According to Noble, "students resisted being made a captive market for company products while faculty responded to the lack of faculty consultation and threats to academic freedom and their intellectual property rights" (DD3, 2–3).

It would seem then that university and college administrations around the country and in Canada have been struck with "technophilia"—the other side of "bibliophilia"—and that the technophilia is spreading. "Technophiles" might be characterized as those who believe that computer-mediated discourse will supercede print-mediated discourse; that the day is near at hand where the "print age" will give way to the "digital age"; those who find in this future a utopia liberated from the "book." I don't think though that this is the case.

The intervention of computer and informational technology in higher education is not merely a story about technological transformation and two fundamental reactions to it. Moreover, it would be misleading and a mistake to suggest that differences concerning the intervention of digital technology in higher education can or should be reduced to merely a debate between technophiles and bibliophiles; between those who tend to see the growth of computer-mediated discourse and wired classrooms through a dystopian vision and those who view this future as a utopia. The significant issues lie elsewhere even if many couch the debate as one between bibliophiles like Proulx and Hillis Miller, and technophiles like Grusin and UCLA's administration. Issues like the ability or nonability to be able to read a book in bed and the digitalization of library collections, and whether the new technology will allow for this, only draw our attention away from the real issues: the commercialization of higher education.

I tend to agree with David Noble's comment that "universities are not simply undergoing a technological transformation." If they were, then the debate between technophiles and bibliophiles would be the significant one, for both are deeply concerned with the ways in which the future of discourse is contingent upon the technologies that mediate it (in the current case, print versus digital) as well as in the ways that technologies of mediation develop to the point where they are eventually completely supplanted or superseded by newer technologies of mediation. While this technological change is important to follow, something more relevant is going on "beneath that change," as Noble says, something that is "camouflaged by it"; namely, "the commercialization of higher education. For here as elsewhere technology is but a vehicle and a disarming disguise" (DD1, 2). The issue of the commodification and commercialization of higher education shifts the terms of the debate from whether the future liberated from the book will be a utopia or a dystopia to one on the "profit" of education. Nevertheless, this debate is most unlike any that we have heard before on the profit of education. It is not about intellectual profit for the student or on the ways in which students can translate an education into a financially successful career but rather one about how much money corporate-funded universities can make by marketing courses taught at their university over the internet; one in which the next generation should rightfully ask will "this kill that?"—will the commodification and commercialization of education kill higher education as we have known it?

## THE NEW GENERATION AS THE POSTTHEORY GENERATION

A few years ago, I argued in a special issue of the journal *symploke* that the next generation is really a posttheory generation by virtue of its unique approach to theory, and discussed as well their interest in the profession as itself an object of criticism.[12] I still agree with most of this assessment, and would like to review some of it now in order to lay out the terms of the next generation's response to the increasing intervention of computer and information technology in higher education.

The next generation seems to be more professionally self-aware than previous generations of scholars.[13] They treat the profession itself as an object of critical scrutiny, and strive to read it in much the same way that they would read any other literary or cultural text. This keen sense of academic self-reflexivity is quite remarkable given that this emerging generation of scholars are members of an institution sometimes exclusively devoted to the study of literature. I have little doubt that future generations of scholars will regard their work as one of the most indepth analyses of the profession as text ever undertaken by its practitioners. As such, the next generation will surely be deeply concerned and involved with controversies and debates concerning the increasing role of new technology in higher education if only to the extent that its intervention impacts the next generation's academic and professional interests.

This emergence of interest in issues concerning the profession and metaprofessional discourse by the next generation comes not as a supplement to the projects and discourses of the cultural studies models that have dominated the profession since the late eighties, but rather as a substitute for them. One might view the emergence of this discourse by the next generation as a spin-off of the theories of culture that challenged and finally displaced the formalist theories of literature that dominated the profession in the late seventies and the early eighties. The increasing significance and impact of work by the next generation may even mark a turn from cultural studies to theories of the "academic condition" even though one could equally argue that rising interest in metaprofessional discourse by the next generation is only a refocusing of the cultural studies agenda toward the profession. While this may be true, it seems that there is an important difference between the two bodies of discourse: cultural studies discourse is theoretically defined, whereas metaprofessional discourse is significantly less so.[14]

The best term to describe the approach that the next generation seems to be taking toward their activity is *posttheoretical.* As such, it seems more appropriate and accurate to refer to the next generation as the "posttheory generation." In general, the posttheory generation appears to be more willing and ready to use theory than the cultural studies generation. Posttheorists are looking less to work out new theoretical models or to expand the ones already in place than to employ preexisting theory to position their work both on and off campus. They may be moving toward a new eclecticism in that they often resort to anything and everything that suits the purpose at hand. Theirs is a pragmatic approach to theory which leads them to assess various theoretical models on the basis of the sociocultural and political understanding that they further. Nevertheless, a posttheoretical approach does not involve an antitheoretical position. In addition to resorting to theoretical sources, posttheorists frequently critique extant theories, interrogating their cultural and political effectiveness. Posttheoreticism is metatheoretical as well as pragmatic.

Posttheory critics complete the progression of postmodern skepticism about "grand narratives." While they share with the cultural studies generation a healthy diffidence to all metanarratives, they tend to part company with it insofar as part of its project still evokes (a) an idea of novelty—the notion that bringing about "new" alternatives to formalist approaches such as poetics, poststructuralism, and so forth, is an end in itself for critics; and (b) a modernist metanarrative—the neo-Marxist paradigm, for example. Most importantly, posttheory critics today are wary of adopting *in toto* theoretical models established in completely different historical and cultural-political contexts.[15] Their skepticism regarding metanarratives is even more pronounced than that of their immediate predecessors. Once again, they reject the self-sufficiency of theoretical novelty and strive to understand the institutional structures that perpetuate this belief.

In order to examine properly the response of the posttheory generation to the intervention of computer and information technology in higher education, it is useful to divide their metaprofessional discourse into five major zones of focus: (1) pedagogical innovation and reform; (2) the politics of tenure and placement; (3) the rhetoric and meaning of visibility, (4) the logistics of publication; and (5) the significance of public accountability. It is fair to assume that their investigations into and positions on these five areas of concern both differentiate them sufficiently from previous generations of scholars and mark to a great extent the "center" of their interrogation of the academic or professional condition. Let's now examine the posttheory generation's response to the new technology through the lens of these five discourse zones.

## The Posttheory Generation Meets the New Technology

One of the fundamental areas of professional concern and metaprofessional discourse for the posttheory generation involves pedagogical innovation and reform. To this end, the posttheory generation, more than many past generations of scholars, aims to more perfectly integrate teaching with research. One of the ways in which they achieve this goal is by turning the undergraduate classroom into a more "theory-friendly" environment by "democratizing" theory. They seem eager to take the challenge of rendering theoretical approaches and refined critical tools effective in undergraduate education. They try to share their own research as much as possible with students of all levels—even if in so doing they risk "watering down" their own positions. Furthermore, they make an effort to convince their students that theory is something for them to *use*, and not just to be studied in itself. They do not believe that theory is the crown jewel of the profession, something reserved only for graduate students or advanced undergraduates. What may be sacrificed in rigor and completeness is overshadowed by the high level of respect students may acquire for a posttheory classroom that sheds new light on students' relationships with literature, society, and ultimately themselves.

Thus, because posttheorists are willing to alter the traditional teaching-learning complexes when they seem to be in the student's best interests, they will be anxious to work with new technology in the classroom to the extent time and circumstance allow. The promises held out by many for new technology within the classroom will be appealing to the posttheorist, though their response will fall more on the side of "enthusiastic speculation" rather than "technological determinism and utopian myopia." In particular, they will be curious about and eager to investigate the claims by some, like Richard A. Lanham, that the new technology makes the democratization of the humanities a real possibility.

According to Lanham—professor Emeritus of English at UCLA—the new technology (along with rhetorical theory) offers ways of solving a problem that has been on the agenda of liberal arts educators at least since the Yale Faculty Report of 1828: How can we democratize the liberal arts without trivializing them?[16] "Up to now," writes Lanham,

> our answer has been the 1828 Yale answer: don't really democratize them; it can't be done; proceed as we always have—what else can we do, eternal verities being our principle product?—and let all these "nontraditional" students learn our ways as best they can. Political and economic pressures have now become too insistent for this. We are required to find really new ways to widen access to the liberal arts without trivializing them. Digital technology and rhetorical theory offer the new ways we need. (1993, 103)

But what are the new pedagogical techniques that this new technology is offering to students "whose talents," says Lanham, "are not intrinsically 'literary,' people who want, in all kinds of intuitive ways, to operate upon experience rather than to passively receive it" (1993, 105)?

These new pedagogical techniques are revealed to us by Lanham through the scenario of how an undergraduate might read Shakespeare's *Love's Labor's Lost* assisted by the new technology. "Imagine her [the student that is]," says Lanham,

> charting the rhetorical figures, displaying them in a special type, diagramming and cataloguing them, and then making hypertext animations of how they work. She'll use another program now on the market to make her own production, plotting out action, sight lines, costumes, etc. And then a voice program to suggest how certain lines should be read. Or she can compile her own edition, splicing in illustrations of cheirographia from the contemporary manuals. Or make it into a film. Or simply mess around with it in the irreverent ways undergraduates always have, mustaching the *Mona Lisa* just for the hell of it. (1993, 105)

The computer-mediated pedagogical idea that Lanham is getting at here is that if students do not possess the tools to comprehend a Shakespeare drama in "traditional" ways, then digital technology offers ways to present plays like *Love's Labor's Lost* to them which can appeal to an almost infinite variety of "nontraditional" approaches. And if by "democratize" Lanham means something like "to render otherwise inaccessible material accessible to students," them it seems as though this line of thinking is on track with the posttheoretical generation's line of practice and thought.[17]

Close reading and critical thinking are more important to the posttheorist generation than the texts one adopts and the method one selects to "read" them.[18] And, while unconventional, if Lanham's suggested method of reading Shakespearean drama will get otherwise uninvolved students "involved" with the text, posttheorists will surely want (when the technological conditions of their academy allow) to give it a try. This approach to texts is line with both the posttheorist's position that literature is just one textual practice among many as well as with their desire to address and work with emerging types of literacy such as visual and auditory.

It seems as well that Lanham's suggested use of digital technology to facilitate readings of Shakespeare for the "unconventional" student has just as much if not more to offer to the "conventional" student. In addition to the things mentioned above, one can imagine (and probably even find), hypertext editions of plays which allow "serious" students to follow the dialogue on the screen along with a dramatization of the play. One might then have links from words or lines in the dialogue to historical, lexical, sociological, philosophical, and other sources of relevant information. And, of course, the technological fantasies (and realities) might be multiplied.[19] These uses of the new technology will as well appeal to the posttheory generation even if the distinction between "unconventional" and "serious" student does not.

Furthermore, the posttheorist will recognize that the real and imagined effects of this type of new technology in the classroom go well beyond its (alleged) democratizing effects. They will note that bringing these new and emerging technologies into play in the posttheory generation classroom will further help to bring about a transformation in our assumptions about and practices as teachers and learners.[20] Moreover, the potential reconfiguration of the identity of institutions of learning resultant upon the intervention of this technology in the classroom will intrigue them. The potential the new media classroom holds for transforming teachers, as Landow says, into more of an "experienced partner in a collaboration than an authenticated leader" (1992, 123) should appeal to the posttheory generation even if some of their colleagues will not be as excited about this prospect.[21] This latter scenario is not difficult to imagine. Think of the professor who has been teaching *Love's Labor's Lost* for the last twenty-five years or so relinquishing some (not all) of her lecture time to the type of activities Lanham describes above. Her role as professor has been altered by this new technology as well as the expectations for her from her students.[22]

The difficult thing here for the posttheorist is not the change of professorial identity in the classroom that might transpire or even the necessary change in teaching-learning complex resultant upon the introduction of this new technology into the curriculum. Furthermore, neither should any of the promises of and prospects for new media in the classroom pose problems or be objectionable to the posttheorist: new media makes the classroom a more "transactional" space; facilitates more collaborative learning and group work; makes students more active shapers of the knowledge; establishes a stronger sense of a "community of learners"; encourages integration of different materials and associative thinking; adjusts to different learning styles and abilities; and so on. In fact, it seems to me that the posttheory generation will be most interested in pursuing and testing these claims. The difficulty will come though when administrators pressure the posttheory generation to take the next step; namely, to turn their attention from the physical classroom to the virtual classroom in the ways in which UCLA Initiative suggested.[23]

While the virtual classroom might provide, among other things, for more flexibility in university and student schedules as well as "free learners from constraints of scheduling without destroying the structure and coherence of a course" (Landow 1992, 132), it will also add pressure on the posttheory generation to become digital out of necessity rather than choice. This pressure will be most evident and the dilemmas most pronounced through tenure and placement policy initiatives.

Tenure and placement policy proves to have a strong impact on both the academic (public) and personal (private) identity of posttheorists. Most definitely, this new generation of academics view the professional world not as an oasis, but a desert through which they are doomed to roam for years after receiving their Ph.D. Moving from one short-term appointment to another has become a commonplace rite of passage. Placement and job-market conditions spawn a kind of nomadic identity which was the exception in the golden age when tenure-track positions were more readily available.[24] The metaprofessional discourse of the posttheorist problematizes this institutional nomadicism, and helps us understand its sociocultural and political ramifications in a profession where academic and personal identities tend to be more and more constructed in transit. The introduction of new technology into higher education will surely add another chapter to this metaprofessional narrative: one which will surely point out the double-edged sword of the new technology with regard to tenure and placement policy.

One the one hand, new technology opens up employment alternatives to the posttheory generation in the shape of newly funded positions with concomitant duties in some traditional area of scholarship and new technology. Many departments are looking to establish computer-based curriculums and will need faculty with expertise in this area. Computers and composition, for example, is a burgeoning field, with many more opportunities for the candidate with technology and composition expertise than merely composition expertise. The other side of this equation though is that those without the preferred computer and information technology training will have fewer opportunities than those without these skills. Furthermore, the number of cases are building of new hires *just* on the basis of computer and information technology skills, and as such, denying more "traditionally" qualified applicants employment opportunities.[25] But the story does not stop at placement—one still needs to ask what are the implications for tenure for those without the newly necessary computer and information skills.

From all indications, departments are increasingly interested in both hiring technologically advanced candidates and in "wiring" their departments.[26] As such, faculty will increasingly be pressured to not only integrate the new technology into their classrooms but also to make their classrooms available online—a position which many find to be not only an infringement of their academic freedom but also exploitative if they are not offered additional financial compensation for putting their courses online. In this situation, it seems as though untenured faculty will be under more pressure than tenured faculty with respect to integrating the new technology, for their job security is more likely to be at risk. If we take this situation into account with the fact that university administrations are increasingly interested in making their curriculums more technologically based and marketing courses over the Internet, then it seems that the integration of new technology in higher education puts the posttheory generation in a most difficult position. Pressures to go digital not only stem from their pedagogical initiatives but also from departmental and universitywide mandates. Nevertheless, it is still one thing to go digital for pedagogical motivations and another to go digital for job security based on the corporatization of the university. And the choices do not become any easier for the posttheorist when we take into account the final three zones: visibility, publication, and public accountability.

We know, for example, that posttheorists place a new type of emphasis on professional visibility in all of its forms.[27] Many are exploring and exploiting new modes of linking up their work and the "social text." They prospect new avenues of social impact and transacademic communication such as electronic media and cyberspace in hopes of increasing the quality and quantity of the social presence publicly associated with teaching and research. Much of their metaprofessional discourse is devoted to exploring the potential held by new forms of scholarly visibility. With this in mind, it undoubtedly will be more difficult for the posttheory generation to resist the demands placed on them to integrate the new technology into their professional lives. Putting their courses on the web, for example, seems to be a reasonable extension of their general interest in visibility as well as their desire to be pedagogically progressive. This, of course, makes them ideal candidates for exploitation by universities seeking to commodify their curriculums.

The situation for the posttheorist does not get any clearer when one considers as well that posttheorists show a strong interest in creating new arenas and instruments of expression as well as in using channels that have traditionally been ignored. In the past few years they have founded new journals—journals which aspire to be a forum for critics who share similar beliefs about the field.[28] There is also a growing trend among posttheorists to publish in more popular and publicly accessible venues such as *Harper's* or *The Village Voice* or even on the WWW.[29] As such, their views on the politics of publication seems to indicate as well a willingness to integrate the new technology into their professional world.

Finally, we must take into account the fact that posttheorists are especially concerned with the reconstruction of the whole notion of academic and public accountability. First, posttheorists believe that what goes on in the profession must be accountable both inside and outside the profession. One of the ways in which they are achieving this goal is by moving away from using the arcane, publicly inaccessible lingo of theory. Posttheorists tend to replace this difficult terminology with a *lingua franca* accessible to a less specialized audience. This *lingua franca* places the public in a better position to grasp what is going on in a profession that has in the past hidden behind a cloud of terminology. Second, the reconstruction of accountability entails an attempt to demonstrate that various models of critical reading can be successfully applied to "public discourse" at large, including political discourse, media representations of everyday life, advertisements, and various cultural environments. Posttheorists show how sophisticated instruments can work to utilize and enable nonacademic subjects, help them with their own social and political position.

It might be argued then that their concern with public and academic accountability will steer them in the direction of actively integrating new technology rather than against. One might claim for example that satisfying increased student expectations to learn about and use the new technology at the university as well as making their courses and course materials (if not even their lectures) public over the Internet are in line with the value that the posttheory generation places on public and academic accountability.

## DILEMMAS OF THE NE(X)T GENERATION

The posttheory generation is facing a host of new problems from university administrators who are not only aggressively coercing faculty (as in the case of UCLA) to integrate new technology into the classroom but also increasingly attempting to run higher education like a business. While the integration of new technology in the class is in line with some of the values and practices of the posttheory generation, the intersection of encouraging faculty to use new technology in the classroom, and the corporatization and commodification of higher education will raise dilemmas for the posttheory generation. It seems to me that the posttheory generation will want to make a distinction between *using* technology in the classroom as well as part of their new professional identity, and being the subject of university exploitation through the use of technology to sell their courses. Instances of moves similar to those of UCLA's Instructional Enhancement Initiative are becoming more familiar in the academy as is resistance to them by the posttheory generation and others.[30] Furthermore, moves not as extreme as the UCLA Initiative but useful in setting the stage for future implementation of such initiatives are in the works as well.

Recently, for example, a draft of the new California State University System Cornerstones Implementation Plan (CIP) calls for all faculty to reevaluate the use of classrooms in higher education by calling for faculty to "determine when student learning can be effectively served by the classroom context, the use of distributed learning technology, community service learning, and other learning methodologies" (Section B, Sentence 3, Draft CIP). On the surface, this should be an agreeable suggestion to posttheorists, given their openness to pedagogical innovation, especially when one considers that the entire CSU Cornerstones Implementation Plan is intended to "create a truly student-centered university" (Introduction, Draft CIP). But, when one considers CSU's past track record, particularly the California Educational Technology Initiative mentioned earlier, one hears big business, corporatization, and commodification marching between the lines of the CIP, rather than the growth of a student-centered university. These and similar scenarios will raise deep dilemmas for the posttheory generation.

The posttheory generation is finely aware of recent attempts by university administrations to run higher education as though it were a corporation. This generation generally believes that cost-based management cripples curriculums and pedagogies established in what, for lack of a better term, might be called "education-based" models of university management. They recognize, as well, that library and research budgets seem to be decreasing at a rate inversely proportional to the rate at which class sizes and teaching loads are increasing. These pressures and others leave their departments desperate for ways to not only decrease teaching loads and increase research budgets but also to gain a voice as a legitimate and progressive unit within the incorporated university. As I see it, this situation leaves the posttheory generation stuck between a rock and a hard place.

While increasing library and research budgets and reducing class sizes and teaching loads are high on their agenda, so too are pedagogical innovation, job opportunities, visibility, new mediums for publication, and public accountability. This puts the posttheory generation in a very difficult position. Supporting integration of the new technology into higher education is tantamount to supporting, for example, lower library acquisition budgets and the commodification of their courses through virtual universities. As the new technology opens up opportunities for employment in a weak job market, so too may it cut down on employment possibilities, especially in the future, if administrators deem that Internet-based education is just as effective, if not more effective than the traditional classroom. This scenario has the possibility of short-circuiting the political efficacy of the posttheory generation because it will be difficult for them to build not only a strong case *against* the new technology, but also *for* the new technology. By having to qualify their positions for and against based on seen and unseen uses and abuses of this new technology in higher education, the posttheory generation risks losing their political agency. One only hopes that the consequence of this situation is not a regression to bibliophilia and technophilia as positions for response among the posttheory generation.

Regardless though of the difficult political situation in which the posttheory generation is placed, the technological enhancement of higher education will continue, as will the concomitant experiments in pedagogical innovation. All in all, this situation will necessarily generate a need for professors who can deploy these technologies within their professions. Given that more and more departments are looking to "incorporate" new technologies into their curriculum, there will continue to be a new hiring demand for assistant professors who are capable and comfortable working in this area as well as a need for faculty (especially untenured) to alter their teaching to accommodate the push for a new technologically based pedagogy. This presents the posttheory generation with yet another set of problems.

First, for the most part, most of the posttheory generation's pedagogical background was formed in and through a nontechnological teaching/learning paradigm.

The adoption of a technological paradigm of learning requires that the posttheory generation must in effect again become students in their attempt to assimilate their nontechnological background to the emerging technological one. Many of their assumptions about teacher-student interaction and the role of the classroom will need to be reevaluated. And while they will be amenable to this reevaluation, it will require some patience and willingness to experiment on their part. Secondly, the posttheory generation was trained to teach literature, and one of their implied goals was to help students to "get" literature, that is, to understand better its social, political, economic, rhetorical, and ethical dimensions. Teaching students about the new technology—as well as how to use it—will become increasing important in the academy and will require a major shift in focus by the posttheory generation, as will showing them how the new technology is shaping and reshaping out understanding. Finally, given that their academic background was grounded in a different curriculum, the next generation will have to find ways to accommodate it to the demands that the new technology places on them.

This chapter has indicated some of the ways in which new technologies can change higher education as well as affect the posttheory generation. It also reveals how the intervention of digital technology into the profession can alleviate some of the fiscal pressures they are now facing as well as suggesting some of the impact that this will have on a specific characterization of the next generation—the posttheory generation—which now is even more appropriately entitled, the "net generation." While the posttheory generation is nothing if not adaptable to new situations and pragmatic in the utilization of resources, still the demands of the new technology call for a radical shift in identity and value. It should be clearer now how the posttheory generation feels about the possibly radical transformation of the profession brought about by technological, pedagogical, and educational innovation, even if it is still unclear whether they think that the price will be too high. It seems to me that the posttheory generation, perhaps more than any before, will be able to adapt to these situations. They have been through the theory wars and culture wars and are now veterans of the job wars. As such, they seem well suited to meet the challenges of the "new technology wars." And while the institutional and political structures that emerge from this situation will be most unlike anything that they have experienced in the past, I am confident that they will find ways to adjust to them and regain the political agency that I have suggested will be temporarily stunned by the increasing role of new technology in higher education.

*Notes*

1. See, for example, the findings of the CCS 1998 survey [http://ericir.syr.edu/Projects/Campus_computing/1998/] discussed below as well as other surveys done by CCS for information on the growing use of computer and information technology in higher educa-

tion today. See also, the website "Building a Web-Based Education System" [http://webclass.cqu.edu.au;Why/Why/index.html] for links to various postings on this subject. Finally, David Noble's "Digital Diploma Mills: The Automation of Higher Education" [http://www.firstmonday.dk/issues/issues3_1/noble/index.html] and "Digital Diploma Mills, Part III: The Bloom Is Off the Rose" [http://webclass.cqu.edu.au/Why/Why/digital3/] provide much information on the various ways faculty in Canada and the United States have been pressured by university administrators to incorporate computer and information technology.

2. See Williams (1995). This article by Jeffrey Williams in a special issue of *symplokē* entitled *The Next Generation* (vol. 3, no. 1) introduced me to this phrase as well as to a set of reasons why the next generation should be regarded as the posttheory generation.

3. See, for example, Collins and Berge's *Computer-Mediated Communication and the On-line Classroom* (1995), Ellsworth's *Education on the Internet* (1994), Kearsley, Furlong, and Hunter's *We Teach with Technology* (1992), McLure's *Libraries and the Internet/NREN Perspectives, Issues and Challenges* (1994), Maurer's *Educational Multimedia and Hypermedia* (1995), and Steen et al. *Teaching with the Internet: Putting Teachers before Technology* (1995).

4. *New York Times,* 5/26/94, A13. Internet version.

5. "Colleges Struggle with IT [Instructional Technology] Planning." http://ericir.syr.edu/Projects/Campus_computing/1998/. Visited 1/19/99. Page 1.

6. Findings of the CCS 1998 survey are posted at http://ericir.syr.edu/Projects/Campus_computing/1998/. Visited 1/7/99.

7. Guernsey, Lisa. "Georgia Tech's Former English Department Combines Multimedia Training With Theory." *The Chronicle of Higher Education.* 11/5/97. Information Technology Section. Internet version.

8. Guernsey's article states that "Georgia Tech's former English department is an example of a breed of programs on new media that are cropping up at colleges across the United States. Some are based in art departments and focus on computer graphics and design. Others are causing ferment in library schools, which have tailored their courses to help future librarians filter the information glut on the Internet."

9. David Noble, "Digital Diploma Mills: The Automation of Higher Education." Cited hereafter as DD1.

10. The events at UCLA are reported by David Noble in DD1.

11. David Noble, "Digital Diploma Mills, Part III: The Bloom Is Off the Rose." Cited hereafter as DD3.

12. See Di Leo and Moraru, "Posttheory Postscriptum" (1995). This essay appeared in a special issue of *symplokē* entitled *The Next Generation,* ed. Peter C. Herman. See also Di Leo and Moraru, "Posttheory, Cultural Studies, and the Classroom: Fragments of a New Pedagogical Discourse" (1997). Our work on the posttheory generation in these two essays and elsewhere grew out of, in part, our response to essays by Peter C. Herman, Jeffrey Williams, and David Galef in the same issue of *symplokē*. See Herman (1995), Williams (1995), and Galef (1995) for further statements on the posttheory/next generation.

13. While the next generation did not originate this academic self-reflexivity (see, for example Gerald Graff's *Professing Literature*), the number of books and articles devoted to this

topic from members of this group is extraordinary. See, for example, Michael Bérubé's *Public Access: Literary Theory and American Cultural Politics* (1994) and *The Employment of English: Theory, Jobs and the Future of Literary Studies* (1998); Michael Bérubé and Cary Nelson's (eds.), *Higher Education under Fire: Politics, Economics and the Crisis of the Humanities* (1995); Bruce Robbins's *Secular Vocations: Intellectuals, Professionalism, Culture* (1993); David Shumway's *Creating American Civilization: A Genealogy of American Literature as an Academic Discipline* (1994), as well as the recent series of volumes of the *minnesota review* on "The Institution of Literature."

14. The claim that cultural studies is theoretical is highly controversial. Many, like Cary Nelson (1997), vigorously argue that it is not. In "Policing the Borders of Birmingham: Cultural Studies, Semiotics and the Politics of Institutionalization" and elsewhere I present extensive arguments against this proposal.

15. See Peter C. Herman's introduction to this volume.

16. Lanham 1993, 103. The Yale Faculty Report of 1828 argued that undergraduate education is the responsibility of the individual student, and that a liberal education should be broad and human, and not narrow and specialized. It also stated that there should be a core curriculum, and that the junior year is the proper time for students to specialize in a subject. The report recommended raising admission standards as a means of democratizing education. See Lanham 101–103 as well as excerpts from the Yale Report of 1828 in Hofstadter and Smith (1961, 275–91).

17. While Lanham is decidedly not "next generation" by the terms set in Herman's introduction to this volume, I think that some of his ideas speak to the interests of the next generation and deserve our attention.

18. This, of course, is a hotly contested point. See, for example, William Cain's "A Literary Approach to Literature: Why English Deparments Should Focus on Close Reading, Not Cultural Studies" and Bérubé's response to it in *The Employment of English,* pp. 5–9. Bérubé asserts, contra Cain, that every one of his department's recent hires "knows how to read a text carefully" (8) and is theory smart.

19. I have seen a quite impressive pilot version by Gregg Van Hoosier Carey, Ellen Strain et al. of D. W. Griffith's film *The Birth of a Nation.* Their intermedia project allowed for easy frame-by-frame analysis of much of the film accompanied by links to useful historical, cultural, and social information. I have no doubt that students from all backgrounds would benefit from such "remediations" of classic films and dramas.

20. For a more complete assessment of the implications of the posttheory position on pedagogy, see Di Leo and Moraru, "Posttheory, Cultural Studies and the Classroom" (1997).

21. In *Teaching to Transgress: Education as the Practice of Freedom,* bell hooks writes that "Making the classroom a democratic setting where everyone feels a responsibility to contribute is a central goal of transformative pedagogy" (39). I agree with this aspect of her pedagogical theory, and find that most of my posttheory generation colleagues do as well. One of the consequences, though, of this type of pedagogy is a shift in the role of the teacher to something like what Landow describes in the quote above.

22. In addition to Landow (1992) and Lanham (1993), there are, of course, many other

ways that the teaching-learning complex can potentially be affected by digital technology, and fortunately, many good sources that discuss these in much, and, sometimes, enthusiastic detail. See the journals *Computers and Composition, Academic Computing* and *Writing on the Edge* as well as Bolter's *Writing Space* (1991), Delany and Landow's *Hypermedia and Literary Studies* (1991), Hawisher and Selfe's *Evolving Perspectives on Computers and Composition Studies* (1991), and Selfe and Hilligoss's *Literacy and Computers* (1994) for further discussion of the promises of and prospects for digital technology in the profession.

23. Some universities have even gone further than the UCLA Initiative. For example, Florida Gulf Coast University was recently established as a university of the future. FGCU has no tenure system, and aims to be a testing ground for Internet-based instruction.

24. See, for example, Terry Ceasar, "Getting Hired" (1996) and Evan Watkins's *Work Time: English Departments and the Circulation of Cultural Value* (1989).

25. Although the MLA does not keep numbers on this sort of thing, one sees more and more academic employment opportunities in the MLA Job List for people with expertise in the new technologies, particularly in composition studies, business writing, and technical writing.

26. Many English departments, for example, have a home page that is overseen by a faculty member. Many departments supply their faculty with computers linked to the Internet and maintain as well email lists for faculty, students, and staff. Some, like the University of Illinois at Chicago, even have computer composition labs/classrooms. Furthermore, faculty are increasingly assumed to be on the net by students and other faculty. The CCS 1998 study uncovered another surprising set of numbers: 45 percent of the undergraduates surveyed said that they use the Internet at least once a day compared to almost 52 percent of faculty. This is surprising because the popular conception is that students are more wired than faculty.

27. This is linked to the recent trend toward "academic stars" who are known more by reputation and the amount of money they ask for a keynote address than by a close study of their work.

28. The journals *symplokē, the minnesota review,* and *journal x,* are, for example, good evidence of this trend.

29. One of the effects and evidence of this is that finding an article, say, by Andrew Ross in the *Nation* or Michael Bérubé in *The Village Voice* is not a surprise—furthermore, it is almost expected of them.

30. See Noble (DD3). In addition to the situations at York University, CSU, and UCLA mentioned already, others might be added. For example, Acadia University faculty recently threatened to go on strike if their administration did not back off unilateral demands for online instruction; Simon-Fraser University faculty have recently challenged their universities' major attempts to create a virtual university; Florida Gulf Coast University faculty have protested against some effects of the schools' Internet-based instruction including increased workloads and intellectual property issues related to handing over their courses to the FGCS; and faculty at the University of Washington in Seattle recently signed a letter of protest against the state's plans to digitize education—seven hundred signatures were gathered there in a mere two days, with another two hundred added later.

*References*

Bérubé, Michael. *Public Access: Literary Theory and American Cultural Politics*. London: Verso, 1994.

——. *The Employment of English: Theory, Jobs and the Future of Literary Studies*. New York: New York University Press, 1998.

——, and Cary Nelson (eds.). *Higher Education under Fire: Politics, Economics and the Crisis of the Humanities*. New York: Routledge, 1995.

Bolter, Jay. *Writing Space: Computer, Hypertext and the History of Writing*. Hillsdale, N.J.: Lawrence Erlbaum, 1991.

Cain, William. "A Literary Approach to Literature: Why English Deparments Should Focus on Close Reading, Not Cultural Studies." *Chronicle of Higher Education* (13 Dec. 1996): B4–B5.

Ceasar, Terry. "Getting Hired." *minnesota review* 45/46 (1996): 225–45.

Collins, Mauri, and Zane Berge. *Computer-Mediated Communication and the Online Classroom*. Three Volumes. Cresskill, N.J.: Hampton Press, 1995.

Culler, Jonathan. *Literary Theory: A Very Short Introduction*. New York: Oxford University Press, 1997.

Delany, Paul, and George Landow. *Hypermedia and Literary Studies*. Cambridge, Mass.: MIT Press, 1991.

Di Leo, Jeffrey R. "Policing the Borders of Birmingham: Cultural Studies, Semiotics and the Politics of Institutionalization." *Semiotica* (2000). Forthcoming.

Di Leo, Jeffrey R., and Christian Moraru. "Posttheory Postscriptum." *The Next Generation*. Ed. Peter C. Herman. *symplokē* 3. 1 (1995): 119–22.

——. "Posttheory, Cultural Studies, and the Classroom: Fragments of a New Pedagogical Discourse." *Class Issues: Pedagogy, Cultural Studies and the Public Sphere*. Ed. Amitava Kumar. New York and London: New York University Press, 1997. 237–46.

Ellsworth, Jill H. *Education on the Internet*. Indianapolis, Ind.: Sams Publishing, 1994.

Galef, David. "The Return of Rhetoric." *The Next Generation*. Ed. Peter C. Herman. *symplokē* 3. 1 (1995): 77–85.

Graff, Gerald. *Professing Literature: An Institutional History*. Chicago: Univerity of Chicago Press, 1987.

Guernsey, Lisa. "Georgia Tech's Former English Department Combines Multimedia Training with Theory." *The Chronicle of Higher Education*. 11/5/97. Information Technology Section. Internet version.

Hawisher, Gail E., and Cynthia Selfe. *Evolving Perspectives on Computers and Composition Studies: Questions for the 1990s*. Urbana, Ill.: National Council of Teachers of English, 1991.

Herman, Peter C. "The Next Generation: '60s Theory/'90s Critics." *The Next Generation*. Ed. Peter C. Herman. *symplokē* 3. 1 (1995): 45–54.

Hofstadter, Richard, and Wilson Smith (eds.) *American Higher Education: A Documentary History*. Volume 1. Chicago: University of Chicago Press, 1961.

hooks, bell. *Teaching to Transgress: Education as the Practice of Freedom*. New York: Routledge, 1994.

Hugo, Victor. *Notre-Dame de Paris*. London and Boston: The Edinburgh Society, N.D. (no date).

Kearsley, Greg, Mary Furlong, and Beverly Hunter. *We Teach with Technology*. Wilsonville, Ore.: Franklin, Beedle, and Associates, 1992.

Landow, George P. *Hypertext: The Convergence of Contemporary Critical Theory and Technology*. Baltimore: Johns Hopkins University Press, 1992.

———. "Twenty minutes into the Future; or, How are We Moving beyond the Book?" *The Future of the Book*. Ed. Geoffrey Nunberg. Berkeley and Los Angeles: University of California Press, 1996. 209–38.

Lanham, Richard A. *The Electronic Word: Democracy, Technology and the Arts*. Chicago: University of Chicago Press, 1993.

Maurer, Hermann, ed. *Educational Multimedia and Hypermedia, 1995*. Charlottesville, Vir.: AACE, 1995.

McClure, Charles, et al. *Libraries and the Internet/NREN Perspectives, Issues and Challenges*. Westport, Conn.: Meckler, 1994.

Miller, J. Hillis. "What Is the Future of the Print Record?" *Profession 95*. New York: MLA, 1995. 33–35.

Nelson, Cary. *Manifesto of a Tenured Radical*. New York: New York University Press, 1997.

Noble, David. "Digital Diploma Mills: The Automation of Higher Education." http://www.firstmonday.dk/issues/issues3_1/noble/index.html. Visited 1/13/98.

———. "Digital Diploma Mills, Part III: The Bloom Is Off the Rose." http://webclass.cqu.edu.au/Why/Why/digital3/. Visited 1/13/98.

Nunberg, Geoffrey. "Introduction." *The Future of the Book*. Ed. Geoffrey Nunberg. Berkeley: University of California Press, 1996. 9–20.

Robbins, Bruce. *Secular Vocations: Intellectuals, Professionalism, Culture*. London: Verso, 1993.

Selfe, Cynthia, and Susan Hilligoss. *Literacy and Computers: The Complications of Teaching and Learning with Technology*. New York: Modern Language Association, 1994.

Shumway, David. *Creating American Civilization: A Genealogy of American Literature as an Academic Discipline*. Minneapolis: University of Minnesota Press, 1994.

Steene, Douglass R., Mark R. Roddy, Derek Sheffield, and Michael Bryan Stout. *Teaching with the Internet: Putting Teachers Before Technology*. Bellevue, Wash.: Resolution Business Press, 1995.

Watkins, Evan. *Work Time: English Departments and the Circulation of Cultural Value*. Stanford: Stanford University Press, 1989.

Williams, Jeffrey. "The Posttheory Generation." *The Next Generation*. Ed. Peter C. Herman. *symplokē* 3. 1 (1995): 55–76.

# EIGHT

# THEORY AFTER THE "THEORISTS"?

## Neil Larsen

### MOCK HEROICS

It's become a fairly common perception that the emergent generation of North American literary-critical intellectuals and academics lacks any one, dominant theoretical "voice" or paradigm of its own. The heroic years of "high theory" having passed—so the story goes—into the institutionalized reign of a few academic superstars, everyone else must apparently be content to be a postmodern consumer in the supermarket of "theory": free to chose the brand one prefers, but, especially with a disastrously shrunken academic job market, uncertain about what to buy and how to use it—assuming one will ever get the chance at all.

The perception is surely accurate as far as it goes, and it raises in turn the important question of what economic and political realities conditioned the rise of the theory generation in the first place. In "The Posttheory Generation" (1995) Jeffrey Williams speculates that the cohort of literary scholars who are now either junior faculty or are just entering the job market differs markedly from its immediate predecessor. While it too has been trained in high theory, the diminishing prospects of ever getting paid to teach it in turn make it much less sanguine about theory's possible pleasures and/or virtues. Williams nicely unpacks the social irony at the core of theory: that having vanquished the older, more belle-lettristic (and/or new critical) regime of the early Cold War, thanks, perhaps, to its conjunctural overlap with the sixties revolts, theory becomes ensconced in a new elite-academic stratum and, in all but words, fails to speak to the social and political ills of younger academics.

But there is still a further irony here, at least from my perspective. I should clarify before saying more that my own generational profile probably places me somewhere between the now thinned-out and entrenched theory generation posited by Williams and the purportedly post-theoretical one. Ph.D.'ed in 1983 in Comparative Literature, I got my first strong dose of theory as an undergraduate in the early 1970s, at a time when names such as Roland Barthes or Michel Foucault were known practically only in French departments. My early fascination for Barthes, in fact, nearly resulted in my being denied a bachelor's degree in philosophy, an academic discipline that, in most of North America, had and still has little use for French thinkers (or any other continental philosophy) after Descartes. That was enough to send me into graduate studies in comparative literature, where I was able to witness firsthand the swift approach and swifter triumph of what John Guillory (as well shall see below) aptly calls the "theory canon." Midway through that interlude—about 1979—I became disenchanted with what had by then become the hegemony of deconstruction and post-structuralism in theory courses and began a serious involvement with the critical tradition of Marxism, one that has lasted ever since. Employed, since 1983, as a Latin Americanist in Spanish departments, I have, in fact, never been a direct party to the theory wars as they raged through English in the 1970s and 1980s. Moreover, having spent nearly fifteen years teaching very rudimentary literature courses at the undergraduate level, I have only relatively recently, by what I regard as an incredible stroke of fortune, gained entry to that upper stratum of graduate seminars and research institutes in which one does, at last, teach and generally engage in theory. I thus am not quite sure which pronoun—*we* or *they*—to use when speaking of the posttheory generation. But to get, finally, to the point I have in mind: my cusplike perspective, perhaps intergenerational, makes me somewhat skeptical when, whether for celebratory *or* critical purposes, the sixties and the theory generations are presented as either correlatives or, at the very least, co-evals. What this correlation risks overlooking are the precise but subtle ways in which theory in its dominant instance as structuralism/poststructuralism rushed in to fill a kind of vacuum left after the last political wave of revolt subsided with the end of the Vietnam War. As Aijaz Ahmad has argued, it is

> arguable . . . that dominant strands within . . . "theory," as it has unfolded *after* the movements of the 1960s were essentially over, have been mobilized to domesticate, in institutional ways, the very forms of political dissent which these movements had sought to foreground, to displace an activist culture with a textualist culture. (1)

It is illuminating, moreover, to consider the circumstances under which theory made its entrance in social and political settings other than those of North America and metropolitan Europe. The Brazilian critic Roberto Schwarz, for instance, has noted that structuralism made its debut in Rio de Janeiro and São Paulo only in the wake of the military coup d'etat in 1964, displacing the incipiently Marxist intellectual culture that had grown up in the preceding years after the latter's representatives were eventually either forced into exile or physically liquidated. (35) But the lesson I am trying to adduce here from my own intergenerational history is that of the risk involved, when proclaiming the existence of a posttheory generation, of inadvertently propagating—as if the démarche noted by Ahmad, Schwarz, and others were merely an irrelevant detail—one of the most potent myths that theory has built up around itself: that of its "revolutionary credentials."

## De Man: "Theory" against Theory

But there is even a further and still less advertent risk in positing a posttheory moment or generation, and this is to regard the current sense of theoretical indeterminacy or even impasse as somehow separable from problems and flaws intrinsic to theory itself. We need to consider whether, and to what degree, the posttheory condition, while a product of the extrinsic, sociological factors cited by Williams (e.g., the Reagan counterrevolution, the jobs crisis, and the resulting academic star system itself) is not, on a more radically social and historical plane, a further development in an ideological crisis of which theory was already a local phase, or symptom. That is, in debunking the quasi-religious myth(s) that theory has tended to create for itself, the possibility persists that one will fall into the opposing myth—that of theory as merely a question of institutional or personal politics in the most instrumental and superficial sense. However emergent critical practice is to define itself with respect to theory, it needs, in addition to coming to grips with the institutional realities, to draw the connection between its own apparently posttheoretical moment as experienced in overtly social and political factors and the instrinsic, ideological content of theory.

To demonstrate what I mean here more concretely, I want to examine one of the more systematic and thoughtful historico-sociological accounts of theory, John Guillory's *Cultural Capital,* taking, like Guillory, the theory produced by Paul de Man (especially de Man's manifesto like "The Resistance to Theory") as exemplary of theory in both its extrinsic/institutional and intrinsic/ideological forms.

In chapter four of *Cultural Capital* ("Literature after Theory: The Lesson of Paul de Man), Guillory in essence argues that the advent of the "age of theory"—and the entrenching of its "canon" and its "syllabus"—is to be explained as the drive to preserve the professional and even the departmental autonomy of the "literary" canon and syllabus in the face of the rise of the New—or "professional managerial"—Class and its corresponding forms of "techno-bureaucratic labor" in the academy. De Man's formula for a literary theory resting on a purely "impersonal" and "technical" process of rhetorical or deconstructive reading, but embodied in the charismatic figure of the master-theorist (de Man himself) as reverently perceived (and transferentially imprinted) by his disciples, adjusts the discipline of "literature" to the new institutional reality, while making a bid to preserve at least the aura—or "charisma"—of its older status as "cultural capital." As Guillory sums it up himself: "The increasingly technobureaucratic organization of the professional field of literary criticism was a condition for the emergence of theory, which we can understand in retrospect as the reassertion of charismatic authority in the face of that technobureaucratic domination." (256)

Little to nothing of what Guillory claims here strikes me as false per se, and his long dissection of the de Manian theory-machine and its psychosocial complexities is surely one of the most painstaking sociologies we have of what the moment of theory was and why it could not be prolonged and made the rightful inheritance of succeeding generations. But it leaves unanswered, even unposed, some fairly pressing questions. If the role of the literary theorist has now been reserved exclusively for the "master" who brandishes the "canon of theory" before the disciples gathered in his/her graduate seminar, what does that leave for the "post"-disciples, for the emergent cohort of literary-critical intellectuals and academics who may not be content simply to adapt themselves to the new 'technobureaucratic' academy (say, by resigning themselves to teaching composition) and who, having in fact been instructed in the canon of theory, regard themselves as both entitled and enabled to deploy it in some way?

Must we simply bend to the current institutional realities and sell off our old copies of de Man, Derrida, and Kristeva—not to mention, Freud, Saussure, and Marx? Are we, after all, not only naive in our aspirations to do theory but also, as it were, guilty of our own quixotic desires for the thrills of charismatic mastery?

To attribute such cynical advice directly to Guillory would of course be unfair. For the positive critical spirit of *Cultural Capital* is to make us come to grips with the necessity to alter these institutional realities if we are to find our way out of the post-theoretical impasse that obliges most of us to sit by and watch as the fortunate few undertake the "reassertion of charismatic authority in the face of technobureaucratic domination." (Guillory 25) To proceed as though theory could be innocent of the so-cial conditions of its own reproduction, or as though, to be more precise, the aspira-tion to theory in its most progressive sense could afford to formulate itself apart from an aspiration to reform or even revolutionize academic structures and power relations is sure folly, and it is one of the considerable virtues of *Cultural Capital* to have ex-posed the grounds of such folly so exhaustively.[1]

And yet, as anyone who has become involved in the effort to reform, much less revolutionize institutions such as the university knows, such efforts are notoriously complex, refractory and, it sometimes appears, rather futile. To spend more than a few years in the academy and devote time and energy to progressive reform—say, for ex-ample, to the creation of remedial classes for working-class and minority students, or the establishment of a more equitable distribution of graduate courses among junior and senior faculty—is to learn how quickly everything one has worked for can come to naught with the single stroke of an administrator's pen. Moreover, anyone able to remember what the academy was like before the sixties rebellions—or able to fend off the constant efforts of right-wing revisionism to rewrite this history by attributing to the sixties all present-day ills—knows that only massive, extramural movements of so-cial rebellion and protest have had much success in reforming the academy, and that even then the gains become endangered as soon as the streets grow quiet. The point here is that to explain the theory canon as an effect of shifts in institutional structure, although valid in and of itself, nevertheless begs the question of the larger social and economic structure—the totality—into which that institution is inserted, and of the relation between part and whole. Although Guillory would be the last to deny the im-portance of this question, his Bourdieuan, socioinstitutional account of theory rests implicitly on the idea that the whole—the entire "ensemble of social relations"—bears on the problem under scrutiny (theory) only via the institutional part, or mediation, outside of which the problem itself ceases, apparently, to be theoretically meaningful. "Extrainstitutional 'interests' can be expressed within a given relatively autonomous institution only as they are mediated by the self-interests of that institution" (250). It is, in fact, according to *Cultural Capital,* the distinctive ideology of theory to suppose that it is autonomous of the institutional reality that calls theory itself into being. But if, in fact, the part cannot be truly transformed or superseded without, on some level, transforming the whole as well, doesn't this require us to think about the problem not only in full awareness of its institutional mediacy but also in light of its own precise "relation to totality"? What if theory, in addition to being all the things Guillory says it is, were at the same time the manifestation of important changes on the level of the social totality as such? Indeed, doesn't the logic of "mediations"—if it is to remain faithful to the dialectical perspective from which it ultimately stems—oblige us to think through this relation? And if we do think it through, might we not find, inscribed in the rise and fall of theory, a process whose historical and critical lessons cannot be confined to the terms of a neo-Weberian sociology of bureaucracies and "charisma"—or to a narrative of job markets and "academostars"? Might not, then, the aspiration to theory, even as it partakes in the reproduction of an institutional rationality, also, however unconsciously, signal the presence on a deeper level of a social, ideological crisis impossible to glimpse within strictly institutional parameters?

To further illustrate my point here, let us look directly back to de Man in "The Resistance to Theory." In Guillory's reading, to reiterate, de Man's two-fold recipe for a literary theory—according to which all nonlinguistic categories must first be jettisoned for their "cultural and ideological" normativities and the linguistic itself then merged with the rhetorical, leaving grammar and logic by the wayside (de Man, 6)—registers the same, extraliterary change in the conditions of intellectual work associated with the rise of the "professional managerial class" and a "technobureaucratic" division of labor. Again, there is considerable plausibility to this critique. Anyone having experienced firsthand their rise in the literary academy can intuitively confirm the strong initial impression that structuralist and poststructuralist theory had finally supplied literary criticism with the rigorously technical methodologies it had previously lacked, even in the most formalistically demanding new criticism.

But, more carefully considered, Guillory's sociological critique of "The Resistance to Theory" can be shown to rest on a dangerously abstract analogy: "Theory's constitutive 'impersonality' was achieved not simply by the deconstruction of illusions of autonomous agency but by the transformation of the work of reading into an *unconscious mimesis* of the form of bureaucratic labor" (257). But what, then, in turn, would explain or make necessary such an "unconscious mimesis"? (De Man as the Frederick Winslow Taylor of literary criticism?) What is more: if the real, perhaps unconscious purpose of de Man's regime of theory was to rationalize literary criticism along technobureaucratic lines, leaving only the figure of the master himself to perform the necessary "cathexis of routine," how, then, to explain de Man's unabashed skepticism that the object of such a theory exists at all :

> If there is indeed something about literature, as such, which allows for a discrepancy between truth and method . . . then scholarship and theory are no longer necessarily compatible; as a first casualty of this complication, the notion of "literature as such" as well as the clear distinction between history and interpretation can no longer be taken for granted. For a method that cannot be made to suit the "truth" of its object can only teach delusion. Various developments . . . reveal symptoms that suggest that such a difficulty is an inherent focus of the discourse about literature. (4)

Or how, if de Man's mission was to introduce a narrowly technical rationality to literary criticism, to explain his final relegation of theory to "the resistance into theory,"
to "the universal theory of the impossibility of theory" (p. 19)? How, that is, to square
the evident analogies in "The Resistance to Theory" to technobureaucratic rationalization with the no less evident, final embrace of a standpoint of sheer indeterminacy
and *aporia?* To suggest that this is merely the trump whereby the technobureaucratic
master is left holding all the cards, that this newly rationalized technique called "theory" must finally slip from our grasp *deus-absconditus* fashion, so as to keep the disciples salivating, is to stretch the sociological/psychoanalytical/literary analogy to the
breaking point.

A defense of theory premised on the rejection of all extralinguistic (in fact, ex-
trarhetorical) "phenomenalistic" categories—cultural, historical, aesthetic—but which
is obliged, in the end, to concede theory's purely irrational basis; a bracketing off of
all content as merely the effect of a formal mechanism ("language") to which, however, the condition of a purely unknowable and inscrutable thing-in-itself must be
conceded: should not this remind some of us who were taught the canon of theory
(at least those who share what I believe to have been my good fortune in turning from
Barthes and Levi-Strauss to Marx, Lukács, and Benjamin, rather than to Derrida and
de Man) of something? I am thinking here of the concept of the commodity fetish,
and even more particularly of the general forms of conscious corresponding to it, what
Lukács in *History and Class Consciousness* called the "reified structure of consciousness." In the latter book, Lukács propounds the fundamentally "antinomial" structure of reified thinking, best epitomized in the classical epistemology of Kant, for
which the drive to the complete rationalization of the forms of knowledge necessarily (and tragically, given classical philosophy's fundamentally dialectical aspirations)
produced an object of knowledge—a thing-in-itself—unavailable to any rational
knowing, severed from all such rational forms. Without rehearsing Lukács's critique
of "reified consciousness" at any greater length here (and acknowledging its still controversial status, even among Marxists) I want to propose that it is only by reading de
Manian theory as ensnared in the antinomies of a "reified structure of consciousness"
that its mediate relation to society and history can even begin to be reconstructed. For
if, as I had argued earlier, the question of theory qua institutions, academostars, and
contemporary intellectual experience generally cannot be adequately explored without attempting to supply the mediations connecting it to transinstitutional social and
historical realities themselves, the consideration of theory qua reification will turn out
to be an essential step in this process.

Consider, for instance, the following passage from "The Resistance to Theory":

> Literary theory can be said to come into being when the approach to literary texts
> is no longer based on non-linguistic, that is to say historical and aesthetic con-
> siderations or, to put it somewhat less crudely, when the object of discussion is
> no longer the meaning or the value but the modalities of production and of re-
> ception of meaning and of value prior to their establishment. ( 7)

What is remarkable in such a claim—and what, as Guillory rightly asserts, makes de Man's work "symptomatic" of "literary theory" as a whole—is not simply its requirement that the linguistic dimension of literature undergo prior or independent scrutiny. Formalism and new criticism had, after all, already demanded as much. Rather it is the absolute separation or "antinomy" that it enforces between literature as a historical, aesthetic, or hermeneutical object and literature as "language." De Man mitigates this absolutism only slightly by leaving open the apparent possibility that theory, by first examining "the modalities of production and of reception of meaning and value prior to their establishment," might eventually find its way back to literature as a translinguistic object. But one would then have to ask, In just what time and space do such "modalities of production and reception" operate if not the "nonlinguistic" dimensions of the historical and social, in which case the claims for theory turn against themselves? By the end of "The Resistance to Theory" however, as already noted, de Man is quite content to concede the final irrationality to which his conception of theory commits him, and language has become what it is for Derrida and poststructuralism generally, that uniquely "objective" category that is nevertheless not an object at all, but an endless and indeterminate movement of différance. The thing to be stressed here, however, is that de Man not only takes as his theoretical point of departure the antinomy of form and content, an antinomy in whose terms the literary object must appear to all "reified consciousness." Eschewing all (or almost all) half-way measures, equivocations, and eclecticisms, he affirms this antinomy with complete cynical awareness of what are, in essence, its antitheoretical consequences. Symptomatically read, this betokens something rather more, I think, than the rise of the professional managerial class in the institutional structure housing literature. By conceiving of theory in such a way that the latter's very impossibility must stand as the one truly valid theoretical deduction, "The Resistance to Theory" confirms, as a sort of literary-ideological barometer, that any efforts to reverse or even to relax the antinomial law whereby not only literature but language itself is to be mercilessly stripped of all human content must fall short of the rigors and impersonality of the theortician. In failing to account for this dimension in "The Resistance to Theory" *Cultural Capital,* in a sense, slights de Man, whose thinking here, for all its pernicious implications, carries within itself a kind of historical, ideological necessity. One might even go so far as to suggest that *Cultural Capital* cannot perceive the operations of reified thinking in de Man's theoretical manifesto because it too, like "The Resistance to Theory," succumbs to a reification insofar as it is the Bourdieuan "institution" here rather than language that comes to seem impervious to the praxis of human subjects.

But Guillory's reading aside, I think we are now in a position to perceive how the lesson of Paul de Man may be read as a warning to the posttheory generation: that theory can find its way back to literature—and thus become a universal, rational, truly democratic pursuit—only by incorporating within itself the critique of the whole—of capitalist social existence in its present form—that itself generates the reified theory for which de Man formulated the literary *ultima ratio.*

## Cultural Studies and "Post"-Theoretical Fetishisms

Sensing oneself, or one's generation as posttheoretical should not, then, from this perspective, become a pretext for rejecting theory outright as merely the institutional prerogative of a few academic superstars. If, in fact, theory has now become a form of cultural capital so highly concentrated in a few hands that its loses all connection with the intellectual and academic rank and file, its repudiation by those same literary-critical "proletarians" indirectly ratifies the deeper social and ideological malaise. Nor should it be taken as a signal to begin picking and choosing theoretical models as one wishes in a spirit of unapologetic eclecticism. Perhaps the posttheory generation *has* earned the ironic privilege of the theoretically disinherited: that of surveying the seemingly broad array of theories now in currency without the onus of having a dead theoretical ancestor to worship. But the conviction that one paradigm is as good as another seems to me to be only the flipside of the rigorous, fetishized indeterminacy promulgated by "The Resistance to Theory." Coming on the scene "after theory" should, rather, prompt an aspiration to supersede what de Man proposes in "The Resistance to Theory": not to exchange narrowly "empirical" forms of literary study for a literary theory as "language about language," but to overcome all narrow, reified categories (including those advocated by de Man) as the methodological basis for knowledge, and to approach theory in it fully critical—even revolutionary—meaning as a methodological commitment to the category of "concrete totality." The point, indeed, the challenge that the present historical-intellectual moment presents is neither to continue the literary-theoretical enterprise in its presently canonical form nor to reject it in favor of seemingly more pragmatic and empirical pursuits. It is to grasp and take up the more universal and at the same time more concrete problem of critical *method* that foregrounds the theoretical question itself. The question, in other words, is not whether we "do literature" (or "culture") or "do theory"—as if such an opposition were legitimate in the first place—but what new methodological forms of mediating the literary and/or cultural object we are left with after theory?

What might these new methodological forms be, then, and what critics or theorists can be looked to for examples of their practical realization? To answer these questions at length would exceed the scope of this chapter. But in brief, I would propose, somewhat paradoxically, that while the traces of a new method are already detectable in a broad array of contemporary criticism—from feminism to cultural studies to new historicism—they remain, at present, an inadvertent presence, and that the posttheory generation's search for direct models within the above-named critical schools has poor prospects.

Take the case of cultural studies. The mere fact that, under the theoretical aegis of this trend, the contemporary critic no longer senses any obligation to literature or the canon in their narrowly formalist, aestheticist, or civilizational forms, and is free to focus her critical attentions on anything from science fiction to soap operas to legal codes, indicates that, from an implicitly methodological standpoint, the concept of the social totality has taken on a much greater urgency. This is precisely the result that de Man, in his last ditch effort to isolate literature within its own self-generative and self-regulative sphere, had sought to prevent.

But the social totality of cultural studies as presently practiced is itself the ultimate reification: a rigid, empirical positivity that is merely the sum of its parts. In being merged into culture, literature just reverts back to the narrowly empirical and positivistic form that the theory revolution had originally, if largely blindly, sought to overcome. From Raymond Williams to Stuart Hall to Andrew Ross, the price of breaking free of the provincialized aesthetics of traditional "English literature" is typically, despite (or perhaps, in keeping with) the occasional flirtation with Althusser or Foucault, a methodological reincorporation within positivist, late-bourgeois social science and its "sociology of culture."

I'll offer just one brief example of what I mean here: Andrew Ross's still controversial essay on "The Popularity of Pornography" in his 1989 work, *No Respect.* [1] In it Ross cautions against what he regards as the intellectually elitist condemnation of pornography, even on feminist grounds, arguing that such condemnation fails to account for the real popularity and "autonomy" of the "desire" that leads to the consumption of pornography. According to Ross, the proclivities of critical intellectuals to "vanguardism"—the same that manifested themselves in the "theory canon"—run the risk of dictating what is and is not a legitimate form of pleasure, even to those "sexual minorities" who might find in pornographic countercultures the only quasi-public sphere available to them:

> What if the pleasures of pornography . . . however complicit with patriarchal logic, prove to be resistant to *direct* pressure from a reformist agenda? Nothing seems more alien to the vanguardist function of the intellectual, trained, educated and committed to raise the consciousness of others, and to redeem ordinary people from what she or he sees as their ideological servitude. And yet nothing seems more certain than that the . . . pleasure of pornography . . . *is* autonomous; that it is not a false, spurious, displaced or addictive substitute for a more "authentic" world of social and sexual relations. (193)

We're certainly a far cry here from "The Resistance to Theory." Or are we? The "cultural studies" that Ross arguably exemplifies has clearly left de Man's strictures against the "nonlinguistic" far behind. The all-seeing eye of reading is here trained on a text that has reabsorbed all those troublesome "normativities" that de Man had sought to sheer off, even down to offbeat sexual tastes. Theory now surveys the world, or at least everything that can be qualified as culture—and that does seem to be just about everything. But note that this same theoretical and critical amplitude and generosity also caution us against looking at this cultural totality from the perspective of a "more 'authentic' world of social and sexual relations." We are to look at culture—or desire, and so forth—only as what they *are*—which is to say, as the reifications and alienated relations they are in the present form of social existence. The exit from theory in the de Manian version leaves behind only its *linguistic* or *rhetorical* fetishism, not the "reified structure of consciousness" that stamps it. Cultural studies takes the classic one step foward, two steps back. Not coincidentally, Guillory's *Cultural Capital,* like the neo-Weberian sociology of Bourdieu that informs it, risks suffering the same fate.

The task, if the initially radical impulse of cultural studies is not to be squandered, is, in my view, to find a way to talk about culture—or literature—on the level of the social totality without loosing sight of the negativity that this relationship to contemporary society must entail. What if, as Marx always believed, there is something historically intrinsic to literature or even culture—social forms whose origin predates capitalism—that makes them finally incompatible with a capitalist existence? Even the most penetrating and nuanced analysis of, say, hip hop as an expression of "resistance" loses its critical force if it fails to consider the deeper, methodological question of *what general form culture itself assumes* in a world driven to reduce every last shred of humanity to its commodity form. The object of critique, that is, has to find its place in a totality that is itself understood as subject to—and deserving of—negation.

The dialectical tradition of critique that stretches from Marx through Lukács to the Frankfurt School did, in fact, regard this as its task, but, with few exceptions, did so out of loyalty to a traditional, canonical sense of the literary or the aesthetic that contemporary experience requires us to rethink. My most hopeful outlook for the posttheoretical generation of critics and theorists, then, is this: to redeem this tradition by forcing the negative, even blindly methodological work undertaken by the theory revolution to become socially self-conscious. I can think of only a handful of academostars who answer to this sort of demand. But pending the time when this socially self-conscious form of theory finally grips the masses, we'd be worse off without them.

## Notes

This chapter first appeared in *College Literature* (26, 3 (1999): 115–27.

1. "It seems highly unlikely that a theory of political practice can be generated out of the terms of any particular academic discipline or discourse. The hypertrophic demand upon literary criticism to adumbrate such a practice is clearly not capable of being satisfied by the literary curriculum alone. It is only a certain kind of pressure exerted from without the discipline of criticism that can impose upon the discourse and syllabus of criticism such a task of political articulation" (Guillory, 237).

2. For a more extensive discussion of cultural studies and of Ross's work in particular, see my own essay "The 'Secularizing' of Poststructuralism; or, Cultural Studies a Decade On," forthcoming in *Mediations* 22 (1999): 6–17.

## Works Cited

Ahmad, Aijaz. *In Theory: Classes, Nations, Literatures.* London: Verso, 1992.

De Man, Paul. *The Resistance to Theory.* Minneapolis: University of Minnesota Press, 1986.

Guillory, John. *Cultural Capital: the Problem of Literary Canon Formation.* Chicago: University of Chicago Press, 1993.

Ross, Andrew. *No Respect: Intellectuals and Popular Culture.* New York: Routledge, 1989.

Schwarz, Roberto. *Misplaced Ideas: Essays on Brazilian Culture.* (John Gledson, trans.) New York, London: Verso, 1992.

Williams, Jeffrey. "The Posttheory Generation." *symplokē* 3, 1 (1995): 55–76.

# NINE

# WORDS, WORDS, WORDS

## *David Galef*

If the halls of academia can be likened to Wall Street, here's what the market was like in the Eighties: Consider the next generation of emerging scholars as a bunch of neophyte investors. Big Theory was at an all-time high, despite threats of an imminent collapse, not so much from any squabbling in the boardrooms as from disgruntled shareholders. Deconstruction had clearly been oversold and was being either quietly unloaded or liquified into other holdings. Meanwhile, other stocks were rapidly diversifying: feminism branched into gender studies, for example, promoting entire industries in multiculturalism and queer theory. New Historicism was the hot new property, its R&D department gearing up to produce cultural studies, which would eventually swallow the parent company. Composition programs were the unexciting workhorses of the industry, not flashy but dependable and necessary to the enterprise as a whole. Creative writing programs were considered nebulous, a slow-paced version of investing in stock futures.

Over a decade later, there's been a retrenchment if not a breakdown. And the latest players, those who got their advanced degrees any time after 1985 or so, have gotten burned. (Though *generation* used to mean roughly a twenty-five-year span, the term was meant to distinguish between one group of individuals and its descendants. In the academy, we can define a new generation as any group that faces substantially changed conditions from those undergone by its teachers. The current volatility in our field seems to make for a new generation every decade or so.) As with a false prosperity concealing the real poverty of the people, academia's bull market was in theory, not practice. The job opportunities expected to materialize never did, as the postwar generation retired but left few openings. Federal funding was slashed right and left, leaving the Left and the Right snarling at each other over what went wrong. Students actually decreased in number, and the mini-booms here and there reflected a changing population more interested in reading skills than in reading Lacan.

Is it too late to ask for our money back? Should we diversify? Two trends now dominate a flagging market: Americans with declining literacy skills and an influx of immigrants needing standard English has forced a massive expansion in basic writing programs, now called composition and rhetoric. And the onetime cottage industry of creative writing programs has expanded into a nationwide octopus of M.F.A. programs in everything from playwrighting to children's books. Moreover, an interest in innovative methods of teaching writing may eventually lead to a merger in rhetoric and creative writing. Prospective investors, please take note.

### How We Got There from Here:
### A Composition and Rhetoric Primer

The ascension of freshman English to doctoral programs in composition and rhetoric represents a marketing success as much as it reflects the needs of a changing student population. Some decades ago, a course known variously as Freshman English, Weekly Theme, or Basic Composition was the norm in colleges across the country. Students took the class to improve their writing skills, then moved on. The course was de-emphasized during the free-for-all Sixties but re-emphasized in response to decreasing S.A.T. scores in the early 1970s. In truth, the perceived decline owed as much to a greater proportion of American youth applying to college as to an actual drop in writing skills. Still, to see Ivy League schools enforce as much as a year of expository writing was humbling.

Nonetheless, instructing students in composition has traditionally been a lowly calling compared with the teaching of literature. At least, this is what the exiting classes in the 1980s were told. (It is axiomatic that the more essential or immediately useful the subject, the lower the status of its teachers. Consider the example of trade school—an example that many of the Lost Generation of scholars, circa 1970 on, have *had* to consider.) The irony of this was long ago pointed out by William Riley Parker, who noted that modern English departments derive from rhetorical instruction. The advent of Big Theory in literature intensified the problem, for if Theory made the teaching of mere literature seem provincial, it dwarfed the writing classroom.

At one time, the grand theoreticians Barthes and Foucault proclaimed the death of the writer, though the assassination attempt was really just an argument for the importance of historical context. From another angle, the kind of radical reader-response theory espoused by critics like Georges Poulet privileged the *lecteur* over the *auteur* as the producer of textual meaning. (See, for example, Gerald Prince's "Introduction to the Study of the Narratee" and Stanley Fish's "Literature in the Reader: Affective Stylistics" in Jane Tompkin's anthology *Reader-Response Criticism*. Despite the trappings, many forms of reader-response are really a pseudoscientific form of New Criticism.) The actual construction of writing seemed a dreary business, acquiring its techniques similar to mastering the arcane craft of an extinct guild. By the 1970s, many writing courses had metamorphosed into either literature samplers or contemporary issues classes.

Paradoxically, Theory itself eventually gave composition its boost. For some time now, the way to legitimize a field in our profession has been to accord it serious study, to theorize it. Pedagogues like Donald Murray and Peter Elbow wrote about expressivist writing principles, borrowing from Romanticism. Kenneth A. Bruffee's *Collaborative Learning: Higher Education, Interdependence, and the Authority of Knowledge*, along with Peter Elbow and Pat Belanoff's *Sharing and Responding*, justified peer evaluation in the classroom. (For a historical overview of the theory revolution in composition and rhetoric, see James Berlin's *Rhetoric and Reality: Writing Instruction in American Colleges, 1900–1985*, with its distinctions between cognitive or objective rhetoric, subjective or expressivist rhetoric, and transactional or socio-epistemic rhetoric.) No longer was the writing student a mere recorder of objective reality but a subjective register of experience. Expressivist principles also made composition and rhetoric a much easier sell, de-emphasizing grammar, syntax, and even structure in favor of self-expression and other emotive strategies.

Following the example of women's studies, which borrowed eclectically from literature, sociology, history, and other fields, the emerging specialization of composition and rhetoric built itself up from a hodgepodge of linguistics, second-language acquisition, technical writing, and composition theory. The largest recent trend, multiculturalism in the writing classroom, stresses the need to articulate individual experience against one's own cultural background. Any of the new generation hoping for a renaissance of New Critical methods were destined to be disappointed. The history—of both stock trends and academic shifts—tends to be not so much cyclical as spiral, with overlays and add-ons each time around. In the academy new models have arrived on the scene, such as the portfolio system, group learning, and in recent years a merger with cultural studies—as in James Berlin and Michael J. Vivion's anthology *Cultural Studies in the English Classroom,* which shows how to insert social signification in everything from free-response exercises to research papers.

Books like Donovan and McClelland's *Eight Approaches to Teaching Composition,* published by the National Council of Teachers of English in 1980, helped put the new theories of pedagogy into wide circulation. Besides bringing the composition classroom "up to date," these innovations have contributed to classroom praxis, which in turn provides grist for more theory. At the same time, journals like *College Composition and Communication* and *Focuses* (there are now some fifteen journals devoted to composition and rhetoric) provide avenues for publication and further scholarly exchange, along with NCTE and CCCC conventions.

In fact, the situation in comp/rhet (the inevitable shortening that comes with frequent usage) is similar to that of lit crit for our predecessors: expanding theoretical horizons, spurring internecine quarrels, and witnessing a return-to-the-basics backlash, as in Maxine C. Hairston's *Successful Writing* a supremely organized primer for advanced comp that includes grammar, subject-verb agreement, and so forth. This reinvention shows another aspect of generational conflicts: bound to similarity by a form of academic genetics, the next generation often comes to resemble the earlier one in its pursuits while simultaneously trying to free itself from the anxiety of influence.

Of course, no market can flourish without some bearish grumbles. Sherrie L. Gradin's *Romancing Rhetorics: Social Expressivist Perspectives on the Teaching of Writing* is an express (and expressivist) attempt to defend the theory and praxis of romanticist pedagogy against the recent backlash. As Gradin notes: "While expressivism is being hit from all sides, the harshest and most invested criticism are coming from proponents of social-epistemic rhetorics" (9). Though such attacks are not likely to merely die down, the feminist fusion of empathy and politics that Gradin advocates suggests a way to please a greater faction. The numbers speak for themselves: By 1980, over twenty programs devoted to comp/rhet were in existence, as reported in *Rhetoric*

*Review.* Since then, such programs have increased in number nationwide to over seventy, and the number of doctoral students in the field has also increased well over 100 percent since 1986 (Brown et al. 240). Publication in the theory of comp/rhet has exploded, with books covering everything from *l'écriture feminine* in the classroom to postmodern epistemologies as they inform the grading of student papers. What started out as a cottage industry has become big business, as well as a legitimate study: witness Joseph Janangelo and Kristine Hansen's handbook *Resituating Writing: Constructing and Administering Writing Programs,* in which the editors note that nowadays "the concept of writing program administration as a significant expression of academic scholarship comes of age" (ix).

The message is clear: In a time of cutbacks in English departments, universities are nonetheless expanding and diversifying their writing programs, with an emphasis on teaching students how to produce effective prose. Unfortunately, this message came as belated news to those of us schooled in the literary theory practiced by our professors and handed on to us as professionalism. For the past ten years, the *MLA Job Information List* has listed fewer and fewer decent jobs in the old period categories while boasting scores of advertisements for posts in comp/rhet. Clearly this is a gap felt on campuses across the country, as schools struggle to provide writing instruction for students who need it more than ever, and to placate a public increasingly disenchanted with what it sees as irrelevant literature departments. Whether this is a Bad Thing or even an Ironic Thing (given the dependence of comp/rhet's market value on theory) is almost beside the point. The point is that it's out there and it's selling like junk bonds in the early Eighties. In an era nostalgic for crafts, writing has gained a new cachet.

At the same time, other branches of theory have started to include the writer as crucial to the work's message and context. The Sixties wave of critics considered themselves crucial to the work and had tenure to prove it. Our generation, downsized here and unemployed there, has yet to find itself crucial to any enterprise. Not surprisingly, many of us wish to wrest authority from the senior faculty and administration and restore it to authors. Feminists and multiculturalists care deeply about the background of the author: are her or his sympathies in the right place, and is she or he entitled to speak for the character in the story? The unmasking of political agendas puts the writer into an incriminating spotlight, but a spotlight nonetheless: the rebirth of the writer as an active agent. At the same time, the political exigencies of both the right and the left demand art with a message, which suggests a closer look at rhetoric.

Aristotle's *Poetics* is a beginning for this kind of criticism: an astute analysis, not of the meaning of Sophocles' *Oedipus,* but of how such plays wring pity and terror from their audiences. After a long interval of religious concern with exegesis, the Renaissance and eighteenth-century neoclassicism spurred a renewed interest in the secular uses of discourse. Though one generation is often at odds with its immediate forebears, it often finds concordance with older antecedents. Just as T. S. Eliot and Ezra Pound skipped the Romantics in favor of Renaissance and classical authors, many of us have grown tired of the posturings of Barthes, Foucault, Lacan, Derrida, and their standard American bearers and have begun looking further back to an era when none of these figures was sacred. To put it in Freudian (not Lacanian) terms: one way to kill the father is to go back to a time before he was born.

Given the ever-accelerating pace of history, we need not look back that far. Wayne Booth's *The Rhetoric of Fiction* in the 1960s was a modern version of this sub-merged interest in rhetoric, and it made Booth's career. Kenneth Burke's *A Rhetoric of Motives* a decade earlier presented a similar argument from the perspective of semi-ological ontogeny. To put it unadornedly, *how* one says something is as important as *what* one says. Or, as Jane Tompkins observed in "The Reader in History: The Chang-ing Shape of Literary Response," what links the age of classical rhetoric to current the-oretical concerns is "the common perception of language as a form of power" (226). In other words, the literary hegemonies taught in theory courses have joined forces with comp/rhet to focus no longer on the production of meaning but on the means of production. The real, unaddressed perplexity is how techniques from the Greek age of reason apply to the postmodern age of relativity. Gnosticism, *pace* Harold Bloom, is not the same as what Camille Paglia labeled the "new paganism," an eclectic ado-ration of power icons in America.

Still, comp/rhet principles are beginning to inform literary theory. A hint of the new direction can be seen in a work like Francis-Noël Thomas's *The Writer Writing*, with its emphasis on technique. Rather than a recursive exercise on intertextuality, *The Writer Writing* is a sustained focus on "the power and scope of commonplace con-cepts of agency, intention, and purpose" (xix). Thomas has rediscovered that authors can mean what they say and convey these ideas to their readers. This kind of empha-sis is particularly useful for studying writers like George Bernard Shaw, for whom the text is a means of specific inculcation, or Marcel Proust, whose prose is devoted to-ward equally particular evocation.

The distinction Thomas raises between these two different writers has much to do with the power of rhetoric. Whereas Shaw is devoted to scientific interpretation, advocating a large social theory to support his drama, Proust is more involved with what Thomas, borrowing from the historian J. H. Hexter, calls "processive explana-tion," or an incremental level of observation that depends on an accumulation of in-cident to account for psychological change, rather than on any grand unifying hy-pothesis (59–63). In a sense, these two categories correspond to what Berlin terms objective versus subjective rhetoric (6ff.). In both cases, however, the writers advance a definite *Weltanschauung* that Thomas examines in terms of rhetorical strategies, con-scious choices of word and scene functioning as persuasive arguments to how the world works. These issues of how a writer can promulgate ideology were generally passed over by graduate schools in the Eighties in favor of how ideology could prom-ulgate writers. Significantly, Thomas has gone on to co-author a handbook called *Clear and Simple as the Truth: Writing Classic Prose*, focusing on the elements of style.

Thomas B. Farrell's *Norms of Rhetorical Culture* presents another argument for the forceful effects of style, outlining how verbal communication works in society. Tracing the breakdown of language from modernism to postmodernism, Farrell reclaims rhetoric as a legitimate method of inquiry, "*an acquired competency,* a manner of thinking that invents possibilities for persuasion, conviction, action, and judgment." (16). Fusing matters of style and politics, analyzing literary texts as well as political speeches, Farrell finds underlying laws of efficacy in the rules of discourse. His subjects are as varied as "Recalling the Public Sphere" to "Topoi for Rhetoric in Conversation." Allied with dialectic, rhetoric is a potent—to coin a term—*aesthipolitical* force. At its highest level, it can even produce epiphany. As Farrell observes: "almost everyone admits to having occasionally been seized and transported by a discourse which changed or influenced their lives and priorities" (230). Such is the potential inherent in a field that is both art and criticism.

The heuristic impulse also cannot be ignored: Just as schools of rhetoric once flourished, many classes are now teaching the substance of individual style and voice, such as Martin Luther King, Jr., compared to Malcolm X, as well as how one movement adopts and alters another's rhetoric. In this era of renewed emphasis on issue-oriented pedagogy, perhaps the most telling signals are not new books on theory but the flyers sent out by the textbook publishers catering to the trade. A mailing from St. Martin's Press, for instance, advertises an anthology called *Writing Lives: Literacy and Community,* as well as the second edition of the handbook *The Writer's Presence: A Pool of Essays.* Besides being good business, this may be a clever way to circumvent The Critics' Presence; i.e., the words of those who taught us to salute the theory boom of the Eighties.

The new rhetoric should therefore also bring about a sense of return, whether historically distant as Ciceronian tactics, or merely a closer look at T. S. Eliot's *objective correlative,* a pairing of text and response that has never been adequately addressed. In this era, where everything seems "retro," the current generation can at least rediscover and reclaim older ideas of empowerment. Voices from the previous generation bemoaning what's happened to their field may come in helpful here. In *The Rise and Fall of English: Reconstructing English as a Discipline* (103ff.), Robert Scholes advocates a return to the old trivium of classical studies, grammar, dialectic, and rhetoric, with an emphasis on direct applicability and performance instead of analysis of specific works: "This modern trivium, like its ancestor, would be organized around a canon of concepts, precepts, and practices rather than a canon of texts. In particular, each trivial study would encourage textual production by students in appropriate modes. Since this is a modern trivium, such production would include, where appropriate, not only speaking and writing but work in other media as well" (120). In place of the textual idolatry for which anti-canonists pilloried an earlier generation, a healthy respect for the power of one's own words might take over.

One disturbing outgrowth of this empowerment is the link between rhetoric and propaganda, but this is a connection to be studied, not espoused. As Edward P. J. Corbett points out in his rhetoric text for the classroom, "The term *propaganda* was once a neutral word, signifying the dissemination of truth" (30); i.e., foul use is what has corrupted the term. The resurgence of the Republican Party, for example, may suggest to liberals how useful slant and spin can be, but those who oppose such tactics should wish to study rhetoric if for no other reason than to unmask one's opponents. Corbett further observes that interest in rhetoric escalates during sociopolitical upheaval (21)—which is to say, welcome to the new millennium. One heritage we can never shake is a profound postmodernist suspicion of words.

In the political arena of the future, *rhetoric* will no doubt continue to mean "lack of substance." In the other direction, however, one can trace rhetoric to its origins in *rhēma* ("word") or note that *rhētor* is "a teacher of oratory." What started in the second century B.C. as a means for a newly democratic citizenry to reclaim confiscated property in court eventually came to be codified in Cicero's time as an entire system, from finding appropriate arguments to rehearsing proper delivery. Modern rhetoric involves such commonsense tactics as argumentation, exposition, description, and narration (see Corbett 20ff., 540).

But in this anti-essentialist era, one need not be that structuralist. As Aristotle's *On Rhetoric* notes, rhetoric is simply "an ability, in each case, to see the available means of persuasion" (36). Moreover, for those still anxious over the ends of persuasion, one may emphasize "see" over "ability," just as one may criticize a text without being able to write it. Moreover, even a casual glance at Aristotle's treatise reveals a concern with the good and the true, rather than a twisting of facts. The danger of sophistry is more linked to the Isocratean school of rhetoric, which Aristotle accused of teaching mere flattery. Isocrates, in turn, accused Aristotle of eristic methods, but contentiousness has its uses, both in society and the academy. Perhaps a better definition of rhetoric is "a combination of analytical knowledge and knowledge of characters" (53); i.e., it borrows as liberally from sociology and psychology as many recent literary theories. George A. Kennedy's translation of *On Rhetoric,* from which this material is taken, is subtitled *A Theory of Civic Discourse,* further suggesting the importance of this vision in an era of politically charged criticism.

The recent intersection of academic and public discourse hints at another reason that rhetoric is becoming increasingly important. In an era when Camille Paglia could become a superstar for warmed-over Freud and Frazier served up as cultural polemics, the appeal of flashy writing is obvious. (In fact, those toting around Paglia's *Sexual Personae* when it first came out tended to be more from the student population and lay public than from the ranks of faculty. This is to be expected: those who have built their professional existence on specific beliefs are not eager to embrace the anti-Christ. Then again, this is exactly what much of the next generation is waiting for: the Second Coming, or some opposite but equivalent setting to rights.) Yet this is simply the ever-growing tip of a phenomenon older than Stanley Fish: say something strongly, with just the right mix of self-assured overstatement, and the critical world will begin to read you and probably even footnote you. Every age-group of scholars desires recognition, but the current generation is additionally burdened with the need to forge an identity, even as the dogma from previous critics stamps them. Just as they dutifully read their professors at school, they now crave to be read themselves, and though a cloned version of the previous generation may result in publication, it won't guarantee distinction. This is the burdensome question we now face: in the increasingly blurred thicket of journals and reviews, what will ensure some visibility?

In a *New York Times* article a few years ago, "Journeys from Ivory Tower," the journalist Janny Scott made the point that many academics want a forum more public than the *PMLA* Forum. Critics whose role models were content to publish in scholarly quarterlies are now seeking acceptance in *Harper's* and *The New Yorker.* Again, this aspect of publishing is not confined to younger voices: those selfsame role models, with greater reputations, are also crossing academic boundaries, and to just as great acclaim. Do we follow them, or do they follow us?

In any event, the need to go public is more pressing than mere aggrandizement. Since English departments arrogated all of society as their focus of study, society seems to have repaid the favor by scrutinizing the academy with a rigor unheard of since the McCarthy days. As Jeffrey Williams, an English professor quoted in Scott's article, claims: "When I was coming up, it was the cool thing to be a theorist. "Now, the need is to justify and legitimate ourselves to a broader public" (A13). To accomplish the transformation from professorial pundit to public intellectual, the current cadre of academics is going to have to pay more attention to its prose, a topic of some concern in the academy. Anyone who has helped a colleague write a more concise, snappier letter to the editor can testify to the pressing need for teaching rhetoric on all levels, from remedial on up.

## How We Got Here from There:
## A Crash Course in Creative Writing

Concomitant with comp/rhet's ascent as a discipline is the rise of creative writing programs, to the point where most colleges in the United States now have at least some form of fiction or poetry workshop. According to a study issued by the AWP, the Associated Writing Programs now comprise well over three hundred undergraduate and graduate-level creative writing programs nationwide. As AWP's director D. W. Fenza understates, "Much has changed since a baker's dozen of writing programs formed the Associated Writing Programs over two decades ago" (*AWP Official Guide* vii). For job-seeking academics, such expansion may be inspiring. Yet because colleges and universities are increasingly run as straight business operations, the motives aren't quite what they used to be.

Like comp/rhet, what started as a gallimaufry of writing workshops, literature courses, language and translation classes, and pedagogy, creative writing programs now have their own core curricula and degree requirements—for the A.A. and B.F.A. at the undergraduate level, the M.A., D.A., and M.F.A. at the graduate level, and occasionally the Ph.D., offered at places like Iowa and Southern Mississippi. More recent offshoots of the basics include drama, screenplays, creative nonfiction, and even advertising copy. As in other academic fields, the degree of specialization gets ever more refined. For example, Vermont College was the first in the nation to develop an entire M.F.A. program around writing for children, even as Goucher College in Maryland spearheaded a low-residency M.F.A. in creative nonfiction.

This oversimplification is distorting, of course, but some of it has become received opinion, and in any market, buyer perception is what drives sales. Also, given that even some of this description approximates what has happened over the last quarter century, one must acknowledge the ever-increasing popularity of creative writing (though "cr wr," the acknowledged written short form, never caught on as a label because of its unpronounceability). Here again, the link to comp/rhet is significant, especially through the expressivist teaching of composition. That is, both take their premise from a supposed need for self-expression in the classroom, and of the kind that can be "made up" rather than rely on cultural outrage or victimology. As Berlin notes: "The influence of expressionism in art and of Freudian psychology also encouraged the rise of creative writing courses in high schools and colleges" (79). Beyond that, any etiology must rely on cultural *Zeitgeist:* the exhibitionist Sixties movement and the 1970's Me Decade coming to slow fruition in the inevitable time lag that exists within the academy; the appeal of creative outlets in an era when more and more jobs seem programmed or systematized; the quixotic lure of originality in a society whose current generation cannot top the economic accomplishments of the baby boomers.

In fact, the history of the discipline predates both generations. Creative writing in the academy started with the Iowa program, begun in 1922 with the acceptance of creative work for advanced degrees and formally inaugurated as a program in 1936 as a workshop of poets and fiction writers (*Writers' Workshop* 1). Despite distinguished alumnae and alumni like Flannery O'Connor and Paul Engle, for decades creative writing suffered the same ghettoization as comp/rhet, as a poor adjunct to the English department, often staffed by adjunct faculty. If the study of English literature originally suffered by comparison to the classics, at least it was analytic and could boast a tradition. The creative writing workshop, in which students produced original poetry or fiction and subjected it to a circle of peers, seemed unacademic to many: non-rigorous, unscientific, and cultivating a skill that was either unteachable or which smacked of arts and crafts. That English departments looked down on the in-house production of the very material they purported to study was an irony that did not go unnoticed but also did not get corrected. To this day, a tacit war exists between literary critics and writers, though both usually publish and teach within the same department.

The rift widened during lit crit's theory boom as the emergent critical schools began to pay more attention to psychology, linguistics, history, and sociology at the expense of literary technique. As Norman Holland sharply observed in *The Critical I,* Derrida spoke obscurely of what language is and does—without ever acknowledging the necessity of a conscious mind as the language user: "the cognitive scientists would say that we can never know anything *except by our own processes of cognition,*" yet Derrida "*rests our symbolic constructions, not in our psychological processes of construction, but in the differences, hence the 'forces' of language*. . . . Derrida makes the same mistake as Saussure. He confuses two senses of 'meaning.' He confuses 'meaning' as one element in a formal description of language with 'meaning' as a psychological event in somebody's mind" (158, 162). In other words, the text is not active; the mind is.

On the other side of the critical spectrum, the trinity of race, gender, and class spent more time on context than on text, as politics and the hegemonies of discourse crowded out the so-called literary (or writerly) qualities of a sonnet or a novel. In the quasi-Marxist shift from individuals to history, writers became an effect rather than a cause. The advent of popular culture studies administered the final blow by devaluing literature altogether, going so far as to brand such distinctions old-fashioned and elitist. Writing literature nowadays is a profession on its way toward the quaintness one associates with blacksmithing or lute-playing. In the academy, some faculty have retreated to an earlier concept of literary values by joining the ALCS, the Association of Literary Critics and Scholars, which now boasts a membership of about twenty-five hundred, a journal called *Literary Imagination,* and even an annual convention. Others have turned to creative writing workshop techniques as a means of pursuing old-style lit crit in the classroom. Before his retirement, the Modernist scholar A. Walton Litz at Princeton became head of the school's creative writing program. He said that he appreciated the emphasis on primary texts there, and he likened the work they were doing to monks preserving manuscripts during the Dark Ages. As with so many rearguard pronouncements (to shift metaphors), this one leaves the newly trained troops at a loss. This problem will intensify over time and no doubt lead to the succeeding generation of academics looking nostalgically back upon our era.

Yet even in a cynical age that knows the importance of spin, marketing, and audience, the aura of the isolated artist continues to shine among the general populace. If much of this feeling is misguided, the enthusiasm of dilettantes, it nonetheless drives enrollments up. Robert Wincour, a lawyer devoted to copyright law, puts it best: "As writing is one of the desperate professions, it has universal appeal, especially for those who are not engaged in it" (7). As Auden observes, somewhat more harshly: "How often one hears a young man with no talent say when asked what he intends to do, 'I want to write.' What he really means is, 'I don't want to work'" (7). Perhaps the idea of something for nothing, of creation seemingly *ex nihilo,* is leading droves of students to sign up for fiction workshops.

As composition classes encourage imaginative writing while fiction workshops allow mixed-genre documentary novels and autobiography, the traditional dividing lines between these two disciplines have started to blur. The differences remain largely the myth of the artist in the creative writing program, somewhat denied those who are teaching their composition students the technique of loop-writing.

The twin ascension of comp/rhet and creative writing splits into two peaks after a while, in any event, especially in their recent acquisition of academic cachet. Both were for a long time inimical to the larger machinations of literary criticism, and even today the bulk of criticism regarding creative writing has largely concentrated on exercises and anthologies: see, for example, such classics in the field as John Gardner's *The Art of Writing* and Robert Pack and Jay Parini's *Writers on Writing,* or recent efforts like Madison Smartt Bell's *Narrative Design: A Writer's Guide to Structure.* But if comp/rhet has surrounded a crucial skill with a wall of pedagogical theory, creative writing has begun to isolate a comparative luxury within the airless walls of professionalism. Over the last fifteen years, a recognizable workshop product has emerged, both in fiction and poetry. As Christopher Beach asks rhetorically in "Careers in Creativity: The Poetry Academy in the 1990s": "Does the entrenched network of academic poetry constitute an elitist and reactionary front, a wall of vested power and institutional status that marginalizes alternative poetic cultures and discourages the participation of groups from outside the mainstream?" (5). Many others have inveighed against the burgeoning of MFA programs, some famously—see, for example, John W. Aldridge's *Talents and Technicians: Literary Chic and the New Assembly-Line Fiction,* Bell's "Less is Less: The Diminishing American Short Story," Joseph Epstein's "Who Killed Poetry?" or Dana Gioia's "Can Poetry Matter?" Nonetheless, the numbers in workshops continue to rise.

As with comp/rhet, the trend is economically driven: creative writing is a cash cow, a popular offering with a low overhead and a big return. It's even self-generating. As one professor with a foot in both literary criticism and creative writing cynically commented: "All you need to start is a copy machine and an instructor with a few poetry publications under his belt."

Still, as with stock prices that continue to rise despite gloomy prognostications by economists, creative writing is clearly a hit among education consumers. In any event, the danger of over-expansion here is not that the bottom will drop out of the market but rather that a more subtle form of devaluation will occur. The need for creative writers to publish has spawned hundreds of little magazines, journals, and reviews, with the result that the market share of each is minimal. The more there are, the less each matters individually—or as Yogi Berra once said of a popular restaurant: "That place is so crowded that no one goes there anymore." The same situation happened to cable television when it expanded to umpteen channels, just as the same scenario is replaying itself as the World Wide Web beckons to every face in front of a computer screen. In all these cases, the embarrassment of riches is embarrassing only to those offerings more or less ignored. What seems like a surfeit resembles a vast banquet at which the majority eats from only a few dishes. Some of the food has a distinctly institutional flavor, but few go truly hungry in this land of plenty, where blandness is always safe. The urge to scribble now almost seems like an American right: life, liberty, and the pursuit of self-expression.

The latest in creative writing and rhetoric, the current craze for memoirs, has finally attracted the literary theoreticians. Some of the all-too-well-established critics are now busily explicating the text of themselves. Frank Lentricchia, once the "bad boy" of literary criticism, has since written memoirs and novels and repudiated his previous role "as an historian and literary polemicist of literary theory, who could speak with passion, and witout noticeable impediment, about literature as a political instrument" ("Last Will" 59). Eve Kosofsky Sedgwick has migrated from masturbation in Jane Austen to a self-involved brand of poetry. To some extent, a focus on oneself is a focus on the force of personal style. As Adam Begley noted in a *Lingua Franca* essay called "The I's Have It" (55), narcissism and self-expression are often linked. Since narcissism knows no age limits, rhetorical excess can be any generation's property. Still, to watch one's mentors abandon their critical moorings cannot help but be somewhat disheartening, even as the next generation gamely tries to jump ships. We are still an impressionable bunch, and if Julia Kristeva once exposed the text of herself, and Jane Gallop bared even more, we feel that perhaps we should, too. In response to this growing trend, the October 1996 *PMLA* Forum dwelt entirely on the use of the personal in literary scholarship. N.B.: some creative writing programs, ever-alert to an opportunity, now offer memoir workshops.

One irony remains: Though creative writing once offered a refuge from the wars of political correctitude, many composition classes and creative writing workshops are now afflicted with the same problems that disciplines like postcolonialism have pointed out. Gayatri Chakravorty Spivak's "Can the Subaltern Speak?" has been translated to the creative writing instructor's dilemma, "Is It Okay to Write Like an Afro-American If You Aren't One?" The stakes may be somewhat higher than in the politically charged sociology *cum* literary criticism classroom because in there, at least, students are encouraged to question received values and label cultural products as an essential process of critical reading, whereas such strategies have rarely been thought crucial to writing fiction. The policing of creative writing presents another reason for the popularity of the memoir, with the self as the source of authority, as well as the focus on minorities and working-class concerns to show one's social merit badge. As the author and creative-writing teacher Barry Hannah has remarked, "If you want to get taken seriously these days, you've got to write about trailer parks."

Another problem has to do with the two-tiered academic society arising these days based on the tenured class versus the temps and adjuncts. The sorry economics behind this situation are as unfair as they are unlikely to change in the near future. The recent political action taken by the Graduate Student Caucus at the MLA conventions—making its voice heard and gaining access to MLA committees—is heartening but unlikely to change the economics of the game. Still, if creative writing and composition were once the undisputed property of the subordinate instructors but have now acquired real status, as cultural studies acquires ascendancy over all, perhaps straight literature classes will become the new workhorses for the underclass—along with remedial writing and TESOL instruction. Creative writing and comp/rhet are no longer the awkward rough spots in the literary prospectus. In fact, these days they may be sliding smoothly up the ranks in mainstream English departments, for some of the best and worst reasons.

Will there be any change in the near future? A slowdown in certain areas is inevitable. As *Rhetoric Review* editor Theresa Enos observes of comp/rhet programs, "What we see now is not the growth between 1987 and 1994 but maturity and diversification." And though she talks of "consolidation" and "sophistication," seven fewer programs responded to the latest survey. AWP's Fenza sees a rise in creative writing programs, but notes that the numbers more reflect an integration of creative writing into lower levels, such as a poetry-writing emphasis in a B.A. degree. Already, some are seeing a plateau reached and perhaps the start of a reversal in popularity, which commentators like David Radavich tie to the collapse in the literary marketplace. (110). And no one wants to think about will happen when the stock market collapses. Economic cycles are all too closely tied to educational booms and bursts. By the time it all shakes down—well, that may be a problem for the next-next generation.

*Works Cited*

Aldridge, John W. *Talents and Technicians: Literary Chic and the New Assembly-Line Fiction.* New York: Charles Scribner's Sons, 1992.

Aristotle. *On Rhetoric.* Trans. George A. Kennedy. New York: Oxford University Press, 1991.

———. *Poetics.* Trans. Richard Janko. Cambridge: Hackett Publishing, 1987.

Auden, W. H. *The Prolific and the Devourer.* Hopewell, N.J.: Ecco Press, 1993.

Barthes, Roland. "The Death of the Author." *Image/Music/Text.* Trans. Stephen Heath. New York: Hill and Wang–Farrar, Straus and Giroux, 1977, 142–48.

Beach, Christopher. "Careers in Creativity: The Poetry Academy in the 1990s." *Western Humanities Review* 50 (1996): 4–16.

Begley, Adam. "The I's Have It: Duke's '*Moi*' Critics Expose Themselves." *Lingua Franca* 4, 3 (1994): 54–59.

Bell, Madison Smartt. "Less Is Less: The Diminishing American Short Story." *Harper's* (April 1986): 64–69.

———. *Narrative Design: A Writer's Guide to Structure.* New York: Norton, 1997.

Berlin, James. *Rhetoric and Reality: Writing Instruction in American Colleges, 1900–1985.* Carbondale, Ill.: Southern Illinois University Press, 1987.

———, and Michael J. Vivion, eds. *Cultural Studies in the English Classroom.* Portsmouth, N.H.: Boynton/Cook, 1992.

Booth, Wayne. *The Rhetoric of Fiction.* 2d ed. Chicago: University of Chicago Press, 1983.

Brown, Stuart C., Paul R. Meyer, and Theresa Enos. "Doctoral Programs in Rhetoric and Composition: A Catalog of the Profession." *Rhetoric Review* 12, 2 (1994): 240–51.

Bruffee, Kenneth A. *Collaborative Learning: Higher Education, Interdependence, and the Authority of Knowledge.* Baltimore and London: Johns Hopkins University Press, 1993.

Burke, Kenneth. *A Rhetoric of Motives.* New York: Prentice-Hall, 1952.

Chapman, David W., and Gary Tate. "A Survey of Doctoral Programs in Rhetoric and Composition." *Rhetoric Review* 5, 2 (1987): 124–33.

Corbett, Edward P. J. *Classical Rhetoric for the Modern Student.* 3d ed. New York: Oxford University Press, 1990.

Elbow, Peter, and Pat Belanoff. *Sharing and Responding.* New York: Random House, 1989.

Enos, Theresa. E-mail interview. 9 Dec. 1999.

Epstein, Joseph. "Who Killed Poetry?" *Commentary* (Aug. 1988): 13–20.

Farrell, Thomas B. *Norms of Rhetorical Culture*. New Haven: Yale University Press, 1993.

Fenza, David. Personal interview. 9 Dec. 1999.

———, and Gwyn McVay, eds. *The AWP Official Guide to Writing Programs*. 8th ed. Fairfax, Vir.: Associated Writing Programs, 1997.

Gardner, John. *The Art of Fiction: Notes on Craft for Young Writers*. New York: Knopf, 1984.

Gioia, Dana. "Can Poetry Matter?" *The Atlantic Monthly* (May 1991): 94–106.

Gradin, Sherrie L. *Romancing Rhetorics: Social Expressivist Perspectives on the Teaching of Writing*. Portsmouth, N.H.: Boynton/Cook-Heinemann, 1995.

Hairston, Maxine C. *Successful Writing: A Rhetoric for Advanced Composition*. New York: Norton, 1981.

Holland, Norman. *The Critical I*. New York: Columbia University Press, 1992.

Janangelo, Joseph, and Kristine Hansen, eds. *Resituating Writing: Constructing and Administering Writing Programs*. Portsmouth, N.H.: Boynton/Cook-Heinemann, 1995.

Lentricchia, Frank. "Last Will and Testament of an Ex-Literary Critic." *Lingua Franca* 6, 6 (Sept.–Oct. 1996): 59–67.

McClelland, Ben W., and Timothy R. Donovan, eds. *Perspectives on Research and Scholarship in Composition*. New York: MLA, 1985.

McQuade, Donald, and Robert Atwan, eds. *The Writer's Presence: A Pool of Essays*. New York: Bedford Books-St. Martin's Press, 1994.

Pack, Robert, and Jay Parini, eds. *Writers on Writing*. Hanover, N.H.: Middlebury College Press and University Press of New England, 1991.

Parker, William Riley. "Where Do English Departments Come From?" *College English* 28, 5 (1967): 339–51.

Radavich, David. "Creative Writing in the Academy." *Profession 1999*. 106–12.

Richards, I. A. *Practical Criticism: A Study of Literary Judgment*. London: Kegan Paul, Trench, Trubner, 1930.

Scholes, Robert. *The Rise and Fall of English: Reconstructing English as a Discipline*. New Haven: Yale University Press, 1998.

Scott, Janny. "Journey from Ivory Tower: Public Intellectual Is Reborn." *The New York Times* 9 Aug. 1994, national ed.: A1, A13.

Thomas, Francis-Noël. *The Writer Writing: Philosophic Acts in Literature*. Princeton: Princeton University Press, 1992.

———, and Mark Turner. *Clear and Simple as the Truth: Writing Classic Prose*. Princeton: Princeton UP, 1995.

Tompkins, Jane P., ed. *Reader-Response Criticism: From Formalism to Post-Structuralism*. Baltimore: Johns Hopkins University Press, 1980.

Wincour, Robert. *Literary Property*. New York: Clarkson N. Potter, 1967.

*Writers' Workshop*. Iowa City: University of Iowa Press, 1996.

# Ten

# Contextualizing Contexts: Cultural Studies, Theory, and the Profession—Past and Future

## *Barbara Riebling*

My credentials for membership in the next generation are not entirely bona fide. I am a recently tenured associate professor with a 1993 doctorate in English Renaissance literature, and although not nearly as "job traumatized"[1] as some of my fellow graduate students, I have felt their pain, both personally and by proxy. However, we are not the same age. I was born in 1949 and first attended graduate school at the University of Pennsylvania in 1972, when formalism still reigned and theory was nothing more than distant thunder. I reentered Penn's graduate English program in 1987 while teaching at the junior college that had been my home for over a decade. In the late '80s deconstruction may have begun its decline, but high theory's assumptions, at least at Penn, were still regnant. I have, therefore, a divided, almost prismatic perspective on the questions raised by this collection. My feelings of solidarity are entirely with the next generation, but I cannot claim to be typical or representative. Nevertheless, I will be drawing from my own experiences—being the only ones I have—to suggest this generation's future. This chapter will be a highly personal attempt to make sense of the context within which the newest generation of literary-critical practitioners struggles to survive while forging an independent identity. While it is somewhat premature to be making predictions, I believe that members of the next generation may differ substantially from their teachers and mentors in a number of ways. (1) Drifting away from totalizing theoretical and political claims (much of which rest on extreme antifoundationalism), the next generation will embrace theories that emphasize human agency and responsibility. (2) Continuing to work within the cultural studies context, the next generation will ease its boundaries and make Cultural Studies more inclusive methodologically. (3) Having become intensely aware of how the academy is perceived, the next generation will not speak exclusively to one another but consider the world outside the profession, the public sphere, their ultimate discursive context. (4) Being under siege from powerful political and economic forces, next generation scholars will be cautious about picking fights both inside and outside the discipline, and they will actively value peace and toleration. This chapter is not so much a linear argument about where we are going and where we have been as it is a series of distinct observations about our profession's future and its past. These observations cohere around a central metaphor of circles in which the themes of context (spheres within spheres) and hegemony (spheres contesting spheres) repeatedly emerge.

## Theory, Cultural Studies, and the Next Generation

The title of this collection invites a genealogical analogy. In what follows, I will be drawing on a dialectical model of generational struggle that some may find crudely oedipal. Still, it seems to me ineluctable that all intellectual movements are formed in relation to their heritage. Whether the next generation rebels against or replicates the parent generation's ideas, it cannot stand apart from its diachronic context.

I will begin by joining the majority of profession watchers who assume the probable staying power of cultural studies (albeit somewhat transformed) as the context within which the next generation will do most of its work. However, I would like to reframe the generally accepted genealogy of the profession—which has new criticism yielding to high theory, which in turn yields to cultural studies, which will then yield to an unknown future—to posit a less linear model. In the family tree I envision, high theory did not give birth to cultural studies; their relationship is more that of older and younger siblings. They both rebelled against the formalist and old historical generation of critics and scholars. This does not mean that theory and cultural studies have always shared a unified agenda; siblings can be rivals as well as allies. Cultural studies owes its older brother a great debt: it would have no space within which to operate without the ground clearing accomplished by theory's intraprofessionally successful assault on received authority, essentialism, and the canon. The problematics of the sibling relationship emerge, however, when instead of cleared ground, theory has offered its younger sister scorched earth. The central projects of cultural studies are political, which means they ultimately involve taking a stand. Unfortunately, as many activist scholars have noted, grounded action is seriously weakened if not destroyed by the absolute nature of much of theory's antifoundationalism. Sorting out this conflict will be the responsibility of the next generation, whose greater distance from the movements' origins may give it greater freedom to forge solutions.

The relation of the next generation to both theory and cultural studies is not that of a still younger sibling but that of a child to parents. The next generation was not shaped by the firsthand experience of battle with the formalists that so deeply affected their teachers and mentors. Right now, despite this lack of shared experience, the child appears to be remarkably obedient to its parents' wishes. Whether it will remain so, I will argue, is impossible to determine at this point. Not until the members of the next generation are liberated from their crushing material insecurity will we know what rebellious impulses may be lurking beneath their conformist exteriors. For some very understandable reasons, their subjective consciousnesses remain hidden, and it is, therefore, premature to expect anything like a next-generation manifesto. Indeed, most of what I will be able to offer up as evidence to suggest that this new cohort may be nursing a semidialectical relationship to its formative context are my own responses to that context—as personal and, therefore, unreliable as they may be.

## An Agent in the Wings

The first prediction I will venture is that the next generation will seek out theories that facilitate grounded action and ethical responsibility. As one member of that generation told me recently, "Agency is in." I was delighted as well as surprised to hear it. Essays such as the one written by Susan Johnston for this collection indicate that this young scholar may be onto something. Contexts are certainly key to the construction of identity. But, particularly if those in control demand lock-step obedience from a new generation, their shaping constraints will more often than not be self-defeating, producing oppositional rather than conformist identities. Indeed, as Peter Herman has already noted, this dialectical truism is central to the current establishment's description of its own intellectual genesis as a collective act of rebellion.

The intellectual context of the next generation's formative years was profoundly hostile to individual or group agency: dead author studies, Althusserian notions of subjectivity, Foucauldian models of societal control, and so forth. Perhaps more importantly, the material context within which this generation has been living is one of near helplessness in the face of the job market collapse. To date the most characteristic response to this calamity by next generation scholars is to study their situation intently, using every hermeneutic tool at their command to analyze the forces that are crashing in upon them.[2] These efforts are attempts to assert agency in the midst of very unpromising circumstances. In my experience reading the literature of political persecution, I have found that theories obviating human agency hold little or no attraction for individuals in dire straits. While still a prisoner of conscience, Václav Havel called such theories "degenerate realism" and his own philosophy "the politics of hope."[3] I feel strongly that the next generation has been primed by its formative context and its present exigencies to embrace a Havelian perspective.

## The Foundations of Historical Revision

As a historically oriented Renaissance scholar who has never practiced the new historicism, I am particularly interested in the kind of historical work the next generation will produce. Personally, I would look forward to younger scholars approaching historical work from a perspective that is provisionally but not dogmatically antifoundationalist, one that could acknowledge degrees of uncertainty regarding "fact" and "truth" but not lapse into epistemological and ethical nihilism. Although modern science and philosophy have plunged us all into a world of unpredictability and factual imprecision, we are still obliged to make ethical judgments. How we deal theoretically with "fact" and "truth" has profound implications for the kind of revisionist historical and literary studies that the posttheory generation will produce.

As counterintuitive as it may at first seem, I would argue that it is possible to admit to a fairly large degree of factual imprecision and still be able to base clear moral and ethical judgments on that uncertain body of evidence. Let me cite an example from our own history. By 1800 between ten and fifteen million black Africans had been transported to America as slaves. The death rate during transport is estimated to have run as high as one in every three slaves or as low as one in five—which leaves us with a range of somewhere between two and five million slaves dying at sea during the infamous "middle passage."[4] This is a very large difference in numbers, and any exact figure will probably be forever beyond our reach. Nevertheless, I feel comfortable stating with complete moral certainty that what was done to those men, women, and children from Africa was a crime against humanity. And if tomorrow we had a way of determining that it was indeed two million rather than five million, would it make a moral difference? Would it be less than half the crime? In other words, I can take a strong moral stand on a historical event where I must perforce accept a large degree of factual uncertainty, and furthermore, I believe it is my duty to do so.

Slavery, among other practices, was not always considered a crime. But that does not mean that it should not be considered a crime today. Historical revisionism is, I believe, above all a process of moral reperception. Many will argue that we do not have the right to apply our moral values to the past—either to history or to literature. I would argue that it is both right and necessary to do so, but that it is neither right nor necessary to play fast and loose with the facts in order to do so. Historical revision will continue to be a pressing responsibility of the next generation, and to succeed, I would argue, it should rely on a respect for the facts (as they can best be determined) and be driven by an obligation to bear witness to the truth. One cannot "set the record straight" if there is no real record—if all history is merely a collection of stories manufactured to support whatever group is in power.[5] Further, if historical revisionists concentrate on the reperception of moral questions rather than the wholesale and foundationless rewriting of facts, their ideas enter the field with a far greater degree of credibility.

Sometimes the facts of a particular case have to be researched anew; more often they have merely to be presented within a new context, one that values the lives of "others." Another example drawn from American history that illustrates this distinction is the United States' treatment of the Cherokee and the Creek. In the early decades of the republic, these tribes lived peacefully in what is now Western North Carolina and Georgia having signed a series of treaties guaranteeing their rights to their traditional lands. When Andrew Jackson sought to violate those treaties and "remove" them from their lands, he was joined by the state of Georgia, which passed laws making it illegal for whites to stand in the way of Indian removal. In defiance of these laws a group of white missionaries attempted to aid the Cherokee, appealing their case to the Supreme Court, where they won. However, under executive order, the Cherokee were eventually driven off their land, later to be forced west on a death march in the dead of winter, the survivors ending their journey in what is now Oklahoma. Those who resisted the Act of Removal were hunted through the mountains and killed, and many who marched died of cold, hunger, and disease. In a rare act of courage, two missionaries continued to defy the state of Georgia and stood with the Cherokee; they were beaten, jailed, and eventually sentenced to four years of hard labor.[6] In 1992, 160 years after *The Trail of Tears,* those two missionaries were pardoned by the current governor of Georgia. The facts of the case have never been in dispute. What then changed these two men from criminals to prisoners of conscience? Clearly, it was a shift in our views about America's treatment of its original inhabitants—a shift that, I might add, is still in need of some encouragement since the face of the man most responsible for the murder of the Cherokee still graces our twenty-dollar bill. I would argue that as simple and straightforward as it may seem, the kind of revisionist thinking that prompted the governor of Georgia to issue those pardons derives from a sound theoretical base. A revisionist history constructed from a theory of moral reperception is both flexible and sturdy enough to shape and support the next generation's literary and historical studies. As they move away from the ethical impotence the profession's commitment to extreme antifoundationalism has fostered, their work can claim greater significance as well as wider appeal in the public sphere.

## WHEN VISIBILITY IS POWER

Cultural studies is "a work in progress" in the most positive sense: its acts of expansion, inclusion, and contextualization are permanent contributions to literary studies that make all of our work more interesting (by vastly expanding fields of inquiry and types of evidentiary materials) and more meaningful (by valuing the perspectives of groups that had previously been neglected or deliberately erased). None of what I am saying is new, except perhaps the assertion that these contributions may now be called "permanent."

Strangely, although I believe it, I find this a difficult assertion to make, largely because my own experience of the pre-cultural studies era still weighs heavily upon me. That era is almost impossible to describe to those who never knew it firsthand. As students we lived silently within a strange world of selective invisibilities; it was as if we were haunting our own lives. I vividly remember what it was like to be a woman in a classroom where the professor called us all "lads" and openly lamented the day our university became coed, and listening to that same professor wonder aloud how any non-Christian could be a Renaissance scholar as he seamlessly segued to the recent suicide of a stockbroker, "a Jewish fellow. . . ." I also remember surreal classroom experiences where the mandatory erasure of difference made a coherent reading of certain texts almost impossible. For instance, we actually managed to study Marlowe's *Edward II* without Edward's sexuality ever being mentioned. Shakespeare's *Taming of the Shrew* was a delightful comedy—never mind (never knowing) that in early modern England "shrew" was a legal category carrying with it physical penalties of enormous cruelty. These invisibilities were more than a political issue—although they were and are just that. To this day I resent my undereducation: the intellectual poverty of learning textual analysis divorced from pertinent contexts makes me feel robbed.

I am revisiting this era not only to demonstrate that I have no nostalgia for the pre-cultural studies *status quo ante,* but also to evoke, for those too young to remember, the oppressiveness of invisibility. At the same time, I would argue that while it was in many ways genuinely awful, this status quo ante is now quite harmless. The formerly invisible contexts (race, class, gender, and sexuality) cannot, *will* not, in our lifetime lapse into oblivion. However, to those of us who lived within it, that strange dead world still feels like a clear and present danger, just waiting to be reborn and reerase us all.

The phobia my generation (and here I mean my chronological generation) feels about its past would be of little interest were it not for the fact that these fears are a living context for cultural studies as it is presently practiced. The fear of relapse has caused cultural studies to engage in its own lesser but not insignificant acts of erasure. The group contexts—race, class, gender, and sexuality—have multiplied over the past few years by subdividing, but they have not significantly expanded. In Renaissance studies, for instance, there is a particular aversion to looking at the one context the old-school formalists tolerated—dynastic history. Like close reading, the history of dynastic struggle (including rebellions and risings) as well as the history of political and religious thought have suffered a kind of guilt by association, all of them considered somehow inherently "conservative." Work in these areas is not exactly disallowed, but it is not put in the mix with the rest of the cultural studies' contexts, and it should be.

## WHEN INVISIBILITY IS POWER

The PC and culture wars were a formative context for the next generation's pedagogy. Most of us were teaching assistants while these wars raged, and we often implemented curricula in freshman English programs designed by leading rhetorical and literary theorists, who were admired within the academy while their ideas came under assault from outside its walls. For many of these theorists, the classroom was a political arena of great consequence. Some of us, while left entirely free to design our own introductory courses, witnessed a variety of programmatic attempts to mold a generation's politics. Sharon Crowley's response essay in *Contending with Words: Composition and Rhetoric in a Postmodern Age,* typifies such attempts, and it concludes with a remarkably frank statement regarding the progressive composition teacher's political project:

> Because nearly every student who enters an American college or university is required to take a composition course, this project indeed has potential for bringing about social reform. However, because composition students are in some sense our captives, we must give up our traditional subscription to liberal tolerance if we are to bring about social change through them. We must also admit

that we enact our own hegemonic desire when we use the required composition course to teach our preferred politics.

Of course, teachers everywhere have always used their courses to do exactly that. . . . It remains to be seen whether or not freshman composition can be radicalized in the service of social justice. Some of us seem willing to try. (196–97)

Sharon Crowley's declaration that "we must give up our traditional subscription to liberal tolerance" because our students are our "captives" is more than a howling non sequitur. It is an assertion that radical teachers are obliged to politically coerce their students, thinly justified by the bland contention that teachers everywhere have always done the same. Crowley should speak for herself. The idea that all teaching is always already political control (so let's just replace their hegemonic design with our own) indicts us all—left and right, past, present, and future. *Contending with Words* was published by the MLA in 1991, and this essay is just one product of the heady times in the academy that preceded the disastrous PC wars. It is difficult to imagine a statement as self-damning as Crowley's being made today.

One sign that the profession is now moving away from coercive pedagogy can be found in Gregory Jay and Gerald Graff's recent essay "A Critique of Critical Pedagogy." Even as they celebrate the infusion of multicultural perspectives into the classroom, Jay and Graff mount a powerful argument for "persuasion" and "community" as the basis for student/teacher interaction. They critique the "oppositional pedagogies" advocated by such theorists as Donald Morton and Mas'ud Zavarzadeh, asserting that politicized critical pedagogies that attack a student's "false consciousness" are built on the assumption that "The teacher is not only authoritatively right about the issues, but also justified in assuming the inauthenticity of the student's opinions" (205). Jay and Graff do not want to banish politics from the classroom; they want to transform classroom dynamics to be a truly political, that is to say communal, activity:

> We grant that critical pedagogy has its place at the level of individual teaching practices, at least when it is willing to respect the resistance of students. But as long as education is an institution in an overlapping system of democratic processes, the school cannot and should not enforce a program that commits everyone to a predetermined world-view, however just we may believe it is. Theorizing the practice of entire institutions of higher education means thinking from the viewpoint of conservatives, liberals, and others with whom we work, not just from the viewpoint of radicals. This calls for a model of education in which we engage with those who hold the "wrong" politics and will not take our assumptions for granted, that is, a model in which ideological opponents not only coexist but cooperate. (209)

Whether or not the next generation follows Graff's specific recommendation to "teach the conflicts," I am confident that they already share his and Jay's basic teaching philosophy. The tide has turned against coercive and intolerant pedagogy in the name of utopian politics.

However, for a brief time in the late '80s and early '90s, both Right and Left routinely made startling assertions about what teaching could and should accomplish politically. Both sides had seized on a mission: they would shape the future of the nation by exposing students to the salvational power of the canon or the anticanon. In the grandiose designs of some progressive theorists, students who read carefully chosen emancipatory texts would leave their introductory writing courses with a life-long awareness of systems of oppression based on race, class, and gender. In the lurid fantasies of the Right, Stalinists had captured the nation's classrooms and Western Civilization was about to be lost because classical works of literature and philosophy were now abandoned or condemned.[7] I remember being virtually alone among my fellow graduate students in worrying deeply about the ethics of trying to indoctrinate entering students, whatever the cause, and I was also mildly worried about its prudence. I now feel that my concerns were seriously misplaced. In retrospect, I should have been much less distressed about the students' intellectual freedom and much more concerned about the effect a handful of ham-fisted attempts to mold belief would have on the reputation of the academy, and on our collective futures as the next generation of academics. When attempts at coercion succeed, they create ethical dilemmas; when they fail, the problems they present are prudential. To echo Talleyrand concerning an action taken by Napoleon: "It was worse than a crime, it was a mistake."

All freedoms, intellectual or other, are exercised within spheres of sovereignty. These spheres englobe one another concentrically; in other words, they contextualize one another. In the academic arena, empowered spheres can be said to begin with the internal subjective consciousness of each student and move outward to the classroom, the university, and the society at large. Whether or not the smaller (less powerful) spheres remain free depends in large measure on how penetrable are their boundaries and how visible their activities. Contrary to the pessimism of such postmodern theorists of power as Foucault and Althusser, I would argue that subjective consciousness resides in a "shaded zone,"[8] generally impenetrable, invisible to the searching eye of coercive power, and, therefore, surprisingly free. There are, of course, times when the indoctrination of an individual's consciousness is possible. For instance, it occurs rather easily when someone joins a cult, primarily because s/he enters declaring, "I am an empty vessel—fill my life with meaning." The average student entering an introductory writing class makes no such declaration, explicit or implicit. If the student's presence is saying anything it is more like, "I am an insecure writer—please get me into medical school." The student may seem helpless and eager to please, but this does not equate to being a candidate for mind control.

Subjective consciousness can also be deeply affected by outside forces in another context: in the early stages of a totalitarian regime, where all of the concentric spheres of power vibrate in harmony. In these cases there is no larger sphere with which a resistant individual consciousness can resonate; complete isolation can break the will.

However, as we all know, the emancipatory classroom flourished inside the academy while the country at large was electing Reagan and Bush. In the final analysis the PC professor could not be an effective Stalinist if s/he wanted to—with no real coercive power beyond a letter grade and no support from the society at large, nothing much could happen to the students, especially if they could keep silent and go along to get along.

Although as I have pointed out, cultural studies with its politics of inclusion has a secure and permanent presence within our field, at the levels of both the entering student and the society at large, the brief attempts to mold a generation politically were resented and resisted, and they also helped to feed the media frenzy over PC that still dogs our every move. What was ultimately even more harmful to the future of the academy than high-profile media debates happened among low-visibility state legislators. They eagerly read about "prof-scamming" and "tenured radicals" who were "closing the American mind," while their constituents were staging tax revolts, all of which made for a highly dangerous context for the state-supported university. In their introduction to *Higher Education under Fire*, Nelson and Bérubé point to the dangerous link between fiscal policies and a harsh political climate:

> We do not claim a direct and immediate causal link between attacks on higher education and reduced state funding, but we do claim that these attacks have established a climate in which universities are vulnerable and in which public resistance to cuts is almost nonexistent. There is a consensus in many states that we are no longer a high priority. It is also clear that some legislators believe there is political capital to be gained in attacking us; anti-academic rhetoric is what they believe their electorate will be glad to hear.

In the '80s too many within the profession assumed that their students' minds and wills were more or less transparent and malleable; they were not. Further, they assumed that the classroom was a safe and private space, a "shaded zone"; it was not. Literary academics in that era, despite myriad indications to the contrary, often behaved as if they were visible to one another alone, striking poses in front of mirrored walls that were in reality one-way glass. As each annual article ridiculing the MLA convention should have made clear, we were and are under constant, hostile scrutiny. And it is the next generation of scholars who will pay the heaviest material price for our damaged public image.

Even when their loyalties lie squarely within the academy, members of the next generation who write about the profession are acutely sensitive to matters of public perception. This sensitivity contrasts sharply with writers of the previous generation, who rarely felt obliged to acknowledge the public, its attitudes, its interests, or its power. In *Public Access: Literary Theory and American Cultural Politics*, Michael Bérubé tackles all three. He assesses the dangers created by our negative image as well as our isolation:

This is not simply an academic discussion of the shifting sands of time. The reasons these questions of value and merit come before us with such exigency, the reason we need so desperately to be able to take our case to the public and to the literary public sphere, is that we are facing a drastic shrinking of resources, the defunding of the humanities, the wholesale elimination of entire academic programs and departments that aren't directly helping us compete with Japan. And I believe that our chances, in the humanities, of withstanding this defunding and this retrenchment depend largely on our ability to recognize and win new constituencies among aspiring educators and professionals, new constituencies on the progressive-but-not-poststructuralist left, and, not least of these, new constituencies in what we must help to make a broader and more diverse public sphere. However arcane and "theoretical" some of its manifestations may seem to be, therefore, the struggle over the university is a struggle in which centrists and progressives, inside or outside the universities, have a civic obligation to engage. (112)

I agree with Bérubé's call for strategic alliances between academics and nonacademics and among various progressive groups. I only wish it had come much sooner. Liberal humanists and those who would describe themselves as members of the "progressive-but-not-poststructuralist left" have for years been pointedly (sometimes savagely) excluded from the profession's theoretical and political discussions. Enough damage has been done to relations between the literary establishment and these other groups that it may well take more than a common enemy to win their active support.

Today members of the profession widely acknowledge a public relations problem. Conventional wisdom has it that the arcane language of high theory is one wall that stands between us and the general public. I wish I could agree because that would make gaining credibility and material support for our enterprise a relatively easy task of translation. I would contend, however, that the clearer the messages of theory have become, the more they have eroded our relations with the public. If as is variously asserted, literature departments should no longer be in the business of studying literature, and we as a profession have discovered the death of the author along with the absence of any claim to truth, fact, or meaning, is it any wonder that the general public might hesitate to support continuation of such work? Whether people outside literary studies find these theoretical claims tenable is moot; in either case the enterprise might appear to have a questionable future. Wouldn't it make more sense for taxpayers to fund research on cancer, AIDS, or the environment than something that sounds like the old "Saturday Night Live" routine on Francisco Franco ("It's March 23, 1999, and the author is still dead . . . truth is still dead.")?

To those who have made careers in high theory, such a description will doubtless seem shallow and dismissive. Although there is some justice in this accusation, my point here is not to analyze poststructuralism, but to mimic the response of nonacademics.[9] Whatever their actual value, current theories have not flourished in the public sphere, and further theoretical discussions among academics of the merits of poststructuralism will do nothing to engage those outside the academy. The public has not and never will examine the tenets of poststructuralism via the dense theoretical discourse literary professionals respect. Still, the public's opinion counts; it is, in fact, crucial to our survival. I would argue, therefore, that one of the next generation's most urgent tasks will be to recontextualize the profession's theory, to look at theory from a nontheoretical perspective, and to build bridges from the academic to the public sphere. We should be able to discuss our central theories in ways that can be understood by a wider audience. If we cannot, perhaps it is time for these theories to be reexamined. Poststructuralism is not rocket science; none of literary studies is. If after twenty years we as a profession cannot communicate its basic principles to members of an intelligent lay audience in a way that engages them, then we might begin to look for the faults within the theory, or among the communicators, and cease to find fault with an estranged or indifferent public.

On the subject of theory as well as politics, many members of the previous generation see themselves in the role of a vanguard vis-à-vis the American people. They assume they are leading the culture, and seldom look over their shoulders to see if anyone is following. For some practitioners of high theory, living within a self-contained sphere of arcane discourse, estrangement and isolation from the public are badges of honor: if what they write cannot be understood by outsiders, this is further proof of its brilliance. For many members of the '60s generation of theorists in the humanities, that mule "the public" can be led by the nose, or if not, it deserves simply to be ignored. I believe that members of the next generation are going to be more sensitive than their predecessors when dealing with nonacademics. However unjust, recent attacks on the humanities have taught this generation the necessity of effectively communicating its intellectual mission. If our professional practice is to be supported beyond the level of writing instruction, we cannot afford to stand aloof. We have learned a useful if painful lesson: in a democracy, intellectual elitism is as self-destructive as it is obnoxious.

## OUR NEWEST WAR

Sensitivity to public perception has always carried material consequences for the academy. These days, however, shaping those consequences is a matter of greater exigency. Unlike the crises of the '70s, our current dilemma is a severe job shortage based not on an absence of need but on a lack of funding. We are competing inside and outside the academy with other disciplines for increasingly scarce resources. Thus the model of concentric spheres of power I introduced earlier needs to be expanded upon to include hegemonic struggles within spheres.

In the fierce competition within universities to fund faculty positions, the hard sciences have always had an advantage. By and large, scientists command greater respect in American society than humanists. Representing the most powerful hegemony within the university and linked to powerful market forces outside it, scientists not only attract, but also often control funding—if for no other reason than because they

have their share of academic administrative posts and positions on key university committees. Deconstructive and poststructuralist theorists, as a result of the sweeping nature of their epistemological claims and in conjunction with the sociology of science
movement, have chosen this moment in history to make a radical assault on the scientific method. Many literary scholars insistently proclaim that scientists do not pursue "truth" through objectively gathered "facts," but instead weave the fashion-driven
narratives that will enrich them.[10] I will refrain in this chapter from engaging the
highly complex question of the social context of scientific knowledge. My point is,
once again, not about the theoretical validity of these concepts, but about the wisdom
of attacking scientists and their methods with so much careless invective in a public
forum.

   Scientists are by and large infuriated by the kind of portrayal I have described,
and they are striking back—witness a book like Gross and Levitt's *Higher Superstition*
and the physicist Alan Sokal's hoax in *Social Text*. Sokal's hoax and Gross and Levitt's
book are important signs of the time. Indeed the ill-fated issue of *Social Text* that
printed Sokal's essay was devoted to "The Science Wars," with Andrew Ross's introduction as a stirring call to arms. I do not know about other academic humanists, but
I am not particularly looking forward to this newest battle. Willing or no, we are being drafted into fighting on foreign soil against a determined enemy (who need not
be an enemy), and we are hopelessly out-gunned. Am I alone in wondering how many
more wars of this kind our profession can afford? *Higher Superstition* is an unpleasant
book, hectoring and contemptuous, and Sokal's hoax was arguably an uncivil act, but
they demonstrate that at least some scientists are sufficiently exercised by ideas about
the social constructedness of scientific knowledge to put in a considerable amount of
time and effort to combat them. Gathering together scores of examples selected from
among the most embarrassing works in print on the social contexts of science, Alan
Sokal did his homework in "Transgressing the Boundaries: Toward a Transformative
Hermeneutics of Quantum Gravity," which is more than can be said for the editors
of *Social Text*. Both Stanley Fish and Stanley Aronowitz complained to the *New York
Times* that Sokal's hoax distorted the position of social constructivists to mean that
"reality" is a pure construct (Fish, A 11) and that they are "epistemic relativists"
(Aronowitz quoted in Scott, New York Times, front page). Unfortunately, whatever
the more responsible takes on the social constructedness of reality and the scientific
grounds for modern theories of epistemology may be, there is plenty of material in
print that says exactly what Fish and Aronowitz are denying is being said.[11]

   What troubles me more than the recent visible counterattacks by Gross, Levitt,
and Sokal are the myriad invisible moves against us that such public disrespect will
have provoked. For the most part, the posttheory generation is a victim of economic
forces beyond its control. However, for over a decade, our predecessors have been
tweaking the noses of tigers. Institutional funding for departments is not fixed but dis-
cretionary. Every time we pick a fight or adopt a posture, department lines may hang
in the balance, and who knows how many we may have lost to forays against rivals
whose strength we have not even begun to appreciate.

## WHOSE HONOR? WHOSE SACRIFICE?

Principled conflicts often entail sacrifices. Laying down one's life or one's career for a cause is commonly held heroic. However, because the consequences of political acts are almost always felt by groups and not just by individuals, heroic political action is rarely this simple. It is one thing for individuals to act when dire consequences will fall entirely upon themselves. It is quite another when these consequences fall upon themselves and others. And it is quite another still when they fall upon others alone. In the first case the actions may indeed be called honorable, in the second case reckless, and in the third case reckless and craven.

Recently, I have begun to raise issues of safety when speaking to colleagues about the profession and its future. My friends' responses have not been encouraging. They have politely asked if I might be adopting positions that are, among other things, cowardly, tawdry, unprincipled, Machiavellian, or trivial. And these are my friends. Still, despite such active discouragement, I have decided to persist in this line of argument because I believe that survival is an ethical issue. Safety is trivial to those who have it. I am reminded of the fact that, for some social scientists, women were deemed "ethically immature" because when given values tests, they chose to sacrifice principles rather than people, whereas men would more readily sacrifice people than principles.[12] Machiavelli, whose work I study and admire, must have been a woman at heart; he too had his people's survival as his baseline ethic. Consequently, he insisted that in politics one must study the world as it is, not as it should be. Vulnerable to invasion and wracked by civil wars, early modern Italy was simply too dangerous a site to structure its politics on naive utopian fantasies. To this day, Machiavelli's reputation is stained by accusations of immorality, which, in my opinion, fail to take into account the context that forged his political vision. Similarly, I have decided to risk being dismissed on moral grounds. Regardless of how tawdry arguments about our collective safety may seem, they flow from civic consciousness. Like Machiavelli's Italy, today's academy is a world torn apart and under siege. I feel strongly that under these circumstances we owe ourselves (particularly our youngest professionals) conduct based on the *principles* of mutual protection and prudent choice.

Because they are the ones who will suffer most as support for our enterprise evaporates, members of the next generation might well ask all of us—from the most to the least prominent members of the profession—to take stock of our words and actions in the light of their material consequences. It would be hard to imagine a more prominent member of the profession than Edward Said, and along with a few other well-known academics, he has recently (if belatedly) begun to address the problems the younger generation of professionals are facing and their relation to the actions of his own generation. In his "President's Column" in the spring 1999 *MLA Newsletter,* Said makes exactly the kind of connection between what is happening to those at the bottom and on the margins of the profession and the unfortunate actions of academic "stars," covered so relentlessly by the media. After discussing the exploitation of part-

time, adjunct, and graduate student employees in the academy as well as the trend toward corporatization, he states:

> At the same time, in what appears to be an unrelated development, the media
> have turned their attention to disputes within prominent literature departments
> in English and other languages, disputes that threaten the existence of such de-
> partments all over the country. The *New York Times* a few months ago highlighted
> the factionalism and misfortunes of the Duke University English department
> (Scott), but it is true, I think, that several other departments across the country
> are going through the same travail. It is too often the case that as the opportuni-
> ties for young scholars and teachers either dry up or are converted into exploita-
> tive, poorly paid menial "service" jobs, senior professors who have the luxury to
> be locked in factional strife are unable to vote coherently on junior faculty ap-
> pointments, tenure cases, and curricular needs. This situation plainly hasn't
> caused the crises in scholarly employment, but it certainly hasn't helped. I am
> convinced that we need to turn our attention seriously to the intellectual pass we
> have come to that accompanies the diminished employment opportunities for ac-
> ademic humanists. When reputable, distinguished departments of literature can
> no longer function without terrible, paralyzing disagreement on the smallest as
> well as the largest issues, something is quite wrong. (3)

I agree with Said's analysis, and I would argue that it is for these reasons that we need
to recontextualize our political positions, moving them from realms of abstraction and
hothouse strife into real-world contexts, where we may better insure the welfare of the
weakest and most vulnerable among us. Of course, stars are not the only members of
our profession who squander energy and public credibility through politically
thoughtless action. A friend of mine related an incident that illustrates the sort of behavior I wish to interrogate with an event that occurred at his university. A senior
member of his department was on the verge of obtaining chair endowments from a
wealthy alum when the local newspaper ran a story about its core program, which was
attacked by a department member as sexist, racist, and homophobic. The endowments disappeared. In this particular case the faculty member was untenured, and the
consequences of her imprudence (or courage, depending on how you want to read her
actions) fell upon her as well as her department.

　　More typically, as Said's analysis implies, it is the profession's stars who draw
down hostile fire on their departments and the academy as a whole. Insulated from
the consequences of the public alienation their extreme rhetoric can create, academic
stars operate within a safe and liberated discursive sphere. In contrast, the next generation's professional world is neither free nor secure. The job insecurity academics
are facing now and will face in the future (including the possible elimination of tenure)
cannot be separated from what is happening in the country at large. In a very real
sense, the protective boundaries that once formed our professional sphere are crumbling. It is unlikely that this nation's citizenry will indefinitely afford us a form of job

security they themselves have been so mercilessly denied. As one downsizing consultant puts it: "Full-time permanent employees have become an endangered species. All employees are now, in a sense, temporary" (David M. Noer as quoted in "Does America Still Work?: On the Turbulent Energies of the New Capitalism," 39). In the context of America's economic restructuring, tenure must look to nonacademics like the inherited privilege of an *ancien régime,* ripe for the shaking.

What makes the situation especially thorny is that prominent professionals often reward each other for outrageousness and would, very understandably, resist the chilling effect of self-censorship. To ask the dominant generation to monitor its conduct will be particularly difficult because they have a unique view of themselves as professionals. The gap between the next generation and its predecessors is as much one of *Weltanschauung* as it is ideology or theory. Their differences are reminiscent of the '20s and the '30s, of the vastly different worldviews before and after the Crash—this despite the fact that the '70s were also difficult times in which to find a job. For whatever reasons (perhaps because of their attachment to the '60s), many older generation scholars seem to have a ludic sense of their professional life. Although more than a little gray, they still love to be daring, outrageous, to shock their elders (never mind that these elders are a vanishing remnant, white haired and largely toothless). By contrast, even radical members of the next generation strike me as a serious and sober lot, particularly when they write about the academy. These days no one I know feels much like jumping into a fountain or climbing on a table top to dance the Charleston.

I cannot offer a simple solution that prescribes our collective conduct within this increasingly vulnerable sphere. It might help matters considerably, however, if all of us, no matter how secure our position within the profession, would consider each other's welfare when we speak and remain aware that the world outside the academy is our ultimate rhetorical and material context, and that the language spoken there can be very different from our own.

Despite the popularity of theories that posit multiple discourse communities, humanist scholars have been late recognizing that the rhetoric which plays well inside the academy will not necessarily play well outside it. If nonacademics were, for example, to hear a program's offerings called "racist," they would most likely picture the presence of Hitler's *Mein Kampf,* not the absence of Morrison's *Beloved.* As I argued in the section of this chapter on cultural studies, absence and erasure can indeed be acts of oppression, but outside the context of the academy's lengthy discussions on the subject, such an accusation will sound seriously overstated. When speaking to the general public, we cannot use rhetoric that has been heated by years of ongoing intramural debate unless we provide its context, and that is very difficult in the soundbite world of the media. It makes more sense to me for us to adjust our rhetoric to our audience—if indeed our aim is to persuade the public rather than posture to one another.

Where we draw our battle lines in the incessant wars that beset the academy will also affect the sacrifices we incur. In *Public Access,* Michael Bérubé argues eloquently against the academic Left engaging in endless self-criticism as a means of fend-ing off the cultural Right: "Should we (properly) disavow inflammatory and wrong-headed people like Leonard Jeffries, for instance, the hard right will simply insist that we disavow another black scholar, and another, and then another, ad infinitum" (90). I agree with Bérubé that the assaults of the cultural Right will be relentless and often indiscriminate, but I think that is all the more reason not to draw our front line around salients (in military terms a "salient" is a strategic position that protrudes beyond a defensive perimeter—like the Ypres Salient on the Western Front). Jeffries's positions are intellectually, morally, and strategically indefensible, and they are strategically indefensible *because* they are intellectually and morally indefensible. While Bérubé seems to envision a "domino theory" of conflict and sacrifice, where we are forced to throw one black scholar after another to the wolves, I see the need for strategic and principled retreat. I would argue that on every issue we should attempt to draw our line in the sand at the precise position we will defend with our lives (or livelihoods). Naturally, the position of the line will differ for each individual; nevertheless, if more members of the profession could refrain from the impulse to rush out and defend what they themselves admit is indefensible, we could hunker down and give our attackers a real fight, defending the core of our beliefs not someone else's irresponsible extremes. I agree with Gregory Jay and Gerald Graff who argue that it is now time for the profession to engage in serious self-critique:

> Ironically, the dogmatism of the right made it less, not more, possible to isolate and criticize dogmatism on the left, for the entire left and much of the middle had been heaped together under the PC rubric. But the time has come when some serious efforts at left self-criticism have to be ventured, even if they give some aid and comfort to the enemy. The risk is necessary, for only such self-criticism can save the movement for the democratic transformation of the academy from being undermined by its own advocates. In the long run, this movement will benefit from such self-criticism, which will sharpen our thinking and enable us to answer our critics more persuasively. (201–202)

## IRENIC ADIAPHORISM; OR ALL WE ARE SAYING, IS GIVE PEACE A CHANCE

Members of the next generation, whether or not they feel free to complain, are shell shocked and war weary. Working like demons to stuff their cvs, trying to survive year after year of brutal job searches, keeping body and soul (not to mention relationships) together on a string of temporary appointments, these men and women understandably may want to decline the invitation to participate in yet one more war—Culture War, PC War, Theory War, Science War, whatever.

In the late seventeenth century, after decades of ferocious religious warfare had bled Europe dry, there arose for the sake of peace a general movement to relegate as many matters of faith as possible to the realm of things indifferent (the *adiaphora*). If minor beliefs were no longer invested with salvational power, no one would have to kill or die for them. It was not that irenic adiaphorists were calling for their fellow worshipers to become unprincipled; they simply wanted to stop fighting over whether or not they stood or knelt for communion, and whether or not the church glass was stained or plain. Swift's satire of religious war in Book IV of *Gulliver's Travels* typifies the irenic adiaphorist perspective, as Gulliver explains to his master Houyhnhnm:

> Difference in opinion hath cost many millions of lives: for instance, whether *flesh* be *bread* or *bread* be *flesh:* whether the juice of a certain *berry* be *blood* or *wine;* whether *whistling* be a vice or a virtue; whether it be better to *kiss a post,* or throw it into the fire; what is the best colour for a *coat,* whether *black, white, red,* or *grey;* and whether it should be *long* or *short, narrow* or *wide, dirty,* or *clean,* with many more. Neither are any wars so furious and bloody, or of so long continuance, as those occasioned by difference in opinion, especially if it be in things indifferent. [italics in the original] (234)

According to scores of political pundits, America itself may be entering an era of irenic adiaphorism. Commentators in the popular press are pointing to a significant lesson the recent elections have taught both political parties. Initially the '94 and '96 elections seemed to offer no coherent message. The public first rejected Clinton and his programs, thereby creating the Gingrich revolution, which it then repudiated in short order. Had the American people become wedded in rapid succession to each party's core ideological tenets, or was it being mindlessly whipsawed between two powerful personalities as some baffled experts originally posited? After the impeachment crisis and the surprise victory for the House democrats in the '98 elections, most political writers now feel that the electorate was not moving at all; it was instead expressing a consistent weariness with all "big ideologies." Average citizens, it is argued, had become deeply alienated from the warring extremes of right and left, their grand schemes, along with the general nastiness and governmental gridlock vehement partisanship inevitably produces. They wanted their politicians to grow up, to work together, to focus on small concrete solutions to the nation's problems. According to today's conventional wisdom, congressional Republicans committed a near fatal error when their fanatic devotion to Gingrich and "The Contract" shut down the government. Conversely, Clinton began his miraculous recovery when he declared in his 1995 State of the Union Address that "the era of big government is over," and when he began to focus on a series of small proposals that were at first ridiculed by professional political commentators as trivial, but that played very well with the voters.[13] This intensely anti-ideological stance, accompanied by the mantra to be allowed simply to do the work the American people elected him to do, carried Clinton through a year of scandal and impeachment with stunningly high poll numbers. Meanwhile, as a result of their response to these same events, the radical House Republicans lost their ideologue-in-chief, Gingrich, and watched helplessly, captive to beliefs the general public did not share, as their approval ratings plummeted.

I do not want to imply that I enthusiastically embrace everything I read on the subject of bipartisanship, especially calls for the eradication of ideology. Even as someone dedicated to political realism, I have never believed that ideology can or should be eliminated from politics. I am making two arguments. First, embracing irenic adiaphorism would not mean getting rid of ideology but narrowing its ground, making principled conflicts both important and rare. Secondly, no matter how I feel about the matter personally, there seems to be a growing irenic trend (dialectically generated) that is shaping our current political context. Sooner or later we will all be forced to contend with demands for peace.

To bring matters back to the profession, I have just been reading work in my field, the Renaissance, that indicates literary studies may also be moving into an era of wary toleration. Two recent books describe a critical scene where opposing views coexist in dynamic tension, which is not to be confused with consensus. In *What Was Shakespeare?: Renaissance Plays and Changing Critical Practice,* Edward Pechter takes a detached look at the fragmented state of today's Shakespeare criticism, which he then extends to literary studies in general. Pechter describes our contemporary state of affairs as one in which nearly everyone feels like an underdog, beset from all sides, and where, for all our fighting, no faction has been able to deliver a knockout punch. But he argues that a continuation of our current condition of "dissensus" is not necessarily harmful to our critical practice. If we can learn to live within this contested context without trying to force consensus, we may find it a singularly stimulating intellectual environment. Similarly, Rebecca Bushnell in her recent study of humanism, *A Culture of Teaching,* looks back to conflicts within early modern humanism that can shed light on current controversies about theory and pedagogy within the humanities. Her views about the history of humanism and her own theoretical stance are refreshingly free from the impulse to totalize:

> My primary theoretical category is "ambivalence," or contradiction set into motion—a fluctuation between opposites. This principle of ambivalence differs from a poststructuralist or Derridean textual indeterminacy in which the play of "différance" cancels out the value of opposed terms. Nor does it work like the Foucauldian paradox, in which one gesture or move is subsumed by its apparent opposite; that is, what appears to be a negative gesture is really a productive one. Rather, I read for *functional* ambivalence: to see one tendency of early modern humanist pedagogy always allowed for the realization of an opposite one, without undermining or effacing itself in turn. Implicit in my method is the belief, shared by many scholars, that "humanism" was never a coherent ideology, whether construed in the most general terms as a value system or in the narrower sense of an intellectual and pedagogical practice. (18–19)

Along with describing the status quo and its historic precedents, Bushnell and Pechter are, however tentatively, charting a new direction for our profession. By resisting both onesided dogmatism and those theories that obliterate conflict via collapsing all differences into deconstructed rubble, these scholars are limning a spacious and diverse critical context—not uncontested but tolerant.

It is too early to say for certain, but I believe the next generation may very well become active tolerationists—certainly, they have every reason not to squander their life's blood on meaningless internecine battles. For one thing, they will probably be too preoccupied repelling wave after wave of assault from forces outside the academy to battle one another. My final prediction is both hopeful and grim: for the foreseeable future (even after tenure), the next generation will be doing what it is doing now—standing together, supporting one another, and fighting very hard just to survive.

*Notes*

1. I am borrowing this term from Jeffrey Williams's chapter in this collection. Like most of us who are next generation scholars, Williams is acutely aware that the job market collapse affects every aspect of this generation's intellectual, professional, and personal life.

2. There are a number of astute analyses of our current job crisis and its consequences. Among them are the cluster of articles in the November–December 1995 issue of *Academe:* Cary Nelson's "Lessons from the Job Wars: What Is to Be Done?"; Michael Bérubé's "Standard Deviation: Skyrocketing Job Requirements Inflame Political Tensions"; and Stephen Watt's "The Human Cost of Graduate Education; or, The Need to Get Practical." While I did not agree with all of the specific proposals made by these authors, I was struck by their desire to turn their theoretical insights into actions—immediate, real-world, ethically informed actions. Cary Nelson and Michael Bérubé's impressive essay collection, *Higher Education under Fire,* attempts to understand the current crisis in the academy by looking at its material as well as ideological contexts: its essays aim simultaneously to "articulate the discourses of fiscal policy to the discourses of pedagogy, politics, and the production of knowledge" (5).

3. See especially Havel's chapter "The Politics of Hope" in *Disturbing the Peace,* and his *Open Letters.*

4. See Zinn 23–38.

5. The deleterious consequences of asserting that all representation is misrepresentation have spread beyond our ability to write effectively about history. They have come back to haunt us rather more directly. Reed Way Dasenbrock's essay in *PC Wars,* "We've Done It to Ourselves," points out the practical consequences of embracing contemporary theories of truth that derive from Nietzsche's classic assertion that "truths are illusions of which one has forgotten that they are illusions" (175). Dasenbrock states that because humanities scholars following Rorty or Foucault have continued the Nietzschean assault on truth, they have effectively disarmed themselves when facing right-wing lies about their conduct: "Our commitment to a critique of 'truth regimes' without a compensating substantive vision of truth outside those regimes has been a large part of what has disabled the academy in its response to the outside criticism it has received" (181).

6. See Zinn 124–46.

7. I am thinking, of course, of such reactionary classics as Allan Bloom's *The Closing of the American Mind: How Higher Education Has Failed Democracy and Impoverished the Souls of Today's Students* and Roger Kimball's *Tenured Radicals: How Politics Has Corrupted Our Higher Education*. That these two books became so prominent in the attack against current practices in the humanities has always puzzled me. Bloom's book is one of the most eccentric pieces of scholarship ever written. The only way to understand this opaque work is to study the hermetic philosophy of Leo Strauss, and then one sees just how "democratic" Bloom's ideas are. Without the Straussian key, the work is incomprehensible; with it, it is vile. Unlike Bloom's, Kimball's book is an easy read, but transparently partisan and superficial.

8. I am borrowing this concept from Frank Lentricchia's critique of Foucault, where he argues that "because he leaves no shaded zone, no free space for real alternatives to take form, Foucault's vision of power, despite its provisions for reversals of direction, courts a monolithic determinism" (70).

9. Elsewhere I have engaged in a lengthy theoretical critique of poststructuralist ideas about fact, truth, power, and political action. See my essay "Remodeling Truth, Power, and Society: Implications of Chaos Theory, Nonequilibrium Dynamics, and Systems Science for the Study of Politics and Literature," in *After Poststructuralism*.

10. I am afraid I may be found guilty, along with John Searle, of treating my opponent's ideas about science "only in caricature" (Bérubé, "Truth, Justice, and the American Way," 55). In an ideal world, all of us would be held accountable exclusively for the best and most thoughtful statements of our positions. However, as this world goes, we are more likely to be held accountable for all of them—the careless, the vulgar, the half-baked, and the ignorant right along with the reasoned, the knowledgeable, and the nuanced. The discourse we produce is oral and informal as well as written and formal, and it is more likely that individuals outside our field will be exposed to the former than the latter. Still, even among written and presumably refereed works by humanists on the subject of science, there is more than enough to make one wince.

Recently, when I entered the field of science and literary theory by writing on the implications of chaos and new paradigm systems theory in *After Poststructuralism,* I was saddened to find that the responses I got from many of my fellow humanists were genuinely absurd: pronouncements about scientific knowledge and scientific methods that vulgarized the theories of Kuhn, Heisenberg, and Einstein beyond recognition. Personally, I would recommend Paisley Livingston's *Literary Knowledge* as the best work on the issues raised by modern science for epistemology in the humanities. I would also like to recommend that humanists exercise humility and caution when speaking or writing about science. I've seen far too much foolishness on the subject, and, unfortunately for us, so have many scientists.

11. For example Robert Markley's article in *Genre,* "The Irrelevance of Reality: Science, Ideology and the Postmodern Universe," states that in the context of "radical critiques of science,"

> "Reality," finally, is a historical construct. We can thump our hands on tables and exclaim, "This is real!" just as we can thump our hands to our chests and assert, "I think, therefore I am." But these gestures are not indicative of any ultimate truths. (270)

A work that displays "epistemic relativism," nay nihilism, would be Arkady Plotnitsky's *Complementarity: Anti-Epistemology after Bohr and Derrida,* while Harvie Ferguson's *The Science of Pleasure* presents the history of scientific discovery almost exclusively as a socially constructed narrative.

For Sokal's description of his hoax see *Lingua Franca* May/June 1996; see also Scott's front page article in the *New York Times* of May 18, 1996, and the reply to the hoax, "Professor Sokal's Bad Joke" by Stanley Fish in the *New York Times* op-ed section May 21, 1996; see also Katha Pollitt's essay in *The Nation* for a bemused view of the scandal from what she describes as a non-pomo left perspective.

12. See Carol Gilligan's critique of Kohlberg and Kramer's "six stages of moral development." These psychologists devised a system to measure moral maturity in which the highest stages (four through six) were those where ethical decisions were grounded first on rules and then on universal principles. The higher stages were classified as developmentally superior to stage three, where ethical decisions were based on "helping others." When tested by Kohlberg and his associates, females were routinely labeled morally immature because they based their decisions on stage-three criteria. While much of the rest of Gilligan's work has come into question, her criticism of Kohlberg is still widely accepted.

13. For a discussion of the public's rejection of what he calls the political parties' "howling, tone-deaf partisanship" see Joe Klein's *New Yorker* article, "The Hug" (54). In addition, for an analysis of young voters' political preferences see Leland and McCormick's, "The Children of Gridlock." The authors argue that according to polling data and on-campus interviews, this generation of students is jettisoning what it perceives as the rigid positions and fruitless ideological battles of its parents: "Today's college students have been shaped not by war or Watergate, but by tales of infighting and stalemate" (33). See also *Newsweek's* "The Small Deal," which found a mandate in the '96 election results for small pragmatic solutions to America's problems "at a time when the purer ideologies of the left and right were out of public favor" (127). See Alan Wolfe's *Marginalized in the Middle* for an academic's look at warring intellectual factions. Wolfe calls for discursive practices that transcend ideological dualisms.

*Works Cited*

Bérubé, Michael, and Cary Nelson, eds. *Higher Education under Fire: Politics, Economics, and the Crises of the Humanities.* New York: Routledge, 1995.

Bérubé, Michael. *Public Access: Literary Theory and American Cultural Politics.* New York: Verso, 1994.

———. "Standard Deviation: Skyrocketing Job Requirements Inflame Political Tensions." *Academe* 81–6 (November–December, 1995): 26–29.

———. "Truth, Justice, and the American Way: A Response to John Wallach Scott." *PC Wars: Politics and Theory in the Academy.* Ed. Jeffrey Williams. New York: Routledge, 1995.

Bloom, Allan. *The Closing of the American Mind: How Higher Education Has Failed Democracy and Impoverished the Souls of Todays Students.* New York: Simon and Schuster, 1987.

Bushnell, Rebecca W. *A Culture of Teaching: Early Modern Humanism in Theory and Practice.* Ithaca: Cornell University Press, 1996.

Crowley, Sharon. "Reimagining the Writing Scene: Curmudgeonly Remarks about Contending with Words." *Contending with Words: Composition and Rhetoric in a Postmodern Age.* Ed. Patricia Harkin and John Schilb. New York: MLA, 1991, 189–97.

Dasenbrock, Reed Way. "We've Done It to Ourselves: The Critique of Truth and the Attack on Theory." *PC Wars: Politics and Theory in the Academy.* Ed. Jeffrey Williams. New York: Routledge, 1995, 172–83.

"Does America Still Work? On the Turbulent Energies of the New Capitalism." *Harpers* 292–1752 (May 1996): 35–47.

Ferguson, Harvie. *The Science of Pleasure: Cosmos and Psyche in the Bourgeois World View.* New York: Routledge, 1990.

Fish, Stanley. "Professor Sokal's Bad Joke." *New York Times* 21 May 1996: A 11.

Gilligan, Carol. *In a Different Voice: Psychological Theory and Women's Development.* Cambridge: Harvard University Press, 1982, 1993.

Gross, Paul R., and Norman Levitt, eds. *Higher Superstition: The Academic Left and Its Quarrels with Science.* Baltimore: Johns Hopkins University Press, 1994.

Havel, Václav. *Disturbing the Peace: A Conversation with Karel Hvizdala.* Trans. Paul Wilson. New York: Random House, 1990.

———. *Open Letters: Selected Writings, 1965–1990.* Ed. Paul Wilson. New York: Alfred A. Knopf, 1991.

Jay, Gregory, and Gerald Graff. "A Critique of Critical Pedagogy." *Higher Education under Fire: Politics, Economics, and the Crisis of the Humanities.* Ed. Michael Bérubé and Cary Nelson. New York: Routledge, 1995, 201–13.

Kimball, Roger. *Tenured Radicals: How Politics Has Corrupted Our Higher Education.* New York: Harper Collins, 1990.

Klein, Joe. "Letter from Washington: The Hug." *The New Yorker* 72, 39 (December 16, 1996): 52–57.

Leland, John, and John McCormick. "The Voters: The Children of Gridlock." *Newsweek* 127, 1 (July 1, 1996): 33.

Lentricchia, Frank. *Ariel and the Police: Michel Foucault, William James, Wallace Stevens.* Madison: University of Wisconsin Press, 1998.

Livingston, Paisley. *Literary Knowledge: Humanistic Inquiry and the Philosophy of Science.* Ithaca: Cornell University Press, 1988.

Markley, Robert. "The Irrelevance of Reality: Science, Ideology and the Postmodern Universe." *Genre* 25, 2–3 (Summer/Fall, 1992): 249–76.

Nelson, Cary. "Lessons from the Job Wars: What Is to Be Done?" *Academe* (November–December, 1995): 18–25.

Pechter, Edward. *What Was Shakespeare?: Renaissance Plays and Changing Critical Practice.* Ithaca: Cornell University Press, 1995.

Plotnitsky, Arkady. *Complementarity: Anti-Epistemology after Bohr and Derrida.* Durham: Duke University Press, 1994.

Pollitt, Katha. "Pomolotov Cocktail." *The Nation* 10 (June 1996): 9.

Riebling, Barbara. "Remodeling Truth, Power, and Society: Implications of Chaos Theory, Nonequilibrium Dynamics, and Systems Science for the Study of Politics and Literature." *After Poststructuralism: Interdisciplinarity and Literary Theory.* Ed. Nancy Easterlin and Barbara Riebling. Evanston, Ill.: Northwestern University Press, 1993. 177–201.

Ross, Andrew. "Science Wars, Introduction." *Social Text* 46–47 (Spring/Summer 1996): 1–13.

Said, Edward W. "Restoring Intellectual Coherence" President's Column *MLA Newsletter* 31, 1 (Spring 1999): 3–4.

Scott, Janny. "Postmodern Gravity Deconstructed, Slyly." *New York Times* 18 May 1996: Front Page.

"The Small Deal." *Newsweek* 128, 21 (November 18, 1996): 126–27.

Sokal, Alan D. "A Physicist Experiments with Cultural Studies." *Lingua Franca* 6–4 (May/June 1996): 62–64.

———. "Transgressing the Boundaries: Toward a Transformative Hermeneutics of Quantum Gravity." *Social Text* 46–47 (Spring/Summer 1996): 217–52.

Swift, Jonathan. *Gulliver's Travels and Other Writings by Jonathan Swift.* Ed. Miriam Kosh Starkman. New York: Bantam Books, 1962.

Watt, Stephen. "The Human Cost of Graduate Education; or, The Need to Get Practical." *Academe* (November–December 1995): 30–35.

Wolfe, Alan. *Marginalized in the Middle.* Chicago: University of Chicago Press, 1996.

Zinn, Howard. *A People's History of the United States.* New York: HarperCollins, 1980.

# ELEVEN

# AFTER THE DELUGE: RETHINKING ETHICAL INTERPRETIVE CLAIMS

*Susan Johnston*

## THE BOAT MENDERS

While there have been some recent moves toward recovering agency in literary stud-ies (e.g., Booth, Nussbaum, Taylor, Buell), nonetheless, as Lawrence Buell himself points out in the *PMLA* special topic on "Ethics and Literary Study" (January 1999), "[n]o major ethical philosopher from Aristotle to John Rawls has attracted anywhere near the attention among those currently linking literature and ethics that Derrida and Foucault have attracted (neither of them ethicists in any strict sense), with the ex-ception of Levinas, who might rather be called a metaethical thinker than an ethicist proper."[1] He might have added that neither Derrida nor Foucault can properly be called an ethicist in any loose sense, either: the first, even in such late works as *The Gift of Death,* retains that sense of the other as wholly other which, with Levinas's notions of the priority of the other, enables Derek Attridge's paternalistic conception of the other as a sort of Frankenstein's Monster, the virtual person/text, created in its sin-gularity and individuality by its relation to me, and for which (but not to which) I have a responsibility;[2] the second turned at the last to an assertion of the importance of selfhood which, while countering to some degree the radical constructivism of his earlier work, was instantiated primarily in a defense of solipsism, that is, of a so-called ethics of pleasure.

Not all of the critics Buell collects fall prey to this methodological difficulty of using Derrida to do something I suspect he cannot do. David P. Haney, for example, while relying on Levinas in his argument that ethical interpretive relationships become possible only if the other—conceived of as person or text—resists conceptualization (40), begins with Aristotle and ends, ultimately, with Gadamer's view that the work of art, like the person, is "a unity of means and ends" (43).[3] James M. Albrecht is re-freshing partly because he avoids poststructuralist breast-beating about the engage-ment of both author and work with concepts of liberalism.[4] These essays are in marked contrast to Bradley Butterfield's curious attempt to recuperate Baudrillard and the idea of world as simulacra for ethical inquiry, contending that "[o]pposing the will of theory to categorize the ethical and anesthetize the aesthetic, Baudrillard's negative theory, or what Carroll calls paraesthetics, aims to displace and transform both and to enact the very aporias that are the wellspring of an extramoral sense—that is, of an ethics originating in a space with no closure"[5]—an argument that, once having removed "ethics" from the domain of the moral life, does not go on to tell us what such an extramoral ethics might be.

Finally, then, while I welcome Buell's host of critics engaged in "ethically valenced inquiry" as boat menders and dike builders, eager at last to defend the academy and the literary critical project from the flood I sought to name in this chapter's original incarnation, I cannot share his sense of the efficacy of their tools. Having dismissed, not simply carpentry but the very possibility of wood and water, Derrida and Foucault cannot be used to patch the boat. Yet the first of these at least is everywhere in Buell's special issue. And Derrida remains a "shaping presence" in much literary criticism.

## AFTER THE DELUGE

> The sophists are once again among us. Like Socrates, we need a "true rhetoric." That is, we need a form of discourse about literature that concerns itself with real things of serious human importance and that reveres, in so doing, the recently despised notions of truth, objectivity, even of validity in argument, clarity in definition. For if we are talking about real things, it does matter, and matter deeply, whether we say this or that, since human life, much though we may regret the fact, is not simply a matter of free play and unconstrained making.[6]

I want to begin with a story. This is a story about a graduate student who gave a paper at a conference, and it takes place at a time when the idea that there might be professional skills as well as interpretive ones was still a very new one. A great many good people had decided that if the graduate students wanted professional savoir faire, they would do everything in their not inconsiderable power to further that end. And one of the things they did, but not the only thing, was to hold a special session, which, in the interests of fair play, featured both a graduate student and a professor.

When the day came, our graduate student (who is not the hero but only a vehicle for plot development; this is a modern story and thus wholly without heroes), who had set up a small professional development program herself, gave a paper on how graduate students could coordinate similar programs: where to get funding, where to get speakers, how to advertise, what books to use. Actually, it was less a conference paper than a do-it-yourself manual. But before she spoke, the professor gave his paper.

This paper was carefully considered and carefully theorized, taking on a new and important issue. The professor, schooled in the sixties, argued that the move to professionalization was part of the commodification of the discipline and of the next generation of scholars. Such commodification, he said, robbed the oppositional culture of the next generation of much of its potential to change society by absorbing young scholars into existing practices and structures.[7] Now, this professor was both convincing and probably right. But one problem remained. Without such professionalization, my generation of scholars may remain unabsorbed, but only because we will also remain unemployed.

The question before us is What Next? The question I am asking is What can happen next, if, in the interests of emancipation, power remains in the same hands that now hold it? What can succeed the deluge of scholarship which has heightened the contradictions only to find, as Adorno did in circumstances far more horrific than those which now prevail, that "[t]here is no way out of entanglement"?[8] We late and postbabyboomers have inherited a kind of philosophy of despair, a radically nihilistic sense of resignation that goes by the name of postmodernism; it is the condition and the implications of that resignation that I want to address in this chapter.

As "theoretically" trained and competent scholars, we have inherited a sea of accounts which argue, to varying degrees, the relativist notion that truth is dead. The strong form of this idea argues that, since nothing can be known independently of the knower, there can be no a-priori truths. Because they assume that all truth claims must pertain to these nonexistent and universal verities, postmodernists have gone on to argue that all so-called truth claims are merely standpoints with pretensions to transcendence. Any attempt to argue for the truth of a particular standpoint is both interested and partial, excluding other, equally valid standpoints to ends which profit a particular social group. This view sees interpretive realism as both formally and figuratively coercive, inimical to the project of "decentering the world." It is a dismissal of epistemic criteria that involves a dismissal of moral and ethical claims as likewise embedded, so that those interpretations which go one step further and treat the literary artifact, and the literary critical project, as attempts to answer the question of "How one should live"[9] are particularly heinous, since they are elaborate attempts to gull the global population, through a language of universalizing concepts, into compliance with the interests of a dominant group. On this account, as Jane Flax says, power and power alone is seen as determining the outcome of competing truth claims,[10] and any substantive ethical content must be seen as reflecting and reifying the experiences of one group at the expense of another. Thus it is that, in the interests of emancipation, those thinkers who take their own ends to be ethical and moral and engage in literary practice as a means to these ends are seen as engaged in practices that are invidious, interested, coercive, and deeply oppressive.

While not all postmodernists argue so strong a position, it is fair to say that these assumptions have become the orthodoxy of our discipline. While Flax recognizes that the reduction of all claims to know to competing regimes of power is "a frightening prospect to those who lack (or are oppressed by) the power of others" (42), she is unable to proffer an alternative. Arguing against the standpoint of feminist epistemology advanced by Sandra Harding, among others,[11] Flax nevertheless takes refuge in an appeal to partiality, difference, and a hermeneutics of suspicion, such that "our lives and alliances belong with those who seek to further decenter the world—although we should reserve the right to be suspicious of their motives and versions as well" (56). It is difficult to see an account that privileges opposition or "decentering" claims as a departure from either the perspectivism of standpoint epistemologies or

the conflation of reason and force. Like the tenured academic disturbed by the implications of professional development programs, Flax cannot imagine a critical reflexivity that would undertake to interrogate its own embeddedness.

   Linda Nicholson's attempt to address the liberal contention that postmodernism "allows no distinction between reason and power" is equally unsatisfactory.
She argues that

> [w]e can admit of the postmodern claim that conceptual distinctions, criteria of
> legitimation, cognitive procedural rules, and so forth are all political and there-
> fore represent moves of power and also recognize that they represent a different
> type of power than is exhibited in, for example, physical violence or the threat of
> force. A postmodern feminism could thus both support certain procedural as-
> pects of natural science or other reflexive criteria of validity claims, that is "deci-
> sion procedures to guide choices in theory, research, and politics," while also ac-
> knowledging such support as political and grounded in a particular cultural
> context.[12]

Nicholson's analysis in no way redeems competing claims and beliefs from adjudication by power and power alone; it merely argues what should have been clear for some
time, that there is a distinction between physical and ideological coercion. Nor does
her offer to support certain procedures of adjudication alleviate the situation, since
her notion of criteria of validity (legitimation) is based on an understanding of such
criteria as ideological power moves. Thus, on Nicholson's account, we can accept procedural epistemic criteria in order to expedite our ends. Her claim is not even that our
ends justify our means,[13] but that those ends are incommensurable and equally im-
mune to evaluation.

   Part of the difficulty here lies in the fact that postmodernism has fallen victim
to an endemic conflation of all claims to know. The result has been a misrepresentation of what we do. Surely there can be getting it right and getting it wrong in this
field? We do, after all, as teachers routinely castigate the student who attributes dialogue spoken by Milton's Satan to his G-d, or to one of the angels, or who describes
the fairy tale as a genre originating with Walt Disney. Nor are such examples unimportant. At the very heart of both critical and pedagogical practice lies what Frederick C. DeCoste has described as "a modest belief in the possibility of truth."[14] On
DeCoste's account, this modest belief entails neither a commitment to transcendent
verities, nor a grounding in Archimedean epistemology; rather, "[i]t demands only a
belief in the possibility of adjudication, namely, that it is possible to assess proposi-
tions in terms of reason and evidence" (359). This is to say that, as Annette Barnes
and P. D. Juhl have argued, *we judge,*[15] and such judgments are the condition of our
critical practice, not merely a promulgation of the lies of power.

   Literary criticism is conducted on the assumption that the facts of the matter
are knowable, in principle at least. But the judgment and evaluation necessary for such
knowledge are also the ground of critique, and it is here that I suggest postmodernism

has cut off its nose to spite its face, and that we, its inheritors, are in a position to repair the sphinx. For emancipatory theory, if it is emancipatory, is not relativist but normative. That is to say that it is evaluative in that it proposes criticism of existing society, and it is prescriptive in that it is rooted in a vision of the good society and to that end seeks to determine the ideals and principles that should inform social organization.[16] This is so no matter how inarticulate, pretheoretical, or deeply contested a particular emancipatory stance may be; at minimum, it claims that the way social relations are presently organized is wrong. Indeed, it is not too strong to say that the notion of a nonevaluative emancipatory theory is conceptually incoherent. But to describe the so-called emancipatory project of postmodernism as oxymoronic does not fully capture the implications of such philosophy for our academic practice. If at the heart of critical practice, which I define as the process of critical inquiry and contest,[17] is a belief in reasons and evidence, then at the heart of postmodernism is the rejection of knowledge in these senses (DeCoste 366). Absent reason and evidence, the reasoned adjudication of competing claims is impossible. I am arguing that this is the real lie of power. "For if," as DeCoste points out, "an institution or a society is uncommitted to truth, it must inevitably become committed to power and to all that power finally entails" (390).

The postmodernists argue that, in the absence of a-priori truth, all so-called truths are merely conventions. By this they apparently mean "arbitrary" and historically contingent.[18] Conventions, however, are not only or merely arbitrary, and this is crucial to their role in society. Jon Elster defines conventions as a type of social norms, "noninstrumental rules of behavior maintained by internalized emotions and by the sanctions that others impose on violators"; they are also, he says, a particular type of equilibria, such that when all follow the convention, nobody wants to deviate, and when all follow the convention, nobody wants anyone else to deviate either.[19] Traffic regulations are an only apparently trivial example, since failure to adhere to these "mere conventions" is a major cause of human injury and death in North America. Moreover, while traffic laws are eminently conventional, in the poststructuralist and postmodernist sense of arbitrary and contingent as well as Elster's sense of the term, the example of food and its recognition is less limited. We routinely accept as true in a nonconventional sense[20] what prior authority has determined to be food: failure to do so, as in the case of certain berries and mushrooms, can be fatal, and while their toxicity is unrelated to any social compact, recognition of that quality is made possible by public conventions, specifically, by what constitutes an authoritative standard.

This is not to claim that norms are uninvolved in ideology. "Norms" are rules or authoritative standards of behavior, public and conventional as well as internalized, which enable cooperative and communicative action. As such, they are necessarily part of ideology, but are not necessarily ideological in the limited sense I am using that term. I understand *ideology* in the Marxian sense of false consciousness serving dominant interests through the rationalization of the arrangements from which they draw their privileges. The locus of ideology, in this reading, is in beliefs of political import about social institutions. At its zenith, ideology provides the confidence in a social arrangement that is necessary to make the system work, which is to say that it is so-cially directive, even causal. It is, at the same time, "false" consciousness because it mistakes contingent historical facts for permanent and immutable ones, naturalizing the facts of the matter as a-priori truths.[21] Ideological consciousness is false, too, in the sense that it is distortive in failing to ask important questions, so that the Ameri-can founders can declare "[w]e hold these truths to be self-evident, that all men are created equal" while actively practicing institutionalized slavery. The idea of truth to which this notion of falsity is opposed properly belongs to a coherence model, in which a statement is a member of a system whose elements are related to each other by ties of logical implication, so that truth or falsity consists in whether a statement or judgment coheres or fails to cohere with a system of other statements.[22] Thus, that the statement "all men are created equal" cannot cohere with the legality of slavery is evidence of its falsity. At best, "all men are created equal" is partly true, and its dis-tortive effect consists in this inadequacy.

The falsity of ideological consciousness, in this account, further rests in its role of rationalizing an unjust social arrangement. Here the notion of falsity is counter-posed to an idea of truth as an ideal moral order, to which state false consciousness prevents us from ascending. Truth in this sense is ethical and moral, an "ought" rela-tion rather than an "is" relation, and is closest to the account of truth postmodernism would dismiss out of hand.

It would be counterproductive to argue that the view of norms, interpretive or otherwise, as "ideological apparatus" is merely a bogeyman invented by Althusser, Ly-otard and those who have followed them. Nor is that my intent. I confess to belief in both ideological apparatuses and cooptation, and the advantage of the previous gen-erations of emancipatory theory has indeed been their attentiveness to such phe-nomena. But, as Mette Hjort has remarked in a different context, in such theory as it now stands, the foregrounding of "the warlike or strategic dimensions of human be-haviour [occurs] at the expense of all cooperative or communicative forms of interac-tion" (xii–xiii). I want to argue that literary interpretation that is explicit in its appeal to shared ethical and moral bonds—that is, interpretation now frequently dismissed as unsophisticated at best and, at its worst, arbitrary and deeply oppressive—cannot simply be understood as an attempt to reproduce hegemonic interests. I am claiming that even as literary critical practice that is used to make ethical and moral claims can be used to further distasteful and disciplinary ends, to accuse all such claims simply of ideological production is to abrogate any emancipatory dimension such practice may contain. After all, Anna Brownell Jameson's adoption of the vocabulary of do-mestic femininity in *Shakespeare's Heroines* cannot be said to recapitulate "the falsely universalizing perspective of the dominant group," as Flax might have it (Flax 49). Rather, her ethical interpretation of Shakespeare is the vehicle of Jameson's claim that the condition of women in 1832 is "false in itself, and injurious to them."[23] This is not unimportant. Insofar as interpretation is the effort to understand humanity's rep-resentations of itself, the normative dimension of interpretation, which is concerned with morality and ethics, may be indispensible—and this inevitability may be other than tragic.

Indeed, it may be that the real tragedy lies in the prevalent notion that interpretive practice is or ought to be outside the domain of the moral and ethical. One such potentially tragic formulation is Stanley Fish's claim that theory is "a form of thinking with its own goals and rules, and therefore that theories should be evaluated in terms of the coherence of their claims."[24] According to his account, what is at stake in theory is not meaning but theory itself, which is no longer criticism, nor even meta-criticism, but its own enterprise, wholly without referents and thus wholly independent. His theory is initially attractive for my purposes since it retains, albeit in a very limited sense, the idea of the public and conventional aspects of the interpretive act—that is, the ways in which it is a type of cooperative and communicative social interaction. What is missing is a reasonable explanation of how these separate communities coexist. He says that members of different interpretive communities will disagree, but that these disagreements "can be debated in a principled way: not because of a stability in texts, but because of a stability in the makeup of interpretive communities and therefore in the opposing positions they make possible" (15). How these interpretive communities, despite all their other differences, can nevertheless remain stable enough in their makeup to maintain principled debate remains unclear. Fish apparently assumes that interpretive communities will adhere to the rules of politesse and reason that he believes govern the academy, and in this assumption he is not only ignoring the vituperative debates that have become commonplace in theoretical politics of late, but ignores the way in which, by his own model, the rules of politesse will hold only if a minimum level of agreement has already been reached. The very notion of interpretive communities, each with its own standards of right and wrong and each with its own means of evaluating its own members, obviates the possibility of agreement among communities.

For Fish and others of his school, progressive politics may be a useful theoretical tool, but since the only available standards, according to his account, are local, confining, and contingent, no evaluation and no progression is ultimately possible. Fish's repudiation of extreme relativism, which rests on the internal coherence of theoretical claims, is only another maneuver in the game of theory. If, as Nicholson, Flax, Fish, and others would have it, the only available criteria are local, confining, and contingent, and our entanglement precludes even the search for evaluative criteria, then must we resort to a view of interpretive practice as "only a game" or even a "power game" in which Might, understood as an important publishing contract, makes right?[25]

If such is the case, and theory is only a game, I finally prefer Gadamer's account of play: movement without a goal which brings it to an end, movement which renews itself in repetition.[26] For Gadamer, the movement backward and forward is so central to the definition of a game that it is not important who or what performs this movement; it is the game which is played. "Play" is the performance of the movement as such (93). And games can differ from each other, because the to-and-fro movement that constitutes the game is differently arranged. He says: "The particular nature of a game lies in the rules and structures which prescribe the way that the area of the game is filled. This is true universally" (96). But for Gadamer, what is at stake in the game is not merely the Stanley Cup, not merely the incommensurable ends of postmodernism. He argues that the self-representation of human play depends on behavior tied to the make-believe goals of the game, but that the "meaning" of the game does not depend on achieving these goals. In spending oneself on the task of the game, one is playing oneself out, so that the idea of play as a kind of cultural self-representation depends on the player achieving his own self-representation in playing himself out, as well as the spectator's recognition of that representation (104). Recognition here assumes a species of assent. Gadamer goes on to point out that "[o]nly because play is always representation is human play able to find the task of the game in representation itself" (97).

It is Gadamer's claim that what is at stake in the game is not merely the game nor the contest of power but cultural self-representation. And if this isn't so, if Gadamer is wrong, how do we account for the passion surrounding the Blue Jays after they pocketed their second World Series? How do we understand the hostility of Montrealers as Philadelphia was declared the 1994 champions after the suspension of the season, despite their fourth-place ranking? Can the notion of false consciousness, of ideological apparatus, really provide the only reading of such phenomena? Or is there more at stake, indeed, in the game than the game itself?

If Gadamer's account is correct, and if we can use his notion of game to escape the cul de sac of postmodernism's competing regimes of power, then there is something more at stake here than simply the inscription of one discourse of legitimation among many. Rather, since literary theory is a kind of game and the task of the game is representational, then the hermeneutical task can be evaluated on the basis of its proximity to our own intuitions about our own lives. Nor does this require that we revert to a notion of interpretation as a purely subjective activity, confined to an individual standpoint. Since we become human selves in a community and it is these community-based selves we represent in our play, the public and conventional dimension of representation must be retained. This, I think, accords to some degree with the postmodernist intuition that we are entangled in our historical moment, which is an economic and political one, but because Gadamer assumes the possibility of critical role distance, this account does not see us as simply reinscribing that moment. Moreover, for Gadamer and other hermeneuticists,[27] membership in a community does not preclude communication, cooperation, and agreement across community borders, so that the public and conventional dimension of the act of communication means that interpretive practice is not independent of moral and ethical considerations.

Gadamer argues that

> [w]hat appears with the unconditionality of a moral law cannot be based on a
> feeling, not even if one does not mean an individual feeling, but the common-

ness of moral experience. For the character of a moral law totally excludes any comparative reflection about others. The unconditionality of a moral law certainly does not mean that the moral consciousness must remain rigid in judging others. Rather it is a moral command to detach oneself from the subjective private conditions of one's own judgement and to shift one's ground to the standpoint of the other person. But this unconditionality also means that the moral consciousness cannot avoid reference to the judgement of others. (31–32)

For Gadamer, it is through good taste—which historically has been part of the province of the literary critic—that we can stand back from ourselves and our private preferences (34). Taste, then, is not a private phenomenon but a social one of the first order; it is a mode of knowing which is social (public and conventional) (34) rather than either objective or subjective. Moreover, in my reading of Gadamer's treatment of taste, the province of literary inquiry is not only aesthetic but is closely involved with moral and ethical considerations as well. This is so because it is concerned with the problem of understanding humanity's representation of itself, and that representation must always be concerned at some level with our orientations toward our goods.

Gadamer goes on to describe the workings of taste in terms that closely recall ethical philosophy. For him, we make judgments of taste on those occasions when we try to understand something in its concrete individuality (situations in which we must act, for example, demand this of us); therefore, according to Gadamer, these judgments are always about a special case. This means that in every situation that calls for evaluation, the universal principles which form the basis of that evaluation are amended and supplemented in the evaluative act. The case and the principle are thus codetermining (37). Moral decisions therefore require taste, even though, as Gadamer says, we usually fail to recognize the ideal normative element in the concept of taste and are still affected by the relativistic-sceptical argument about differences in taste (37–38).

There is not room in this chapter to unpack Gadamer's position in full detail. I will remark, however, that the advantage of his position is that it avoids the kind of hermeneutics of suspicion which has come to mark literary inquiry in the past two decades, a mode of interpretation that takes any and all normative interpretive claims as attempts to rationalize the arrangements from which dominant groups derive their power and is prepared to suspend inquiry at that point. My claim is that this suspension not only misrepresents the fundamentally human practice of seeking ethical and moral standards through which cooperative action can be rendered more just, but that it is a self-deceiving, if not a disingenuous suspension. For many postmodernist critics have condemned ethical-moral prescriptive claims in interpretation and in literature precisely in the service of their own ethical-moral ends, and in so doing, they have taken refuge in a house of straw.

To say that literary criticism is not or ought not to be interested is to say that literature is uninvolved with politics. Some of the postmodernists whose work has changed my discipline have made precisely such claims, and some have made these claims in the service, covert or overt, of political goals. It is my conviction that to do so is to take refuge, as Robert Holub says, in "a self-cancelling mechanism of ironic one-up-manship and a spiral of infinitely negative speculation."[28] It is to abandon the belief that what we do is involved in the world.

I am not ready for such abandonment. I believe that as critics we routinely practice normative interpretation to political ends and that the claim that we do not is at best self-deceptive. Feminist and other emancipatory criticisms in particular abandon such literary practice at the risk of both incoherence and irrelevance. But I do not think that normative interpretation will always be practiced to emancipatory and progressive ends, and indeed I am making no such claim. I merely argue that we late and post-babyboomers are no less concerned with emancipation than the tenured radicals who have despaired of it, and that, while we may have inherited a philosophy of despair we need not and ought not retain it.

We have posed the question What next? In response I am claiming for interpreters and readers of interpretation the obligation to consider our means as well as our ends. I have been told that it is imperialistic to extend rights to the other, that to demand attention for famine assumes a transparent notion of reality, that the professionalization of graduate students damages the profession by evitiating potential subversion; I have been told these things in the lip service of freedom by those whose colleagues I hope to become, and I am not making them up. Such reasoning would deny women the vote, describe famine as differently resourced, and leave power in the same hands that now hold it. A belief that evaluation is impossible, that epistemology is bankrupt, and that the self is merely positionality cannot succeed in changing the present world orders. My generation of theoretically aware scholars is no less concerned with the possibility of emancipation than those whose academy we are about to inherit, but we cannot achieve such ends so long as we adhere to a philosophy of depair. I believe that as human selves we are always involved in normative claims and, thus, that we require a theoretical model that does not dismiss or indict such claims, which are in fact the sine qua non of both emancipatory theory and ethical criticism. Without such a model we will indeed be irrelevant.

*Notes*

This chapter was first presented as a paper in a special session entitled "What's Next? The Next Generation of Critics," Modern Language Association Convention, December 27, 1994. It subsequently appeared in *Symplokē* 3.1 (1995): 87–100. In both incarnations, as in this one, it would not have seen the light of day but for the encouragement and commitment of Peter C. Herman. The investigations that provoked this paper were undertaken through the support of a Social Sciences and Humanities Research Council of Canada Doctoral Fellowship. The paper itself was first completed during my tenure as a Principal's Dissertation Fellow at McGill University. I am indebted to both these organizations for their support. I am likewise indebted to conversations with Peter C. Herman, Michael D. Bristol, Marcel DeCoste, Mette Hjort, and Frederick C. DeCoste on this and related issues, without which this paper could not have been written.

1. "Introduction. In Pursuit of Ethics," *PMLA* 114 (1999): 7–19, p. 11.

2. See "Innovation, Literature, Ethics: Relating to the Other," *PMLA* 114 (1999): 20–31.

3. "Aesthetics and Ethics in Gadamer, Levinas, and Romanticism: Problems of Phronesis and Techne," *PMLA* 114 (1999): 32–45.

4. "Saying Yes and Saying No: Individualist Ethics in Ellison, Burke, and Emerson," *PMLA* 114 (1999): 46–63.

5. "Ethical Value and Negative Aesthetics: Reconsidering the Baudrillard-Ballard Connection," *PMLA* 114 (1999): 64–77, p. 75.

6. Martha C. Nussbaum, "Sophistry about Conventions," *Love's Knowledge: Essays on Philosophy and Literature* (New York and Oxford: Oxford University Press, 1990), 220–29, p. 220. This essay first appeared in *New Literary History* 17 (1985): 129–39, with the Stanley Fish paper to which it responds.

7. Donald C. Goellnicht, "From Novitiate Culture to Market Economy: The Professionalization of Graduate Students." 29 May 1992, ACCUTE Conference, Charlottetown. Published in *English Studies in Canada* 19, 14 (1993), 471–484. See especially p. 480.

8. *Minima Moralia: Reflections from a Damaged Life* (1951), E. F. N. Jephcott, trans. (London: Verso, 1974), pp. 27–28.

9. I adopt this formulation from Nussbaum, who takes Plato's remark that "[i]t is no chance matter we are discussing, but how one should live" (*Republic*) as the starting point for her thesis in *Love's Knowledge* that "certain literary texts . . . are indispensable to a philosophical inquiry in the ethical sphere." See "Introduction: Form and Content, Philosophy and Literature," 3–53 in *Love's Knowledge,* especially p. 23.

10. Jane Flax, "Postmodernism and Gender Relations in Feminist Theory." *Feminism/Postmodernism,* ed. Linda Nicholson. Thinking Gender (New York: Routledge, 1990), 39–62; p. 42.

11. Sandra Harding, "The Instability of the Analytical Categories of Feminist Theory," *Feminist Theory in Practice and Process,* ed. Micheline R. Malson, Jean F. O'Barr, Sarah Westphal-Wihl, and Mary Wyer (Chicago: University of Chicago Press, 1989), 15–34.

12. Linda Nicholson, "Introduction," *Feminism/Postmodernism,* ed. Linda Nicholson. Thinking Gender Ser. (New York: Routledge, 1990), 1–16, 11.

13. I use this phrase in full cognizance of its distasteful connotations. My own view, which must wait on another occasion for fuller development, is that our means do finally form our ends, and thus that we must take care what those means shall be.

14. "The Academic and the Political: A Review of *Freedom and Tenure in the Academy,*" *Review of Constitutional Studies/Revue d'études constitutionelles* 1, 2 (1994), 356–90, p. 359.

15. For valuable accounts of interpretive realism, see Annette Barnes, *On Interpretation: A Critical Analysis* (Oxford: Basil Blackwell, 1988); P. D. Juhl, *Interpretation: An Essay in the Philosophy of Literary Criticism* (Princeton: Princeton University Press, 1980); and E. D. Hirsch, *Validity in Interpretation* (New Haven: Yale University Press, 1967).

16. This formulation is adapted from Allison Jaggar's discussion of the goals of political philosophy in *Feminist Politics and Human Nature* (Brighton: Harvester, 1983), p. 15.

17. I am here following Frederick C. DeCoste's articulation of the university as the site of such practice. See especially p. 366.

18. Mette Hjort, "Introduction," *Rules and Conventions: Literature, Philosophy, Social The-*

*ory,* ed. Mette Hjort (Baltimore and London: Johns Hopkins University Press, 1992, ix–xxiii, p. x.

19. Jon Elster, "Conventions, Creativity, Originality," in *Rules and Conventions: Philosophy, Literature, Social Theory,* 32–44, see pp. 32–33. Elster is speaking specifically of artistic conventions, and argues that both views—convention as social norm and convention as equilibria—are accurate in describing part of conventional behavior.

20. Truth here would refer to the facts of the matter on the correspondence theory. I am indebted for this example to Michael D. Bristol, who tells the story of shipwrecked Middle Eastern refugees on the coast of Newfoundland being fed peanut-butter-and-jelly sandwiches by the villagers. In such a case, the refugees must rely on conventions—of hospitality, of good will, and of local authority—in accepting as true that the sandwiches are food.

21. This is not to claim that in the absence of a-priori truths, there can be no facts of the matter; this notion of ideology simply counterposes the one to the absent other.

22. For a fuller but brief and refreshingly lucid explanation of the coherence theory of truth, see Alan R. White, "Coherence Theory of Truth," *The Encyclopedia of Philosophy,* Paul Edwards, ed. New York: Macmillan and Free Press; London: Collier Macmillan, 1967, rpt. 1972.

23. Anna Brownell Jameson. *Shakespeare's Heroines: The Characteristics of Women, Moral, Poetical, Historical* (1832). Rpt. from the 2d, rev. ed. of 1889 (New York: AMS Press, 1971), 13–14.

24. Stanley Fish, *Is There a Text in This Class? The Authority of Interpretive Communities* (Cambridge, Mass., and London: Harvard University Press, 1980), p. 68. I am adopting the version Fish advances in *Is There a Text in This Class?* because it is the most well known. Although Fish makes some attempt in *Doing What Comes Naturally: Change, Rhetoric, and the Practice of Theory in Literary and Legal Studies* (Durham: Duke University Press, 1989) to defend adjudication procedures, he does not repudiate his notion of any and all standards as local and contingent, and insists that it is power—rhetorical rather than physical, although it is institutional as well—which finally resolves contests. See especially "Introduction: The Anti-Formalist Road," 1–33, and "Fish vs. Fiss," 120–40.

25. It is worth noting here that Fish is explicit about this dimension of his argument for institutional authority. See "Fish vs. Fiss" for a discussion of the significance of tenure, salary, and publishing power as determinants of authority, esp. p. 136.

26. Hans-Georg Gadamer, *Truth and Method* (New York: Seabury, 1975), p. 96.

27. See, for example, Seyla Benhabib, *Situating the Self: Gender, Community and Postmodernism in Contemporary Ethics* (New York: Routledge, 1992), and Charles Taylor, *Multiculturalism and "The Problem of Recognition,"* ed. Amy Gutmann (Princeton: Princeton University Press, 1992).

28. Holub goes on to point out that "[w]hat is perhaps more disturbing than this Sisyphean state of affairs, however, is the rather dubious political valence of this radicalness. [Fish and others] make gestures in the direction of progressive politics, but it is difficult to determine whether this gesture is the sign of greeting or of a hasty departure." Robert C. Holub, "American Confrontations with Reception Theory," *Monatscheft* 81, 2 (1989): 213–25, p. 223.

TWELVE

# A CONVERSATION WITH GERALD GRAFF

## Peter C. Herman

PETER C. HERMAN (PCH): I'd like to begin by asking your view on the existence of the next generation. Given that most of the theories presently dominating the profession have their roots in the '60s, what do you see arising from critics who came later?

GERALD GRAFF (GG): Perhaps one way in which what you call the "next generation" could stake out a project that would be very different from that of its elders would be by paying attention not just to whatever defines the cutting edge in scholarship, criticism, and theory, but also to how well such work is understood and assimilated by undergraduates and other nonprofessionals. To put it baldly, what difference will it make if tomorrow's paradigm setters establish some really original new ground if the questions they raise remain as nebulous to 99 percent of American students and other citizens as today's new (or for that matter old) academic work?

One would think such a question would have surfaced more prominently by now in a profession that claims in theory to be dedicated to educating everyone, not just a minority. In my experience, however, few either inside or outside the university, including few who call themselves progressives, really believe that more than a small percentage of the student or adult population is capable of profiting from or becoming interested in academic-intellectual concerns. I think this assumption is becoming anachronistic in an information economy in which humanistic skills of argumentation, analysis, and critical thinking are increasingly recognized to be a crucial form of cultural capital. Here, then, it seems to me, is a big potential opportunity for the next generation, to identify itself with the realization of democratic mass education, in the sense not only of democratic access to a college degree but real access to intellectual culture, which despite all our talk of "empowering" students still remains a minority culture.

To be sure, the academic reward system has notoriously discouraged us from taking education seriously in the way I suggest. But the reward system has always proved capable of being modified and stretched in order to accomodate vanguard trends, so blaming the reward system for our failure to take our educational mission seriously seems an excuse. Historically the academic profession has been very good at telling itself why it can't change, and it will be too bad if the next generation continues such rationalizing.

PCH: The previous generations made much of their impact through theoretical interventions, such as the new criticism, deconstruction, and new historicism. What do you see emenating from the next generation?

GG: Again, I'm proposing that taking education seriously rather than making theoretical breakthroughs is one way the NG can make a name for itself, though this in itself would constitute a theoretical breakthrough. Are your doubts about whether the NG will go in this direction or about whether it ought to? Whatever the case, there are a few signs that it may already be heading that way: a new journal called *Pedagogy* has been established that figures to do a lot to make teaching/learning/curriculum respectable as a research field (and thereby overcome the research/teaching gap), and it would appear to be led by next generation people.

PCH: Clearly, some of the next generation think so. David Galef, in his chapter in this volume, also argues that writing and creative writing programs are the wave of the future. In a sense, both you and he suggest that what theory was to previous generations of critics, teaching will be to us.

GG: I'm encouraged to hear that there are other flakes out there who share my hunch that teaching (and the teaching of writing) may be the emergent paradigm, though the teaching of exposition is far more crucial to me than the teaching of creative writing. I have doubts that "Expressivist" models of writing are ever going to appeal to more than a marginal minority of compositionists, though I admit that I may be succumbing to wishful thinking there.

PCH: Concerning the movement of next generation Ph.D.'s into high schools, one problem is that the hiring track and credentialing for those positions is very different from the one for postsecondary education. For next generation Ph.D.'s to start moving in that direction will start turf wars, as it is likely that the education faculties producing their own students for these jobs will resent and resist giving Ph.D's any ground. Additionally, there is the problem of research as there is little allowance in post-secondary education for scholarly publishing. Certainly, there's increasing outside pressure for postsecondary institutions to become more directly involved with secondary education, mainly, though, from administration. The faculty at UCSD, for instance, rejected the chancellor's proposal to create an on-campus high school by a significant margin.

GG: Thanks for the information about UCSD. I have no illusions about the resistance colleges and universities will put up to involving themselves with high school education. Many university professors would rather dig ditches than have contact with high schools. All I would suggest is that a signficant groundswell of interest in collaboration of various sorts has been developing among college faculty and high school teachers, and that some of the financial and other pressures on both camps make it likely to continue. Though it will be difficult to induce some professors to enter into contacts with high schools, it will also be difficult to prevent those who wish to do so, and these are a growing number. Who knows what the outcome will be, but the mere fact of a conflict like the one you report in San Diego suggests that something is changing. As for the turf wars you predict between education schools and other departments over who gets to do high school credentialing, we are already seeing cooperations between these units. See the new book just published by MLA, *Preparing a Nation's Teachers,* which describes several such projects.

PCH: What do you think has changed in the profession that might cause such a shift?

GG: Outside forces: money, jobs, public pressures. Rumor has it that high school teachers are going to be in great demand, fuelled in part by demographics and in part by the public groundswell for improving secondary education. If such job opportunities are indeed opening up, they are doing so at the moment of an unprecedented surge of interest—backed by foundation-grant initiatives—in both the school and college arenas in curricular and pedagogical mergers. As high school teaching becomes less isolated from the university research culture (and as it continutes to pay well in some schools at least), the attitudes that have stigmatized such teaching figure to weaken. Persuasive challenges to such attitudes are already being made—see the cogent essay in the 1996 issue of *Profession* by Alison T. Smith about the financial and intellectual rewards of high school teaching for people with doctorates.[1]

You say a move toward education doesn't fit the publishing paradigm, but I think that's no longer the case. And though it's true that high school teachers up to now have usually had neither the time nor inclination to publish, I believe this situation is changing as high school teaching is becoming more professionalized and many high school teachers seek to move closer to the culture of the university. New interactions are occurring between high school and college instructors that could vastly redefine the way these roles have been conceived.

For example, I finished a project last year that involved bringing over four hundred high school students and their teachers together with volunteer students from my undergraduate class to debate traditional and colonialist readings of Shakespeare's *The Tempest*. I never would have imagined five years ago that I'd be doing this—it goes against all the supposedly iron laws of the profession that you mention—but I am. Basically, in your response you invoke the old rules, but I think a shakeup is taking place which is changing the rules and I'm dedicated to advancing that process. (And speaking of things I would not previously have imagined, a few months after we concluded this interview I was offered and accepted the position of Associate Dean for Curriculum and Pedagogy at the University of Illinois at Chicago, where a major part of my responsibility will be coordinating teacher-education programs.)

PCH: What about the NG's continuance in the critical pathways of previous generations (for the most part); that is, the lack of a voice that alters criticism's direction the way that Fish, Greenblatt, and Derrida did, might stem from a different set of priorities?

GG: Perhaps you can tell me what priorities you have in mind. To me the "continuance" you mention reflects the tremendous normalizing force of the residual institutional model, which makes it very hard for people to recognize that the model may in fact be crumbling. Despite our well known penchant for casting ourselves as subversives, our profession is deeply wedded to the story that nothing really can change.

PCH: For most of us, the primary, overarching priority in graduate school was not to change the world but to land one of the ever-more-elusive tenure-track positions. Consequently, taking on our teachers in print, going in a completely different direction, entails taking a considerable risk. Also, another impediment to privileging teaching, including going into high school teaching, is the way this profession divies up rewards. Upward mobility in the humanities is made possible through prestigious publications, not through teaching. Doubtless, Professor Graff, you are an exemplary teacher, but my guess is that you moved from your first positions to the University of Chicago in large part because of your exemplary publications, such as *Professing Literature*. Consequently, for the next generation to embrace pedagogy means foregoing the usual means of professional advancement. As for the new journal (which I admit I have not seen), my guess is that it is not so much aimed at English and literature departments as for the nascent field of comp/rhet studies (which is in the fascinating position of just beginning to define itself as a discipline and is presently going through the same processes that you outlined for English in *Professing Literature).*

GG: You say I made my way by publishing *Professing Literature,* not by my teaching. But *Professing Literature* is a book about teaching. And hasn't teaching become a growth industry as a publication and research topic? Many books and essays that formerly would have been solely about literature or criticism are now about teaching as well—books that have done very well like Diana Fuss's *Essentially Speaking* and Jane Tompkins's *Sensational Designs.* The educational debates of the culture war have made teaching a boom subject for journals, presses, and conferences, and while comp/rhet leads the field it does not completely monopolize it, as the names listed above demonstrate.

As for your original question about what's next, I don't think critical work is tapped out, but I do think the next generation ran into a change in the nature of academic-intellectual publishing that I've seen set in during my academic career. I'm thinking of the vast increase in the number of academic books from the late '70s or early '80s on that has made it easier to get published but harder to get attention. I don't have statistics to back me up, but my feeling is that people of roughly my age published our work in a far less saturated and competitive publishing market than those who have come after us.

When I started at Northwestern in 1966 a colleague of mine had the whole yearly output of Princeton University Press on his shelves and he seemingly kept up with it. Nothing like that would be conceivable today in the wake of the publishing explosion of the last few decades. After us the deluge, or so it seems. And it's not just that there have been increasingly more books to compete with but a diversification and fragmentation of the audience, so that it's more difficult today than it once was to write the sort of book that "everybody" in the profession feels he or she has to read or at least know of.

PCH: What do you think the effect of this dispersal will be on the kinds of criticism that the next generation will produce? Do you see next generation critics as deliberately aiming at an increasingly small segment of the general audience? Are they trying to broaden their audience? Or settling for a much smaller one? And what will the effect of the economic downturn in publishing be?

GG: In the old days, when men were men and a field was a field, there were one or two major journals in each period and everybody "in" that period was supposed to subscribe to and read them. In the wake of postmodernism and other detotalizing trends that have undermined or blurred field definitions, there are many more journals but no single one that you can count on everyone reading if you get in it. There's a good essay by the sociologist Howard Becker, by the way, on this phenomenon of journal proliferation in the social sciences.[2]

PCH: I agree that there are many more journals today than in the past. On the other hand, prestige still counts, and I've seen search and tenure committees look askance at articles in very small journals and nonuniversity press books. But granted that there are more outlets for tenure-earning publications, what do you think the overall effect of these smaller, less-read, and less-subscribed-to journals might be on next generation critics. Are we moving into an era of coterie scholarship?

GG: Yes, I guess we are, though members of coteries are obviously less likely to publish if they can't get jobs. True, the prestige of the journal can still make a difference. But historically, hiring, tenure, and promotion committees have eventually yielded to the broadening of what counts as tenurable research and publication. Go back far enough and you'll get to a time when such committees would have looked askance at someone who published criticism in *Kenyon Review* or *Sewanee Review*, or at someone who published creative writing or produced paintings. But gradually, and unevenly, such forms of professional production eventually got counted as "research." (I have an essay on this process of change: "The Scholar in Society.")[3]

PCH: Yet I wonder how the economics of the present situation will affect this. I have in mind the fact that many libraries are cutting back on journal subscriptions rather than keeping, let alone increasing them. So, while it is true that there are an awful lot of new journals out there (e.g., *symplokē*, which first published several of the chapters in this collection), fewer and fewer institutions can subscribe to them. And with no distribution, the journal cannot become known and gain prestige. Which means that the already established journals, like *ELH, Representations,* and *PMLA,* continue, and with increased submissions. Yet also, we are speaking here about print journals, which leaves alone online ones such as *EMLS.*

And that brings me to another question. What do you think the effect will be of the World Wide Web on scholarship? And do you see any differences between critics such as yourself who were trained and established themselves in a pre-Net world, and next generation critics who, for the most part, grew up taking computers for granted?

GG: I guess I can't measure the differences yet, but I'm sure that some are emerging as the use of the Net alters our practices. I know electronic communication has already had a big impact on my own teaching now that my classes are online and students can go on conversing after class with each other and with me.

The Net threatens the basic rule of the academic world, which is I won't mess with what you do (in your class, office, department, etc.) if you don't mess with me. That is, it threatens the structure of carefully programmed ignorance of each other that allows us to tune out colleagues who might say things we don't want to hear and thereby preserves a certain civilized Balance of Mutual Fear, at least among those of roughly comparable power. As the educational historian Veysey put it, the modern university is founded on ignorance, and the Net challenges that foundation by making it much more difficult not to know things about each other.

PCH: OK, but do you think that computers will actually effect a paradigm shift in how we do scholarship, or will they just speed things up—that is, we do the same things, only we can do them much more quickly?

GG: My idea of what a significant "paradigm shift" would be may be different from that of others, since as I noted above my interest is in changing institutional structures and not just "how we do scholarship."

To me, a true paradigm shift would be an institution in which contestation and debate (including that over political issues) becomes the central, everyday agenda instead of being marginalized and channeled into self-reinforcing, self-flattering discourses. Yet the outcome of this contestation and debate would not be predetermined or easy to predict. I think this view puts me at odds with current pedagogical radicals of the Paulo Freire stripe, who in effect say, "It won't count as a paradigm shift unless the good guys (ourselves) win."

In any case, I think electronic technology may in and of itself have a tendency to force academics out of our protected zones and into engagements with those we would prefer to tune out. But it's hard to predict that this will actually happen. Already, as Ellen Willis said at a recent conference at my university, the result of email seems not to be a new macropublic sphere but a proliferation of minispheres that (as I would put it) do not communicate with each other and so reinforce in-group self-righteousness. Do the email exchanges of the National Association of Scholars circulate to the Marxist Literary Group and vice versa? There has recently been an interesting listserve exchange over the "Sokal Text" scandal over "science studies" in which antipostmoderns like Norman Levitt, Paul Gross, and Alan Sokal himself engaged with Michael Bérubé, Bruce Robbins, and others more sympathetic to postmodernism.

Predictably, these debates were not very good—parties talking past one another rather than to one another. Still, I thought the exchange showed that a discussion aross the battle lines could at least be started, but others may have seen it as proof that it can't happen. Whatever the case, the exchange or nonexchange would not have taken place at all were it not for electronic communication.

PCH: To move to another topic, In his article, Jeff Williams puts into question the movement toward increasing public access, arguing that its effect is to create a "star system" that most of us dream about while "at the same time socio-institutional conditions make that dream more and more fantastical." What's your response?

GG: Jeff Williams's attacks on the star system seem to be rooted in a fear that professors will someday become comprehensible to more than a handful of students and others and will then become co-opted by corporations, which will schmooze and disarm us even as they downwsize us. In Jeff's view, evidently, the only thing more disastrous for higher education than being defunded by corporate America is being funded by corporate America. In other words, there's a contradiction or double bind in his argument somewhere.

I much prefer the argument you yourself make in a recent PMLA Forum, in which you write that we academics "need to learn how to justify ourselves in the language of the McDonald's mentality."[4] (Of course what this Egghead McMuffin language would look like is not something anyone can prescribe in advance.) This in a way is all that I was trying to say above when I suggested that the big opportunity for the next generation is to take seriously the mass-education mandate—the democratization of intellectuality—to which American education has always given lip service but never tried to put into practice.

PCH: I think Jeff's point is the power inequity between us and corporations, meaning that there will never *be* an equitable negotiation between partners of unequal power.

GG: This is a council of fatalism, then, since unequal power is a structural feature of all human situations. Jeff and the academic Left want a risk-free situation in which a level playing field is provided before it deigns to enter into a public debate. My assumption, by contrast, is that the only way disempowered groups are likely to level the playing field is by entering into unequal negotiations and then doing whatever can be done to displace and transform their terms.

PCH: My point, though, in the letter, is that we need to start appealing to corporate values (rather than simply denouncing them) in order to further precisely the intellectuality that you are talking about. Which brings us to what I think is the primary difference between the material conditions affecting the next generation and previous generations: the corporatization of the academy—that is, the application of business models and business values to higher education. What's your opinion of this, and how do you think it will affect the next generation?

GG: See what I said above in response to Jeff Williams's blanket condemnation of any compromise by academics with corporatization—as if we even have the option of compromising! I think higher education, which has always been dependent on corporations in any case, has no choice but to seek corporate support. Rather than rail in our ritualistic way against corporatization, we would be wiser to begin distinguishing between retrograde and relatively progressive forms of corporatization. If Christopher Newfield is correct in his essay "Recapturing Academic Business,"[5] corporate culture is itself deeply split between pure bottom-line managers and those who take the public interest seriously. So Critical Corporatism (as we might call it) seems a better option for academics than the knee-jerk bashing of business that either flattens our academic sense of superiority or consoles us for our powerlessness.

PCH: Yet the knee-jerk bashing also comes from the opposite side. For example, *The Chronicle of Higher Education* quotes James F. Carlin, chairman of the state's Board of Higher Education, as asserting that "'Professors should teach more than 12 hours a week,' and 'meaningless research' should be banned; 50 percent of research outside the hard sciences was 'a lot of foolishness.'"[6] Nor are such sentiments rare among administrators, let alone the general public. How do you think this will impact the next generation's teaching and research?

GG: I hardly agree with Carlin, but if the next generation is content just to react defensively to such views or merely to shrug them off it's likely to find itself out-voted. It doesn't take a rocket scientist, as they say, to see that probably more than half of the sum total of humanities research put out at any moment is indeed "a lot of foolishness" (yours and mine excepted, of course), almost by definition. What makes Carlin's complaint unfair is that probably an even higher percentage of the re-search in the hard sciences is even more vacuous and useless than the research in the humanities. This is hardly news to anybody. National Public Radio recently did a feature about a doctoral dissertation in which somebody has calculated the statistical possibilities of your getting a parking space at your local supermarket. Some of our recent race-class-gender-obsessed research in the humanities may be silly, but at least it's being silly about important things. You can't say that about the huge amounts of drivel churned out by the social and physical sciences, in which volumes of statistical data are marshalled to demonstrate stupefyingly trivial conclusions.

So if it comes down to a pissing contest over whose research is more jejune, the scientists should be made to answer for their own well-documented record for empty sterility, and they should feel the defunding axe as much as we humanists do, unlikely though this may be. But it would be better to avoid being defensive about our own record or getting into a competitition with the sciences over whose research is more jejune. I think academics on both sides of the science-humanities gap should start ac-knowledging that academic research can no longer expect to be publicly supported unless it can justify itself in some terms—not necessarily narrow or vulgar ones—that the public can understand and whose relevance to undergraduate teaching can be es-tablished. I think we're going to be held accountable to such a public standard whether we like it or not—so get used to it!

PCH: True, but to return to the earlier point, what I have in mind is less corpo-rate sponsorship of universities as the adoption of corporate models by administra-tors. Part-time workers are obviously a lot cheaper than tenure-track assistant profes-sors (about $1500 a course, no benefits), and according to the *New York Times,* only a quarter of America's 1.2 million professors are tenured, only about 40 percent are tenure track, which is a drop of 20 percent from twenty years ago.[7] Given the creation of this migrant labor force of "freeway flyers," how can the next generation make your program of "teaching the conflict" its project? How can it make *anything* its project?

GG: In most colleges and some high schools, many faculties have enough au-tonomy to implement the sort of cross-course and cross-curricular debate that "teach-ing the conflicts" entails. Nor would part-timers need to be excluded. It can happen, that is, if those faculties—or at least a critical mass within them—can be convinced that this way of teaching is more effective with students, enjoyable, and rewarding, and more stimulating (because more collegial) to their intellectual growth.

I think these teachers, full or part time or what you will, will need to be con-vinced that teaching in a more connected and collective way (as my model entails) is ultimately not in conflict with their long-range self-interest—that is, that the com-munity of debate such a way of teaching can provide will help them get socialized into the profession, stimulate them to more and better publication, and be more effective

as careerists. In other words, the supposedly self-protective, careerist strategy of dealing with administrators who don't respect your teaching by dropping out, becoming
an internal emigre, and tending to "your own work" is not really good careerism.

Also, I would like to think that the kind of solidarity that develops in a faculty
that talks through its differences can make it a stronger collective bargaining force.
The habits of isolation in which most of us are used to teaching may contribute materially to our weakness in labor negotiation. Working within a culture of debate with
our colleagues would figure to make us more effective in arguing for our interests than
we have been. Or so it says here.

*Notes*

1. "Secondary Education: Still an Ignored Market," *Profession* (1996): 69–72.

2. "What's Happening to Sociology?" *Doing Things Together: Selected Papers* (Evanston, Ill.:
Northwestern University Press, 1986), 209–20.

3. "The Scholar in Society," Joseph Gibaldi, ed., *Introduction to Scholarship in Modern Languages and Literatures,* 2d ed. (New York: Modern Language Association, 1992), 343–62.

4. In this letter, I propose that dismissing the corporatization of the academy by blithly saying "That means the triumph of the McDonald's mentality" ("Teaching Literature in the Academy Today: A Roundtable," *PMLA* 112 [1997], 112) dangerously underestimates both the degree to which education has been commodified and the threat this poses to education.
Furthermore, I suggest among other strategies, "we need to explore making the case that our
work is not hopelessly alien to the values and aims of the corporations and marketing consultants hired by many universities. Whether we like it or not, we need to learn how to talk about
literary studies in the language of those who see little use for us except as teachers of technical
writing. Otherwise we risk being 'downsized'" (*PMLA* 112 [1997], 442).

5. *Social Text* 51 (1997): 39–66.

6. Patrick Healy, "A Take-No-Prisoners Approach to Changing Public Higher Education
in Massachusetts," *The Chronicle of Higher Education* 5 (December 1997): A41.

7. Brent Staples, "The End of Tenure?" *New York Times* 29 June 1997: Section 4, p. 14.

# Bringing You the Best Mix of Yesterday and Today

## Michael Bérubé

*In an amazing acceleration, the generations precipitate themselves.*
—Jean-Francois Lyotard

This volume represents the first attempt to theorize the newest generation of literature professors *as a generation,* in the sense that it tries to see the profession's contemporary moment as part of a historical narrative. That narrative is a traditional one—the family plot, so to speak—in which sons and daughters gradually deinfantilize themselves and forge some "mature" position with regard to the achievements of their forebears. But even this most traditional of narratives is fraught, in this volume, with complications: as Peter C. Herman's introduction points out, the "generation" named herein is unified not chronologically but conceptually, as the bunch of people who came to the profession (or came *back* to the profession) more or less after the major theoretical waves of the past thirty years had hit these shores. This sense of "generation" leaves us with a host of conundra, the kind usually associated with being neo- or post-: how, Herman asks, can the first filial posttheory generation rebel against its elders, when those elders made their names in the profession by rebelling against their formalist and old-historicist elders? Attacking the previous thirty years' worth of scholarship, Herman suggests, is itself the foundational gesture of the previous thirty years' worth of scholarship: to rebel in these terms is to conform to the generational model bequeathed us by our parents.

It is a problematic familiar to anyone who, like myself, grew up *after* the upheavals of the 1960s and found generational "rebellion" to have become one of the always-alreadys of the general culture: as the generational cliché has it, when we told our parents that we rejected their narrow bourgeois morality and were striking out on our own to form a cooperative nonhierarchical society, they referred us to our older brothers and sisters, who had rejected their narrow bourgeois morality and struck out on their own to form a cooperative, nonhierarchical society back in '67. By 1978 the eighties were already in place: the natural-foods movement had become an upscale marketing niche, mainstream rock-and-roll was bloated, turgid crap like Kansas or Supertramp, and the drug culture, moving from hallucinogens to CNS stimulants, was less about turning on and tuning in than about honing that competitive edge, whether at Studio 54 or in the offices of Lazard Freres.

This generational cliché is both so shopworn and so accurate that it continues to define my own relation to punk, the music of *my* neogeneration's neorebellion, the rejection and transformation of the music industry that it has become impossible to repeat without betraying. The emerging theorist-critics of the 1990s, on this model, wind up more or less in the position of grunge musicians who can't so much as write a three-chord thrash without being praised or blamed for their homage to the Clash, the Pistols, the Dead Kennedys, Black Flag . . . and who will emerge, I wonder, as the Cramps or the Germs or the X-Ray Spex of tomorrow? Of course, not every one of my contemporaries will think of themselves as postpunk: when in 1991 I published an essay titled "Public Image Limited," *not a single one* of my English Department colleagues at Illinois knew that it was an allusion to the name of a punk band—and not just *any* punk band, either. But then, as far as I'm concerned, part of being postpunk is that most of your cohort doesn't know they're postpunk: punk's heyday is already more than twenty years in the past, but there's no way "Blitzkrieg Bop" or "White Riot" is going to show up on the playlist of your local oldies station or your local best-mix-of-yesterday-and-today, devoted as these stations are to playing cuts from *Rumours* and *Hotel California* in perpetuity.

Herman's introduction—wisely, perhaps—avoids mapping the recent history of criticism onto the recent history of rock. His musical gambit, instead, is to liken the current generation of literature professors to jazz musicians after Coltrane—that is, after the passing of the last of the universally acknowledged giants of the bop-and-post-bop-and-hard-bop-and-cool-jazz generation, after the harmonic and rhythmic possibilities of jazz seemed to have been explored so fully that only the strangled-duck sounds of free jazz remained (and we'll just pretend "fusion," a.k.a. Fuzak, never happened). The purpose of the analogy, I think, is to urge on the current generation of scholars something like the historicist eclecticism of a Wynton Marsalis, steeped in the past but not burdened by it. But jazz is itself an overdetermined field, and appeals to the history of how it has dealt with its history cannot avoid replaying some of the anxiety-of-influence logic that made Miles Davis, Thelonious Monk, Charles Mingus, and John Coltrane each try to swerve from Charlie Parker in as distinctive a way as possible, such that by the mid 1960s, jazz was as anxious about its influences as any Bloomian could desire, an agonistic field of Oedipal and almost exclusively male one-upsmanship (the history of the vocalists is another story). If jazz history is to serve as a model for the history of criticism and theory in the present generation, then it's hard to imagine how we (we of this generation) can avoid the sense that everything has indeed been done that needs to be done, and all that remains is for us to decide how we'd most like to go back, Jack, and do it again. To bring you the best mix of yesterday and today.

But whatever analogy this posttheory generation adopts for itself—and we should be so lucky as to be half as cool or charismatic as the most talented jazz and rock musicians of our own day—the brute fact remains that we are living in a profession *created* by the theory generation. It was them what founded the School for Criticism and Theory; them what started publishing *Critical Inquiry* and *New Literary History;* them what rewrote the blueprint for what a successful career in literary and cultural studies would look like. Yes, there may be newer and more interesting journals popping up in the past ten years, different institutes, innovative conferences. But in the wake of what Christopher Jencks and David Reisman called " the academic revolution" of the 1960s, in which professors were freed from "vertical review" by administrators and subjected to "horizontal," discipline-based, peer review instead, the model for the successful academic career has been based largely on the achievement of national recognition, and national recognition has in turn been based on publications and plenary addresses, the machinery of national visibility. That model has persisted, as numerous contributors to this volume note (with varying degrees of cynicism, bemusement, outrage), even into the era of academic downsizing and adjunctification wherein nearly half of all college teachers are part-timers and only one-third of the professoriat actually enjoys the benefits of tenure: as Herman puts it, ours is the era in which the ideal of the scholar as frequent flyer sits cheek by jowl with the reality of scholar as freeway flyer.

The result is a profession that looks more like the lifeworld of *Soylent Green* than any exciting (if anxious) postpunk or postbebop landscape: a handful of super-rich living quite comfortably, thank you, far above the teeming streets; below, a planet overfull with the lumpenproletariat and depleted of natural resources. Why *Soylent Green* rather than any other dystopian postwar sci-fi fable in which the corporate world is utterly insulated from the consequences of its scorched-earth policies, like *Blade Runner* or *Neuromancer?* Because we so assiduously avoid asking where our profession's basic foodstuffs actually come from, that's why.

But since this is a theme amply sounded by the contributors to this volume, let me conclude by offering a few reasons why, even in the world of *Soylent Green,* it's worth thinking of the current cohort of more-or-less—younger literature professors in terms that suggest one form or another of collectivity. It may be, as Herman suggests, that this generation is distinctive precisely in that it has no sense of itself as a generation. But that's not the only thing that distinguishes us from our theoretical forebears. The previous generation of scholars gave us not only new models for success but also a few new models for egregiously bad behavior, whereby self-absorption, hauteur, and primadonnadom were raised to the level of professional principle. One of the professional psychodramas on display in the wake of the abortive 1995–96 graduate student grade strike at Yale, for instance, was the collision between an older generation's sense of entitlement and privilege and a younger generation's sense of betrayal, registered by, among other things, its wholesale rejection of the increasingly hollow rhetoric of professional "apprenticeship." And the resulting spectacle, in which full professors whose vitae were full of "counterhegemonic" books and essays wound up turning in their own graduate students for disciplinary proceedings and possible expulsion, was among the ugliest scenarios any post-Freudian theorist could ask for (the appropriate model, perhaps, being not Sophocles' Oedipus but Goya's Saturn). Admittedly, the current generation does contain a few folks here and there who have somehow, by dint of great diligence, managed to match or exceed their elders in self-absorption, hauteur, and primadonnadom. But for the most part, we're defined structurally by our lively sense of how precarious the whole enterprise is, how likely we are to be—in the words of one of my contemporaries, Larry Hanley, who earned his Ph.D. in the watershed year of 1990—part of the last generation of college professors. The last generation, that is, whose members generally expect or hope to earn a living wage, to enjoy good working and teaching conditions, and to be protected from laissez-faire, right-to-work economics (and economists) by the institution of tenure.

The next generation, or the last generation? What, indeed, will it take for the next to avoid becoming the last? Since I was asked to write an epilogue, I get to twist this question in my usual way, so: first of all, young and youngish and almost-young scholars in literary and cultural studies need to see themselves not only as members of a distinctive generation, the postwar posttheory postpunk almost-posttenure generation; we need to see ourselves also as citizens—citizens of departments, citizens of disciplines, citizens of the professoriat in general, and citizens of our states and nations. The least of these citizenships is the most immediate, and not necessarily the most trivial: on the contrary, the widespread and notorious breakdowns in major departments, so widespread and so notorious as to make the phrase "dysfunctional English department" a redundancy in all too many Research I institutions, can be attributed in part to the erosion of the sense of departmental or disciplinary citizenship. But we would be mistaken to see our obligations as *civitates* solely or primarily in terms of department and discipline; we should also think of ourselves, no matter where or when or how we teach, as college teachers. Everyone who can reasonably afford to do so should replenish the ranks of the AAUP, which is growing older each year, not attracting enough junior scholars to replace its retirees. Everyone who joins the AAUP, and everyone else, should also support the unionization of graduate students *as college teachers,* since so many of them are in fact precisely that: teachers of college students. Some of us may want to affiliate with Scholars, Artists, and Writers for Social Justice (SAWSJ), some with the reborn and reinvigorated Teachers for a Democratic Culture (TDC), some with our counterparts in the K-12 system through the National Council of Teachers of English (NCTE). Never much of a joiner myself, I now belong to all four organizations. But, in the interests of full disclosure, I do not receive any union kickbacks or recruitment fees for urging people to join me in joining.

Besides, the specific form of your aspiration to collectivity is up to you. But the problem is general and applicable to us all: how to make generational thinking (in which, I confess, I'm as steeped as anyone), into organizational thinking. How to make higher education into a vehicle for critical thinking and critical citizenship rather than a vehicle for mere vocationalism. How to imagine tenure not as a bizarre exception to the employment-at-will rule but as the desideratum for all forms of lifelong workplace commitments. How to make sure the next generation isn't among the last, and our current generation isn't among the lost. And perhaps our distinctiveness from previous generations will someday be seen to reside in this, that although we did not develop so many new and dazzling modes of critical inquiry and new literary history as did our predecessors, we succeeded in applying the fruits of our (and their) knowledges to the very institutions in which we found ourselves—to the betterment of those institutions, and to the benefit of future generations.

# NOTES ON CONTRIBUTORS

CRYSTAL BARTOLOVICH is an assistant professor of English and Textual Studies at Syracuse University. She has published essays in *Cultural Studies* and *Early Modern Studies,* and is completing a book, *Boundary Disputes.*

MICHAEL BÉRUBÉ'S pop/new wave band, Normal Men (1982–83), once opened for the Ramones at Columbia University's Wollman Auditorium in a complex performance of belatedness, but that has almost no bearing on his current position as professor of English and director of the Illinois Program for Research in the Humanities at the University of Illinois at Urbana-Champaign.

TERRY CAESAR is professor of English at Mukogawa Women's University in Japan. He is the author of two collections of essays on academic life and politics, *Conspiring with Forms* (University of Georgia Press, 1992) and *Writing in Disguise* (Ohio University Press, 1998). A new collection, *Traveling through the Boondocks,* is forthcoming from SUNY Press.

JEFFREY R. DI LEO teaches literary theory and cultural studies in the department of English at the University of Illinois, Chicago. He is the editor of *symploke,* and is currently working on a number of articles that examine the philosophical, cultural, and pedagogical implications of hypertext and the internet.

DAVID GALEF is an associate professor of English at the University of Mississippi. He is the author *The Supporting Cast: A Study of Flat and Minor Characters* (Penn State University Press, 1993); two novels, *Flesh* and *Turning Japanese;* two children's books; and a translation of Japanese proverbs, *Even Monkeys Fall from Trees.* He has also edited the anthology *Second Thoughts: A Focus on Rereading* (Wayne State University Press, 1998). In addition, he has published a wide variety of fiction, essays, and reviews in places ranging from *The New York Times* to *Twentieth Century Literature* and *The Gettysburg Review.*

GERALD GRAFF, who just recently turned sixty-two, is at work on a book on intellectualism and why everybody dislikes it. He was the director of the Master of Arts Program in Humanities at the University of Chicago, the author of *Professing Literature, Beyond the Culture War* (University of Chicago Press, 1997), and the developer of the "Teach the Conflicts" school of pedagogy which has inspired several textbooks and influenced many courses. In 2000, he became Dean of Curriculum and Pedagogy at the University of Illinois at Chicago.

PETER C. HERMAN is an associate professor of English at San Diego State University and the author of *Squitter-Wits and Muse-Haters: Sidney, Spenser, Milton, and Renaissance Antipoetic Sentiment* (Wayne State University Press, 1996). He also edited several anthologies, including *Rethinking the Henrician Era* (University of Illinois

Press, 1994) and *Opening the Borders: Inclusivity in Early Modern Studies* (University of Delaware Press, 1999), and he is currently working on a book tentatively called "Milton's *Paradise Lost* and the Poetics of Incertitude."

SUSAN JOHNSTON is resisting absorption as an assistant professor in the department of English at the University of Regina, where she teaches genre and Victorian studies. She is the author of *Women and Domestic Experience in British Political Fiction* (forthcoming from Greenwood Publishing in 2001). She has also published on twentieth-century revisions of nineteenth-century texts, and lectured on interpretive genres, Shakespearean adaptations, and Dickens. Her current project involves genres of interpretation and Shakespearean reception.

NEIL LARSEN teaches literature and theory at the University of California, Davis, where he chairs the department of Spanish and Classics and directs the Program in Critical Theory. He is the author of *Modernism and Hegemony* (University of Minnesota Press, 1990) and *Reading North By South* (University of Minnesota Press, 1995). His next book, on narrative, postcolonialism and the national question, is forthcoming from Verso Press in the fall of 2000.

SHARON O'DAIR teaches in the Hudson Strode Program in Renaissance Studies at the University of Alabama where she is an associate professor. She is the author of many essays, co-editor of *The Production of Renaissance Culture* (Cornell University Press, 1994), and her book, currently entitled *Bottom Lines: Class, Critics, Shakespeare,* is forthcoming in 2000 from the University of Michigan Press.

BARBARA RIEBLING is currently an associate professor at the University of Toledo. Along with Nancy Easterlin, she edited *After Poststructuralism: Interdisciplinarity and Literary Theory* (Northwestern University Press, 1993). As well as writing on the implication of Chaos Theory for literary studies, she has published essays on Shakespeare and Milton in such journals as *SEL* and *Renaissance Quarterly.*

JESSE G. SWAN, formerly an assistant professor of English at Eastern New Mexico University, which is one of six institutions marked by receiving the Pew Leadership Award for assaulting the ivory tower, as *Business Week* has noted, currently is assistant professor of English at the University of Northern Iowa. He has been published in the areas of early modern English literature as well as Southern American literature, in journals such as *Milton Quarterly* and *The Southern Literary Journal,* and has written a forthcoming book, with O. M. Brack, Jr., on the influence of Milton's reputation in the eighteenth century entitled, *Milton, Lauder, Johnson: The Politics of Literary Reputation and Forgery.* Swan has added a public role to his professional program in response to his experience serving as Chair of the General Education Committee and Vice President of the Faculty Senate at ENMU.

KALÍ TAL is a professor of Humanities at Arizona International College of the University of Arizona. She had the distinction of being "nonrenewed" in 1997, and then retroactively reinstated to her position following the reorganization of the college. Her most recent book is *Worlds of Hurt: Reading the Literatures of Trauma* (Cambridge University Press, 1996). She has written numerous articles, including popular writings on cyberculture and race for WIRED magazine. Tal runs Burning Cities, a small press. She also administrates the Sixties Project on the Internet (http://jefferson.village.virginia.edu/sixties) and maintains a web site on Afrofuturism (www.afrofuturism.net) in collaboration with other scholars working in the genre.

JEFF WILLIAMS is the author of *Theory and the Novel: Narrative Reflexivity in the British Tradition* (Cambridge University Press, 1998), and the editor of *PC Wars: Politics and Theory in the Academy* (Routledge, 1995). He has also edited *the minnesota review* since 1992 and is an editor of the *Norton Anthology of Literary Theory and Criticism*. He has published numerous articles on contemporary theory in *MLN, Narrative, College English, College Literature, Studies in the Novel,* and elsewhere. He teaches at University of Missouri.

# INDEX

# INCREDIBLE
# ADVENTURE
## AND
# EXPLORATION
# STORIES